Praise from the Experts

"The Little SAS® Book for Enterprise Guide® 4.1 introduces the latest release of the powerful software package. The reader will find plenty of introductory material, good examples, as well as a comprehensive reference section aimed at more experienced users. This book will be of great use to the SAS Enterprise Guide community."

Alex Dmitrienko
Business Intelligence SAS Users Group

"As the development of SAS Enterprise Guide leaps ahead, the need for an easy-to-read handbook for the current version becomes even more important. *The Little SAS® Book for Enterprise Guide® 4.1* continues to fill that niche with relevant and informative tutorials to support even the most inexperienced user. My copy was not "little," but I'd happily trade size for content, which continues to be delivered in this excellent series of user guides. I was especially impressed with the level of detail on customization of the SAS Enterprise Guide client and its reporting, because these are common requests from my clients. I look forward to showing this volume to my clients. Another publication very well done; congratulations Susan and Lora."

David H. Johnson
Principal Business Systems Consultant
DKV-J Consultancies

"Whether you are a novice or experienced SAS user, you will be glad that you have this easy-to-read book as you learn new ways of working as a SAS user. The step-by-step tutorials make getting started with SAS Enterprise Guide easy and fast. The reference section gives you a deeper knowledge and understanding about the product. The chapter on using parameters and the sections on other features that are new with SAS Enterprise Guide 4.1 are very valuable."

Ginger Carey and Helen Carey
SAS Enterprise Guide Instructors

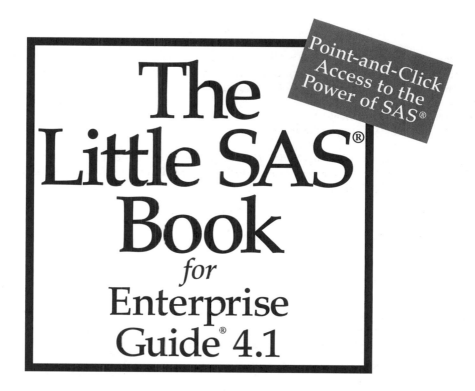

Point-and-Click
Access to the
Power of SAS®

The Little SAS® Book
for Enterprise Guide® 4.1

Susan J. Slaughter and *Lora D. Delwiche*

THE
POWER
TO KNOW.

The correct bibliographic citation for this manual is as follows: Slaughter, Susan J., and Lora D. Delwiche. 2006. *The Little SAS® Book for Enterprise Guide® 4.1*. Cary, NC: SAS Institute Inc.

The Little SAS® Book for Enterprise Guide® 4.1

Contents

About SAS Enterprise Guide

For over three decades, SAS software has been used by programmers, analysts, and scientists to manipulate and analyze data. Today, SAS (pronounced sass) is used around the world in 110 countries, at over 40,000 sites, by more than 4.5 million users. SAS users stay with SAS year after year because they know its broad flexibility and depth of functionality will enable them to get the work done. However, not everyone wants to write programs.

What SAS Enterprise Guide is SAS Enterprise Guide gives you access to the power of SAS via a point-and-click interface. SAS Enterprise Guide does not itself analyze data. Instead, SAS Enterprise Guide generates SAS code and submits it to SAS. Every time you run a task in SAS Enterprise Guide, it writes SAS code. The List Data task, for example, writes a PROC PRINT. The Summary Tables task writes a PROC TABULATE. There are approximately 80 such tasks offered within SAS Enterprise Guide.

You don't have to be a programmer to use SAS Enterprise Guide, but, if you would like to see the SAS code that SAS Enterprise Guide writes for you, you can do that too. You can also edit the programs written by SAS Enterprise Guide, or open an empty code window and write a SAS program from scratch using a syntax-sensitive editor like the one in Base SAS. Then you can run your SAS program, and view the SAS log and output. So, SAS Enterprise Guide meets the needs of programmers and non-programmers alike.

What software you need To run SAS Enterprise Guide, you need, of course, SAS Enterprise Guide software. SAS Enterprise Guide runs in only the Windows operating environment. Because SAS Enterprise Guide writes code and submits it to SAS, you also need a machine on which SAS is installed. That machine is called a SAS server, and it may be the same machine where SAS Enterprise Guide is installed (in which case, it is called a local server) or it may be a separate machine (called a remote server). SAS runs in many operating environments and on many types of computers. Any computer with SAS can be a SAS server as long as you have access to that machine.

SAS has many different products. To run SAS Enterprise Guide, you only need a few. You must have Base SAS software installed on your SAS server. If you have a remote SAS server, you may need a product called SAS Integration Technologies. If you want to run statistical analyses, then you must also have SAS/STAT software. For running econometric time series analyses, you need SAS/ETS software. For graphics, you need SAS/GRAPH software. Except in special cases, you probably won't need SAS/ACCESS software. (See section 2.1 for more information about the types of data SAS Enterprise Guide can read.)

Getting Help We have tried to design this book to answer any questions you are likely to have. In addition, SAS Enterprise Guide has extensive built-in help (described in section 1.14). If you still have questions, you may want to contact SAS Technical Support. With some software companies, very little technical support is available, or the support is available but only for an extra charge--not so with SAS. All licensed SAS sites have access to SAS Technical Support.

There are several ways to contact SAS Technical Support, including via their Web site, **support.sas.com**, or via phone at (919) 677-8008 weekdays, between 9 a.m. and 8 p.m. Eastern time. Before you contact SAS Technical Support you must know your site number and the version of SAS Enterprise Guide that you are running. To find these, start SAS Enterprise Guide and select **Help ▶ About SAS Enterprise Guide**. The About SAS Enterprise Guide window will open, displaying both the version of software and your site number.

About This Book

This book is divided into two distinct but complementary sections: a tutorials section and a reference section. Each tutorial is designed to give you a quick introduction to a general subject. Reference sections, on the other hand, give you focused information on specific topics.

Tutorials section If you are new to SAS Enterprise Guide, you'll probably want to start with the tutorials. Each of the five tutorials leads you step-by-step through a complete project, from starting SAS Enterprise Guide to documenting what you've done before you exit. The tutorials are self-contained so you can do them in any order. People who know nothing about SAS or SAS Enterprise Guide should be able to complete a tutorial in 30 to 45 minutes.

Reference section Once you feel comfortable with SAS Enterprise Guide, you'll be ready to use the reference section. This is where you'll turn when you need a quick refresher on how to join data tables, or a detailed explanation of filtering data in a query. With 11 chapters and 88 topics, the reference section covers more information than the tutorials, but each topic is covered in just two pages so you can read it in a few minutes.

The data for this book The data used for the examples in this book revolve around a theme: the Fire and Ice Tours company, a fictional company offering tours to volcanoes around the world. Using a small number of data sets over and over saves you from having to learn new data for every example. The data sets are small enough that you can type them in if you want to run the examples, but to make it even easier, the data are also available for downloading via the Internet. Appendix A contains both the data and instructions on how to download the data files.

Acknowledgments

Writing about a point-and-click application such as SAS Enterprise Guide is like alligator wrestling—it's a lot harder than it looks. Fortunately, we've had plenty of help.

Among the many people we'd like to thank are our technical reviewers: Vicki Brocklebank, Anand Chitale, Marie Dexter, Beth Hardin, Chris Hemedinger, Iris Krammer, Stephen McDaniel, Gerlinde Schuster, Stacey Syphus, Jennifer Tamburro, Bob Tremblay; our technical publishing specialists: Candy Farrell and Jennifer Dilley; our designer, Patrice Cherry; our marketing specialists: Liz Villani and Shelly Goodin; our copy editors: Caroline Brickley and Amy Wolfe; our managing editor, Mary Beth Steinbach; and Julie Platt , Editor-in-Chief. All these people worked hard to ensure that this book is accurate and appealing.

> And now to our editor,
> we specially credit her
> patience and humor.
> They're not just a rumor.
>
> With Box 1 and Box 2,
> our inquiries flew
> with Pane 3 and Pane 4,
> and windows galore.
>
> From technical questions
> to note box suggestions
> she knew what to do
> and she guided us through.

Thank you, Stephenie Joyner, our acquisitions editor.

Special thanks go to Sam Delwiche for test-driving all five tutorials, and, as always, we thank our families for everything.

TUTORIALS SECTION

Tutorial A

A ▶ Getting Started with SAS Enterprise Guide

This first tutorial will give you a basic understanding of how SAS Enterprise Guide works and how quickly tasks can be accomplished. The following topics will be covered:

- Starting SAS Enterprise Guide
- A quick tour of SAS Enterprise Guide windows
- Entering data into the Data Grid
- Producing simple list reports
- Producing frequency reports
- Graphing data

The data for this tutorial come from the Fire and Ice Tours company, a fictional company that arranges tours of volcanoes around the world. For each tour, the company keeps track of the name of the volcano, the city from which the tour departs, the number of days of the tour, and the price. Because the tours can require some physical exertion, the company gives each tour a difficulty rating: easy, moderate, or challenging.

Starting SAS Enterprise Guide Start SAS Enterprise Guide by either double-clicking the **SAS Enterprise Guide 4** icon on your desktop, or selecting **SAS Enterprise Guide 4** from the Windows **Start** menu. Starting SAS Enterprise Guide brings

Desktop
✓ Double-click SAS Enterprise Guide 4 icon

SAS Enterprise Guide Projects

SAS Enterprise Guide organizes all your work into projects. A project will contain references to all the data that you use, plus all the reports that you produce from the data. You can work on only one project at a time, and all the information for a project is stored in a single file.

up the SAS Enterprise Guide windows in the background, with the Welcome window in the foreground. The Welcome window allows you to choose between opening an existing project or starting a new project. Click **New Project**.

Welcome Window
✓ Click New Project

Welcome to SAS Enterprise Guide ✕

Select one of these options to get started:

Open a project
- SalesQ1.egp
- Volcanoes.egp
- Flights.egp
- Tours.egp
- SeattleSales.egp
- More projects ...

New
- New Project
- New SAS Program
- New Data

Assistance
- ? Tutorial: Getting Started with SAS Enterprise Guide

☐ Don't show this window again

SAS Enterprise Guide windows When you first start SAS Enterprise Guide, your screen should look something like the following. There are several parts to the SAS Enterprise Guide window: some are visible, while others may be hidden or temporarily closed.

Resetting the SAS Enterprise Guide Windows

Does your screen look like this? If not, it may be because someone has already used SAS Enterprise Guide on your computer, and made some changes to the initial settings. To reset the windows, select **Tools ▶ Options** from the menu bar. Then click **Reset Docking Windows**.

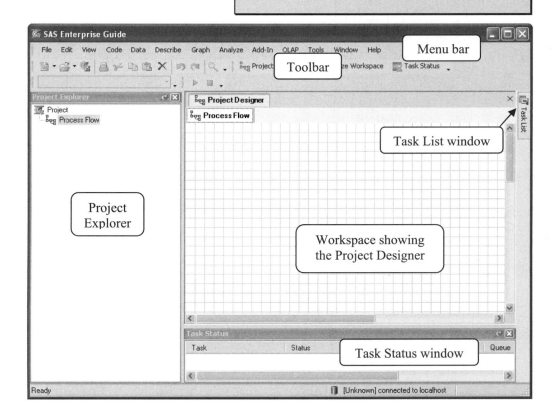

Basic elements of SAS Enterprise Guide

Menu bar: You can access all the tasks and features of SAS Enterprise Guide from the menu bar. Tasks can also be accessed from the Task List.

Toolbar: One-click access to many features of SAS Enterprise Guide can be found on the toolbar. All features on the toolbar can also be accessed from the menu bar.

Project Designer: This is a container that holds the process flows for the project.

Process Flow: A graphical representation of your project is displayed in the process flow. You can have multiple process flows in the Project Designer with each displayed on a separate tab.

Project Explorer: A hierarchical tree-based representation of your project is displayed in the Project Explorer.

Task List window: This window is initially pinned to the right side of the window and looks like a tab. To open the Task List window, simply move the cursor over the tab, and the window will appear. In the window, you can open a task by clicking its name in the Task List. The tasks are arranged by category. You can click the **Tasks by Name** tab to arrange the tasks alphabetically. The tasks listed in the Task List window can also be accessed from the menu bar.

Workspace: This is a container for the Project Designer, results from tasks that you run, Data Grids, SAS code, and Notes. Each item in the workspace will have a tab and you can switch between items by clicking the appropriate tab.

Task Status window: When you are running a task, messages about the progress of the task will appear in the Task Status window.

Menu Bar

✓Select
  File ▶ New ▶
  Data

Entering data There are many ways to get data into SAS Enterprise Guide, and SAS Enterprise Guide can use data from a variety of sources, including SAS data sets, Microsoft Excel files, and plain text files. For this example, you are simply going to type the data directly into SAS Enterprise Guide. To bring up the Data Grid so you can enter the data, select **File ▶ New ▶ Data** from the menu bar.

This opens the New Data wizard.

In the first page of the wizard, SAS Enterprise Guide asks what you want to name the data and where you want to save the data you are about to type. Initially, the location for the data is set to the WORK library and the name is Data.

SAS Data Sets or SAS Data Tables?

A SAS data set and a SAS data table are the same thing. The two terms are used interchangeably. Generally, this book uses "SAS data table" when talking about Data Grids and queries, and "SAS data set" for all other topics.

New Data
Wizard

✓ In Name box
   type **Tours**

✓ Click
   SASUSER

✓ Click Next

Give the new data table the name Tours by typing **Tours** in the **Name** box. Then, because WORK is a temporary storage location, choose an alternate library. For this example, save the data in the SASUSER library. Click **SASUSER** to select the SASUSER library. The SAS Enterprise Guide administrator at your site may have set up the SASUSER library so that you cannot save files there. If this is the case for you, choose an alternate library that is available to you.

New Data

1 of 2   Specify name and location   §sas.

Name: | Tours |

Location: SAS:\Servers\Local\Libraries\SASUSER

```
⊟ ⑦ Local
   ⊟ ⑦ Libraries
        ⊞ ⑦ FAITDATA
        ⊞ ⑦ Local
        ⊞ ⑦ MAPS
        ⊞ ⑦ SASHELP
        ⊞ ⑦ SASUSER
        ⊞ ⑦ WORK
   ⊞ ⑦ Marinosa
```

[< Back]   [Next >]   [Finish]   [Cancel]   [Help]

Click **Next** to open the second page of the New Data wizard.

Libraries

SAS Enterprise Guide and SAS organize SAS data sets into libraries. Libraries are locations, or folders, where data sets are stored. Instead of referring to the folders by their full path, SAS Enterprise Guide gives the folders short nicknames, also called librefs. The WORK library points to a temporary storage location that is automatically erased when you exit SAS Enterprise Guide. The SASUSER library is a permanent storage location. If the EGTASK library is defined for your site, then data sets produced by tasks will be stored in the EGTASK library. If the EGTASK library is not defined, then data sets produced by tasks will be stored in the SASUSER library. Libraries can be created using the SAS Enterprise Guide Explorer or the Assign Libraries task, both available from the Tools menu.

The second page of the New Data wizard is where you assign names and properties to the columns in your data table. As a starting point, the New Data wizard sets up six columns with one-letter names starting with the letter A. All these initial columns have the same properties.

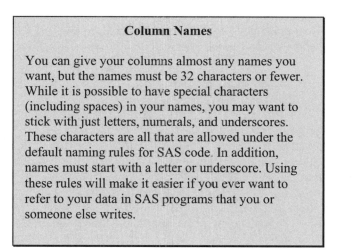

Column Names

You can give your columns almost any names you want, but the names must be 32 characters or fewer. While it is possible to have special characters (including spaces) in your names, you may want to stick with just letters, numerals, and underscores. These characters are all that are allowed under the default naming rules for SAS code. In addition, names must start with a letter or underscore. Using these rules will make it easier if you ever want to refer to your data in SAS programs that you or someone else writes.

New Data
Wizard

✓ In Name
box, type
Volcano

✓ Press Enter

In the Column Properties box, you can assign each column a name, label, type, group, length, display format, and read-in format. The first column will contain the names of the volcanoes, so type **Volcano** in the box next to **Name**.

When you press **Enter**, the name you typed in the Name box will replace the name, in this case A, in the Columns box on the left. Because the names of the volcanoes contain characters, as opposed to numbers, leave the **Type** and **Group** properties as **Character**, and because none of the volcano names are longer than 12 characters, leave the **Length** set to **12**.

Lengths of Character Columns

The New Data wizard in SAS Enterprise Guide gives character columns a length of 12. If your character data are longer than 12 characters, you need to change the length of the column to be at least as long as the longest data value. When you do this, you also need to change the length of the display and read-in formats to match the length of the column. If all your data values are shorter than 12 characters, you can shorten the length for the column. Using shorter lengths for character data decreases the storage space needed for the data table. If you shorten the column length, make sure you also change the display and read-in formats to the same length.

New Data
Wizard

✓ Click Column
B

✓ In Name box,
type
Departs

Now click the column named **B** in the **Columns** box on the left. This column will contain the name of the departure city for the tour, so type the word **Departs** next to **Name** in the **Column Properties** box on the right. Leave the other settings as is.

New Data
Wizard

✓ Click Column
C

✓ In Name box,
type **Days**

✓ From Type
list, select
Numeric

The third column contains the number of days the tour lasts. Give it the name **Days**, and because the values in this column are numbers, use the pull-down list to select **Numeric** for the **Type** property.

Notice that when you set the column type to numeric, the icon next to the column name changes from the red pyramid ⚠ (character) to the blue ball 🔵 (numeric). The length of **8** is the default for all numeric columns and means that the numbers will be stored with maximum precision. Generally, there is no need to change the length of numeric columns.

Character versus Numeric

How do you decide if a column should be character or numeric? If the values for the column have letters or special characters in them, then the column must be character. If the column contains only numerals, then it could be either character or numeric. Generally, if it does not make sense to add or subtract the values, then the column should be character.

Name the fourth column **Price** and give it the type **Numeric**. When you choose the numeric type, you have several options for **Group**: numeric, date, time, and currency. Because Price will contain currency values, select the group **Currency**.

Notice that when you do this, the icon changes from the blue ball to the currency icon.

Numeric Groups

By choosing a group for your numeric column, what you are doing is assigning your column a format. A format is a way of displaying the values in the column. If you choose currency, then when you type a number like 1200, SAS Enterprise Guide will automatically display the number as $1,200. SAS Enterprise Guide has made it easy for you to assign some of the frequently used formats to your columns.

Tutorial A

New Data
Wizard

✓ Click Column
E

✓ In Name box,
type
Difficulty

✓ Press Enter

The final column will contain the difficulty ratings of each tour. The most challenging tours have values of **c**, the moderately challenging tours have values of **m**, while the easiest tours have values of **e**. Give the column the name **Difficulty** and select **Character** as the type.

New Data

2 of 2   Create columns and specify their properties   §sas.

Columns:

Name	Length (in bytes)
Volcano	12
Departs	12
Days	8
Price	8
Difficulty	12
F	12

Column Properties:

Name	Difficulty
Label	
Type	Character
Group	Character
Length	12
Display format	$12.0
Read-in format	$12.0

[New] [Duplicate] [Paste...]

[< Back] [Next >] [Finish] [Cancel] [Help]

New Data
Wizard

✓ Click Column
F

✓ Click Delete
button

Now the properties for all the columns have been set. However, there is one extra column: column F. Delete the unnecessary column by clicking it in the **Columns** box, then clicking the delete button  to the right of the **Columns** box.

New Data

2 of 2   Create columns and specify their properties   §sas.

Columns:

Name	Length (in bytes)
Volcano	12
Departs	12
Days	8
Price	8
Difficulty	12
F	12

Column Properties:

Name	F
Label	
Type	Character
Group	Character
Length	12
Display format	$12.0
Read-in format	$12.0

[New] [Duplicate] [Paste...]

[< Back] [Next >] [Finish] [Cancel] [Help]

By default, SAS Enterprise Guide provides 12 rows for data entry. If you have more than 12 rows of data, then you can press the **Enter** key from any cell in the last row and SAS Enterprise Guide will automatically generate a new blank row for you. Because there are only 10 tours in this data file, you will need to delete the two extra blank rows. Highlight both blank rows by clicking row 11 and dragging the cursor to row 12. Then right-click one of the rows and select **Delete rows**.

Tours Data Grid

✓ Click row 11 and drag to row 12

✓ Right-click row 11 or 12

✓ Select Delete rows

Confirm that you want to delete the rows by clicking **Yes** in the pop-up dialog box.

Delete Rows?

✓ Click Yes

Now the Data Grid is completely filled without any extra rows or columns.

	Volcano	Departs		Days		Price		Difficulty
1	Etna	Catania		7		$1,025	m	
2	Fuji	Tokyo		2		$195	c	
3	Kenya	Nairobi		6		$780	m	
4	Kilauea	Hilo		1		$45	e	
5	Kilimanjaro	Nairobi		9		$1,260	c	
6	Krakatau	Jakarta		7		$850	e	
7	Poas	San Jose		1		$50	e	
8	Reventador	Quito		4		$525	m	
9	St. Helens	Portland		2		$157	e	
10	Vesuvius	Rome		6		$950	e	

Menu Bar

✓ Select
Describe ▶
List Data

Creating a list report Now that all the data are entered, it is easy to produce a simple list report of all the tours. Use the List Data task, which can be found under the Describe pull-down menu. From the menu bar, select **Describe ▶ List Data**.

Describe   Graph   Analyze   Add-I
  Wizards   ▶
  List Data...
Σ Summary Statistics...
  Distribution Analysis...
  Characterize Data...
  Summary Tables...
  One-Way Frequencies...
  Table Analysis...

Opening Tasks and Wizards

You can open tasks by selecting them from the menu bar or by choosing them in the Task List. Use whichever method feels more comfortable for you. In this book, we describe how to open tasks using the menu bar. But it's fine if you want to use the Task List instead.

Some tasks have wizards in addition to the regular task window. A wizard guides you through the task one window at a time and gives access to many of the features of the task. Wizards are available for the Summary Statistics, Summary Tables, Bar Chart, Line Plot, and Pie Chart tasks. Open a wizard by choosing **Wizards** from the **Describe** or **Graph** menu.

Because the data have just been entered into the Data Grid, the following dialog box appears.

Continue?

✓ Click Yes

> **Enterprise Guide**
>
> ? Data must be protected before proceeding. Continue?
>
> [Yes] [No]

Data must be protected before you can perform any task on your data. If your data are not protected, SAS Enterprise Guide will prompt you. Click **Yes**. This opens the List Data task window.

The List Data task window has three pages: Task Roles, Options, and Titles. When you first open the task, the Task Roles page will be displayed. All three pages for the task are listed in the selection pane on the left, with the displayed page highlighted.

> **List Data for TOURS**
>
> Task Roles
> Options
> Titles
>
> **Task Roles**
>
> Variables to assign:
>
> Name
> ⛰ Volcano
> ⛰ Departs
> 🕐 Days
> 💲 Price
> ⛰ Difficulty
>
> Task roles:
>
> 🗒 List variables
>   ☐ <variable required>
> 🗒 Group analysis by
> 🗒 Page by (Limit: 1)
> 🗒 Total of
> 🗒 Subtotal of (Limit: 1)
> 🗒 Identifying label
>
> ...and drop it.
>
> The selection pane enables you to choose different sets of options for the task.
>
> [Preview code]   [Run] [Save] [Cancel] [Help]
>
> The "List variables" role must have at least 1 variable assigned to it.

For every task that you perform in SAS Enterprise Guide, you will need to assign variables to roles. The Fire and Ice Tours company wants a report showing the name of the volcano, the departure city, the number of days of the tour, and the price. Because these variables must all appear in the report, they all need to be assigned the role of List variables. Click the name **Volcano** in the box labeled **Variables to assign** and drag it onto the words **List variables** in the box labeled **Task Roles**. Then do the same for the variables **Departs**, **Days**, and **Price**. If you accidentally assign a variable to the wrong role, simply click the variable's name and drag it to the correct role. You can change the order of the variables in the list by clicking and dragging them to a new location, or by clicking them and using the up and down arrow buttons to move the variables where you want them.

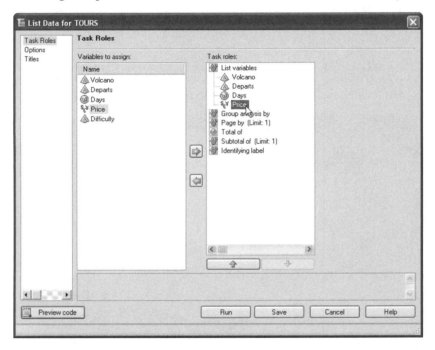

After you have all four variables under List variables, click **Run** to run the task and produce your report.

List Data Window

✓ Click Run

Columns or Variables?

A column and a variable are the same thing. The two terms are used interchangeably, and you will see both terms used in SAS Enterprise Guide. For example, the List Data task uses the term "variable," while the Scatter Plot task (discussed later in this tutorial) uses the term "column." Just remember, a variable is a column, and a column is a variable.

Here is the report that the List Data task produces. This report appears in the workspace of your SAS Enterprise Guide window. You may need to scroll to see the whole report.

§sas. | Enterprise Guide.

The Power to Know:.

Report Listing

Row number	Volcano	Departs	Days	Price
1	Etna	Catania	7	$1,025
2	Fuji	Tokyo	2	$195
3	Kenya	Nairobi	6	$780
4	Kilauea	Hilo	1	$45
5	Kilimanjaro	Nairobi	9	$1,260
6	Krakatau	Jakarta	7	$850
7	Poas	San Jose	1	$50
8	Reventador	Quito	4	$525
9	St. Helens	Portland	2	$157
10	Vesuvius	Rome	6	$950

Generated by the SAS System (Local, XP_PRO) on 31MAR2006 at 11:59 AM

This report has all the required elements, but it could use some improvements. The default title "Report Listing" is not very informative, and the Row number column isn't necessary. Instead of starting over with a new List Data task to create a new report, you can make changes to the List Data task you just completed.

Now is a good time to take a close look at the Project Explorer and Project Designer. Click the **Project Designer** tab of the workspace to view the Process Flow for the project. Both the Project Explorer and the Process Flow show the various parts of your project and how they are related. In the Process Flow, you can see that there is an icon for the Tours data table, followed by the List Data (the List Data task) icon and the HTML - List Data (the results of the List Data task) icon. The arrows show that the Tours data set is fed into the List Data task which produces the HTML - List Data report. The Process Flow makes it easy to see how the different parts of the project are related.

Workspace

✓Click Project
Designer tab

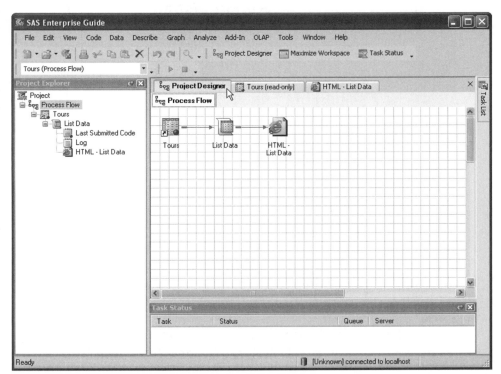

An alternate view of your project can be found in the Project Explorer. The Project Explorer displays the same elements as the Process Flow, except they are arranged in a hierarchical tree diagram. By default the Project Explorer also shows icons for the SAS Code and Log associated with any tasks that have been run. The Project Explorer is always visible, but since the Project Designer is in the workspace, it sometimes gets covered by other items. To bring the Project Designer to the front of the workspace, just click the **Project Designer** tab or the **Project Designer** button on the Toolbar.

Project
Explorer

✓ Right-click
  List Data
  icon

✓ Select Open

To change the List Data task and modify the results, right-click the **List Data** icon in either the Project Explorer or the Project Designer and select **Open** to reopen the task.

Right-click or Double-click?

To open an item in SAS Enterprise Guide you can either right-click the item and choose **Open,** or you can just double-click the item. This book describes the right-click method. If you prefer the double-click method, feel free to use that instead.

Notice that when you reopen the task, all the choices you made are still there. All you have to do is make a few more changes to produce the desired report.

Click **Options** in the selection pane on the left. This gives access to more options for the List Data task.

There are many options listed, including **Print the row number**. By default, this option is checked. To eliminate the Row number column in the report, click the check mark next to **Print the row number** to uncheck this option.

List Data
Window

✓ Uncheck
   Print the
   row number

List Data for TOURS

Task Roles	**Options**
Options	
Titles	

Rows to list

All rows

Heading direction
- ⦿ Default
- ○ Horizontal
- ○ Vertical

☐ Print the row number

Column heading: Row number

☑ Use variable labels as column headings

☐ Print number of rows

☐ Round values before summing

☑ Divide page into sections (no effect on HTML output)

Column width
- ⦿ Default
- ○ Full
- ○ Minimum
- ○ Uniform
- ○ Uniform by

☐ Split labels at:

Includes the row number (Obs) in the output.

Preview code   Run   Save   Cancel   Help

List Data
Window

✓ Click Titles

To add a title to the report, click **Titles** in the selection pane on the left.

The way you modify titles and footnotes is similar for all SAS Enterprise Guide tasks. For the List Data task there are two sections defined: Report Titles and Footnote. Because **Report Titles** is highlighted, you see the default title for the List Data task "Report Listing" displayed under **Text for section: Report Titles**.

List Data
Window

✓ Uncheck
Use default
text

To change the title, click the check mark next to **Use default text** to uncheck this option. When you do this, the text in the box below will change from gray to black and the background will be white.

Now you can click the text and change it to read **Fire and Ice Tours**.

List Data
Window

✓ Type **Fire
and Ice
Tours**

✓ Click Run

List Data for TOURS

| Task Roles | **Titles** |
| Options |
| Titles |

Section:

✓ Report Titles
✓ Footnote

Text for section: Report Titles

☐ Use default text

Fire and Ice Tours

Checked sections will be generated
based on current task settings.

Displays the text that is associated with the selected section in the Section area. You can edit this text.

Preview code   Run   Save   Cancel   Help

Rerun the task by clicking the **Run** button at the bottom of the window. When you do this, SAS Enterprise Guide gives you a choice. You can either replace the results that you generated the last time you ran the task, or you can create new results.

Replace
results?

✓ Click Yes

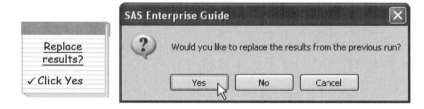

SAS Enterprise Guide

? Would you like to replace the results from the previous run?

Yes   No   Cancel

In this case, there is no reason to keep the old results, so click **Yes**.

Here is what the new report looks like after setting the title and eliminating the Row number column.

§sas. | Enterprise Guide.

The Power to Know.

Fire and Ice Tours

Volcano	Departs	Days	Price
Etna	Catania	7	$1,025
Fuji	Tokyo	2	$195
Kenya	Nairobi	6	$780
Kilauea	Hilo	1	$45
Kilimanjaro	Nairobi	9	$1,260
Krakatau	Jakarta	7	$850
Poas	San Jose	1	$50
Reventador	Quito	4	$525
St. Helens	Portland	2	$157
Vesuvius	Rome	6	$950

Generated by the SAS System (Local, XP_PRO) on 31MAR2006 at 11:59 AM

Producing a frequency report Now the Fire and Ice Tours company wants a simple frequency report that will show the number of easy, moderate, and challenging tours. To do this, use the One-Way Frequencies task. From the menu bar, select **Describe ▶ One-Way Frequencies**.

Menu Bar

✓ Select
  Describe ▶
  One-Way
  Frequencies

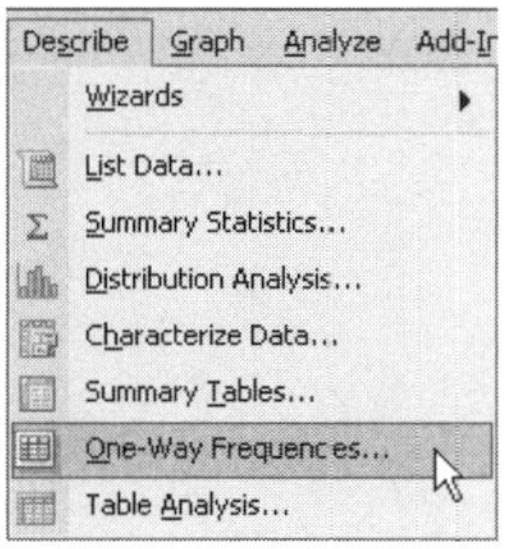

This opens the One-Way Frequencies window. Just as with the List Data task, the first thing you need to do is assign variables to roles.

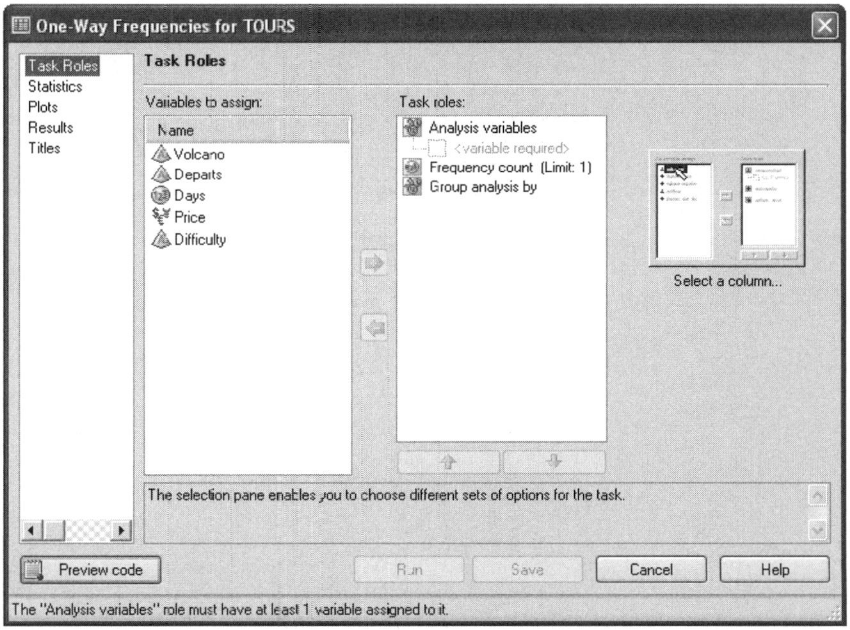

To produce a report with the number of tours in each category of the variable Difficulty, click the variable **Difficulty** and drag it to the **Analysis variables** role.

One-Way Frequencies Window

✓ Click and drag Difficulty to Analysis variables

One-Way Frequencies Window

✓ Click Run

The selection pane on the left lists several other groups of options. There are options for Statistics, Plots, and Results, and, as with all tasks, there are options for Titles. But to produce a simple frequency report, there is no need to make any other changes. Click **Run**.

Here are the results that will show up in your workspace. Two tours are challenging, five are easy, and three are moderate.

SAS | Enterprise Guide.

The Power to Know.

One-Way Frequencies Results

The FREQ Procedure

Difficulty	Frequency	Percent	Cumulative Frequency	Cumulative Percent
c	2	20.00	2	20.00
e	5	50.00	7	70.00
m	3	30.00	10	100.00

Generated by the SAS System (Local, XP_PRO) on 31MAR2006 at 11:59 AM

Click the **Project Designer** tab. Now if you look in the Process Flow, you can see that there are two tasks coming from the Tours data icon, followed by two results.

Workspace

✓ Click Project Designer tab

If you wanted to make any changes to the One-Way Frequencies report, all you would have to do is reopen the One-Way Frequencies task, make any changes, and rerun the task.

Creating a scatter plot The Fire and Ice Tours company wants a graph showing the relationship between the number of days of the tour and the price. To do this, use the Scatter Plot task. From the menu bar, select **Graph ▶ Scatter Plot**.

This opens the Scatter Plot window. Before assigning roles to columns, you need to choose the type of scatter plot to produce. A simple two-dimensional scatter plot is appropriate for this report, so click **2D Scatter Plot**.

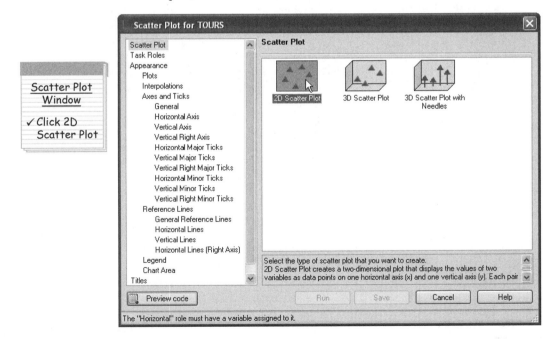

Next, click **Task Roles** in the selection pane on the left to assign variables to roles.

Scatter Plot Window

✓ Click Task Roles

For this plot, the column Days should be on the horizontal axis, and the column Price on the vertical axis. So, click **Days** and drag it to the **Horizontal** task role, and click **Price** and drag it to the **Vertical** task role.

Scatter Plot Window

✓ Click and drag Days to Horizontal role

✓ Click and drag Price to Vertical role

Scatter Plot for TOURS

Task Roles

Scatter Plot
Task Roles
Appearance
  Plots
  Interpolations
  Axes and Ticks
    General
    Horizontal Axis
    Vertical Axis
    Vertical Right Axis
    Horizontal Major Ticks
    Vertical Major Ticks
    Vertical Right Major Ticks
    Horizontal Minor Ticks
    Vertical Minor Ticks
    Vertical Right Minor Ticks
  Reference Lines
    General Reference Lines
    Horizontal Lines
    Vertical Lines
    Horizontal Lines (Right Axis)
  Legend
  Chart Area
Titles

Columns to assign:

Name
△ Volcano
△ Departs
▦ Days
$¥ Price
△ Difficulty

Task roles:

▦ Horizontal (Limit: 1)
  ▦ Days
▦ Vertical (Limit: 1)
  $¥ Price
▦ Vertical (Right) (Limit: 1)
▦ Group charts by

☐ Summarize for each distinct horizontal value

Function
Sum

The column that you assign to this role is the vertical or Y axis variable for the chart.

Preview code   Run   Save   Cancel   Help

The Scatter Plot task has many groups of options, but to produce a simple plot, there is no need to change anything else. Click **Run**.

Scatter Plot Window

✓ Click Run

Here are the results of the Scatter Plot task that will appear in the workspace of the SAS Enterprise Guide window.

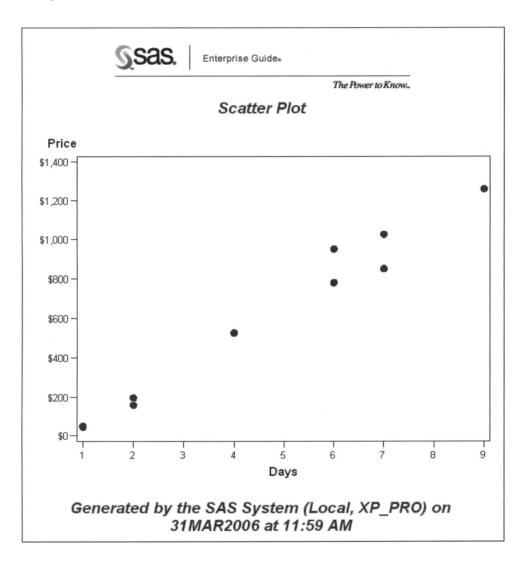

Now click the **Project Designer** tab and take another look at the Process Flow. You can see that the Scatter Plot task and its results form a third path coming from the Tours data icon.

If you wanted to make any changes to the Scatter Plot task results, you could just reopen the Scatter Plot task, make the desired changes, and rerun the task.

By now, you can see how easy it is in SAS Enterprise Guide to produce results quickly.

Adding a note to the project A nice feature of SAS Enterprise Guide is that you can add notes to your projects to document them. To add a note to the project, click the **Project icon** in the Project Explorer so that the note will be associated with the entire project instead of a particular item in the project. Then select **File ▶ New ▶ Note** from the menu bar.

Enter a brief description of the project in the Note window that appears in the workspace.

Note

✓ Type descriptive text

Saving the project SAS Enterprise Guide will always ask if you want to save any changes before allowing you to exit. Of course, you can save your work at any time before exiting. To save the project, select **File ▶ Save Project** from the menu bar.

Menu Bar

✓ Select File ▶ Save Project

SAS Enterprise Guide will ask you where to save the project. You can choose either the local computer or a SAS server. Select **Local Computer**.

<table>
<tr><td>

Save Project To Dialog Box

✓ Select Local Computer

</td></tr>
</table>

What Is a SAS Server?

You don't have to have SAS on your local computer to run SAS Enterprise Guide, but SAS Enterprise Guide does need access to SAS on some computer. The computer where SAS resides is called a SAS server. You can save your projects to your local computer or any of the SAS servers that are connected to your copy of SAS Enterprise Guide.

Navigate to the location where you want to save the project. Give the project the filename **TutorialA** and click **Save**.

<table>
<tr><td>

Save As Window

✓ Navigate to desired folder

✓ In File name box, type **TutorialA**

✓ Click Save

</td></tr>
</table>

Now you can exit SAS Enterprise Guide and all your work and data will be saved. From the menu bar, select **File ▶ Exit** to exit SAS Enterprise Guide and complete the first tutorial.

<table>
<tr><td>

Menu Bar

✓ Select File ▶ Exit

</td></tr>
</table>

B ▶ Reading Data from Files

This tutorial covers reading data into SAS Enterprise Guide from two types of files: SAS data sets and Microsoft Excel files. SAS Enterprise Guide can read other types of files, including delimited data files, fixed-width data files, and files produced by many other types of software. See Chapter 2 for details on reading different types of files. Here are the topics covered in this tutorial:

- Reading SAS data sets

- Reading a Microsoft Excel file as is

- Converting a Microsoft Excel file into a SAS data set

Before beginning this tutorial There are three data files for this tutorial: the Tours SAS data set created in Tutorial A, the TourDates SAS data set, and the Bookings Microsoft Excel file. The Tours data set gives information about the tours offered by the Fire and Ice Tours company. The TourDates data set contains the dates and tour guides for the tours, and the Microsoft Excel file contains information about bookings made by customers for the tours. You will need these files to complete the tutorial. The data and instructions for downloading the files can be found in Appendix A.

Starting SAS Enterprise Guide Start SAS Enterprise Guide by either double-clicking the **SAS Enterprise Guide 4** icon on your desktop, or selecting **SAS Enterprise Guide 4** from the Windows **Start** menu. Starting SAS Enterprise Guide brings up the SAS Enterprise Guide windows in the background, with the Welcome window in the foreground. The Welcome window allows you to choose between opening an existing project or starting a new project. Click **New Project**.

Desktop

✓ Double-click SAS Enterprise Guide 4 icon

Welcome Window

✓ Click New Project

Welcome to SAS Enterprise Guide ☒

Select one of these options to get started:

Open a project
- TutorialA.egp
- Volcanoes.egp
- SalesQ1.egp
- Flights.egp
- Tours.egp
- More projects ...

New
- New Project
- New SAS Program
- New Data

Assistance
- ? Tutorial: Getting Started with SAS Enterprise Guide

☐ Don't show this window again

Tutorial B

When you click New Project, SAS Enterprise Guide will open, displaying an empty Process Flow and Project Explorer.

Tutorial B

Menu Bar

✓ Select
File ► Open ►
Data

Opening a SAS data set from your local computer Using a SAS data set in SAS Enterprise Guide is simple. All you need to do is tell SAS Enterprise Guide where to find it. To open the TourDates SAS data set, select **File ► Open ► Data** from the menu bar.

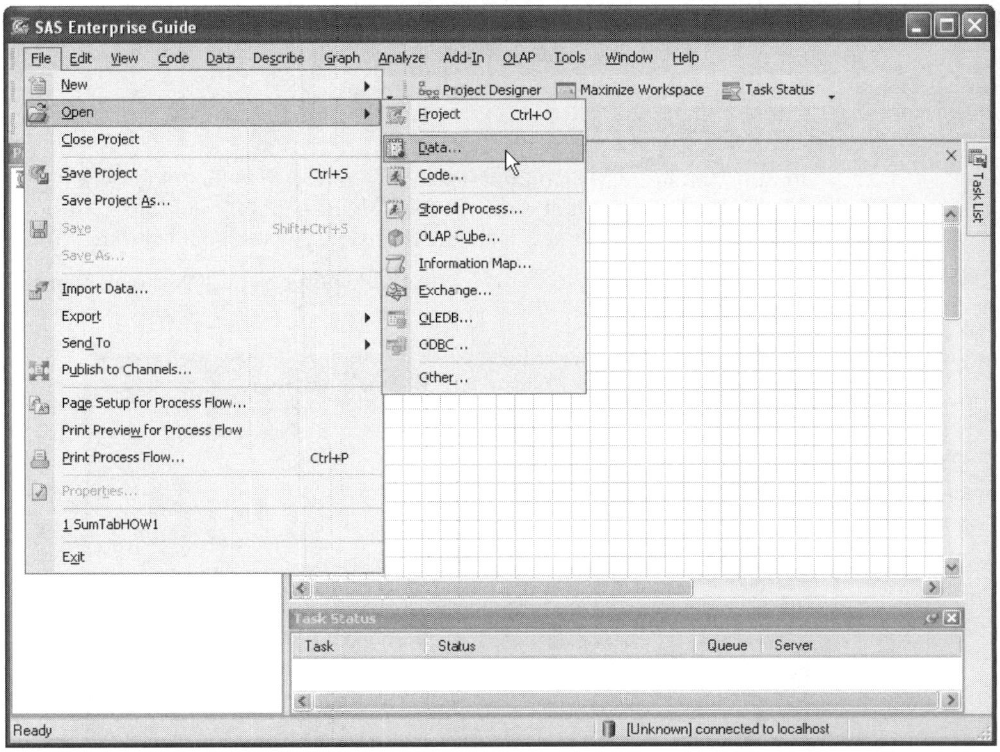

You can open data from either your local computer or a SAS server. Choose **Local Computer**.

Open Data From

✓Click Local Computer

In the Open From My Computer window, navigate to the folder where you store the data for this book. Notice that there are several different types of files in this folder, each with its own icon. SAS data sets have the file extension sas7bdat , and the icon looks like a table of values with a red ball in the lower-right corner ▥. Click the file named **TourDates.sas7bdat**.

Open From My Computer Window

✓Navigate to folder

✓Click TourDates

✓Click Open

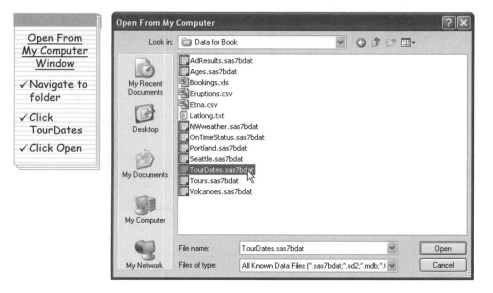

Click **Open** to open the TourDates data set.

Notice that now there is an icon for the TourDates data set in the Project Explorer, and the data appear in a Data Grid in the workspace.

The TourDates data set is now open and ready to use in SAS Enterprise Guide.

> **Read-Only Data Sets**
> When you first open a data set, it is in read-only mode. This means that you cannot make any changes to the data set. If you want to make changes, then you need to switch the data set to update mode by selecting **Data ▶ Read-Only** from the menu bar. To change the data set back to read-only, select **Data ▶ Read-Only** again. Some data sets may be protected such that you cannot switch the data set to update mode.

Opening a SAS data set stored in a SAS library In Tutorial A, you created a SAS data set named Tours and stored it in the SASUSER library (or you might have stored Tours in a different library if your SASUSER library is read-only). A SAS library is simply a folder that has been given a short nickname. To open the Tours data set that you created, you could navigate to the folder for the SASUSER library and open the data set like you did to open the TourDates data set. But, to open a data set this way, you need to know where the SASUSER library is physically located and, depending on your installation, the path to the SASUSER location can be very long. An easier way to open SAS data sets stored in SAS libraries is to look for them in the SAS server list. To open the Tours data set in the SASUSER library, select **File ▶ Open ▶ Data** from the menu bar.

Then, instead of choosing Local Computer, click **SAS Servers**.

The Open From SAS Servers window is similar to the Open From My Computer window, but instead of a listing of the actual file structure of your computer, you get a listing of SAS servers, SAS libraries, and SAS files. A SAS server is a computer that runs SAS and is linked to your copy of SAS Enterprise Guide. This could be your local computer, or it could be a remote computer. It is possible to have access to more than one SAS server. A SAS library is a storage location on a SAS server, and SAS libraries contain SAS files. The following window shows all the SAS files in the SASHELP library on the Local server. Your window may open to a different location in the SAS server/SAS library structure. This is because SAS Enterprise Guide remembers the location where you last opened a SAS file using this method and, the next time you open a file, it automatically goes to the same location.

To get a listing of all the SAS libraries defined for the Local SAS server, click the down arrow on the **Look in** box, and select **Libraries** under **Local**.

Open From
SAS Servers
Window

✓ Select
Libraries
from drop-
down list

What? No Local server?
If you do not have SAS installed on your local computer, then you will not have a SAS server named Local. If this is the case, then look for the SASUSER library on the server where you stored the Tours data set in Tutorial A.

Now you will see a listing of all the SAS libraries defined for the Local server. There are several SAS libraries that come predefined as part of the SAS Enterprise Guide installation, including SASUSER, SASHELP, and WORK. Additional SAS libraries can be defined, so if your list is longer than the one shown here, don't worry. You can store SAS data sets in the SASUSER library unless your SAS Enterprise Guide administrator has set the permissions for SASUSER so that you cannot write to it. If this is the case for you, then there should be an alternate library set up where you can store your data. Click **SASUSER** (or, if you saved the Tours data set in a different library in Tutorial A, click that library).

Open From
SAS Servers
Window

✓ Click
  SASUSER

✓ Click Open

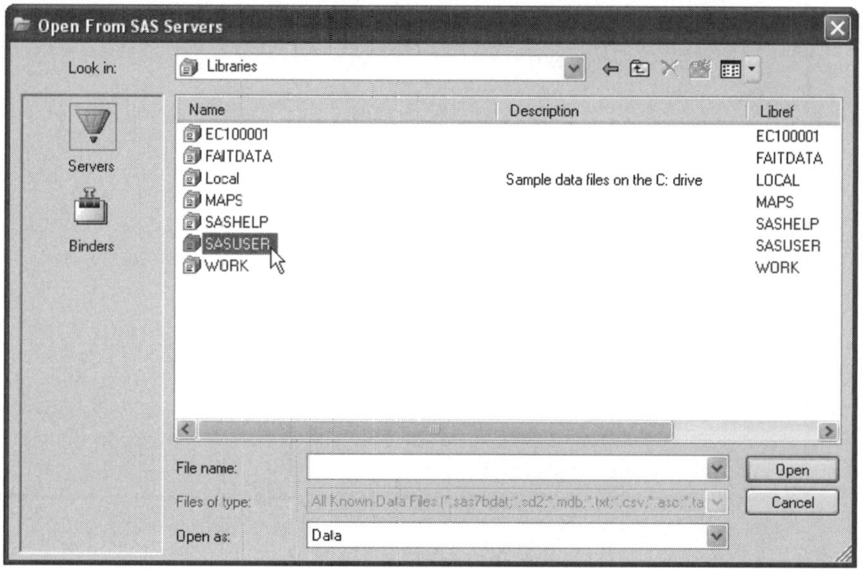

Open From SAS Servers

Look in:	Libraries		
	Name	Description	Libref
Servers	EC100001		EC100001
	FAITDATA		FAITDATA
	Local	Sample data files on the C: drive	LOCAL
	MAPS		MAPS
	SASHELP		SASHELP
Binders	SASUSER		SASUSER
	WORK		WORK

File name:		Open
Files of type:	All Known Data Files (*.sas7bdat;*.sd2;*.mdb;*.txt;*.csv;*.asc;*.ta	Cancel
Open as:	Data	

Click **Open** to view the contents of the SASUSER library.

Now you will see a list of SAS files in the SASUSER library. In the window below, only one file is listed, Tours. Your list may contain more items. SASUSER may be the default storage location for your installation of SAS Enterprise Guide. So, if SAS Enterprise Guide has been used for purposes other than completing Tutorial A in this book, then chances are you will have several SAS data sets already in SASUSER. Click the **Tours** data set to select it.

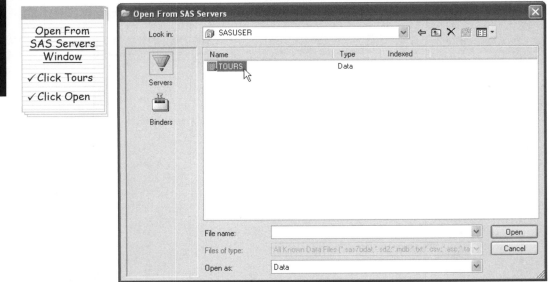

Click **Open** to open the Tours data set.

The Tours data set is now open and ready to use. Notice that there are icons for both the TourDates and the Tours data sets in the Project Explorer. Also, both data sets appear in the workspace. In this window, the Tours data set is in front, and the TourDates data set is behind it. To view the TourDates data set, click the **TourDates** tab in the workspace, or double-click the icon for the **TourDates** data set in the Project Explorer.

Opening a Microsoft Excel file   There are two ways you can use Microsoft Excel files in SAS Enterprise Guide. You can open the Microsoft Excel file and use it as is, or you can convert the Microsoft Excel file to a SAS data set. Both methods have advantages. Opening a Microsoft Excel file and leaving it as is is simple and if the data in the Microsoft Excel file change, SAS Enterprise Guide will automatically read the new data every time you access the spreadsheet (such as when you run a task or open a Data Grid). Converting a Microsoft Excel file to a SAS data set takes one more step, but you have more control over how the data are read into SAS Enterprise Guide, and SAS data sets are faster to process than Microsoft Excel files opened as is.

The following shows what the Microsoft Excel file Bookings.xls looks like opened in Microsoft Excel. Notice that the first row in the spreadsheet contains column headings.

	A	B	C	D	E	F	G	H	I	J
1	Office	CustomerID	Tour	Travelers	Deposit	Deposit_Date				
2	Portland	SL28	SH43	10	425	7/5/2006				
3	Portland	DE27	PS27	6	75	7/11/2006				
4	Portland	SL34	FJ12	4	200	7/19/2006				
5	Portland	DI33	SH43	4	150	7/23/2006				
6	Portland	BU12	SH43	2	75	7/23/2006				
7	Portland	DE31	FJ12	3	175	7/25/2006				
8	Portland	WI48	FJ12	2	100	7/26/2006				
9	Portland	NG17	PS27	5	65	7/26/2006				
10	Portland	RA28	PS27	2	30	7/28/2006				
11	Portland	ME11	PS27	2	30	7/28/2006				
12	Portland	GI08	SH43	8	300	7/31/2006				
13	Portland	HI15	SH43	4	150	7/31/2006				
14	Portland	MA09	SH43	2	75	7/31/2006				

Tutorial B

To open a Microsoft Excel file, select **File ▶ Open ▶ Data** from the menu bar.

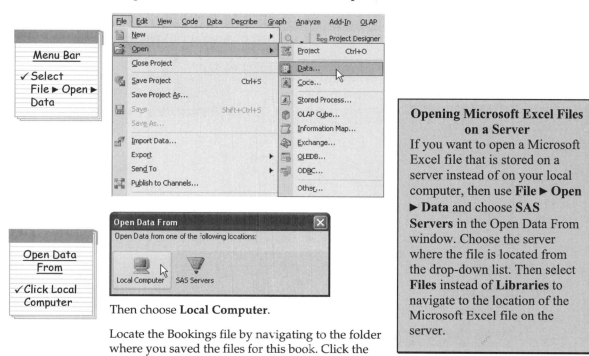

Menu Bar

✓ Select
File ▶ Open ▶
Data

Open Data From

✓ Click Local
Computer

Then choose **Local Computer**.

**Opening Microsoft Excel Files
on a Server**
If you want to open a Microsoft
Excel file that is stored on a
server instead of on your local
computer, then use **File ▶ Open
▶ Data** and choose **SAS
Servers** in the Open Data From
window. Choose the server
where the file is located from
the drop-down list. Then select
Files instead of **Libraries** to
navigate to the location of the
Microsoft Excel file on the
server.

Locate the Bookings file by navigating to the folder
where you saved the files for this book. Click the
Bookings.xls file.

**Open From
My Computer
Window**

✓ Navigate to
folder

✓ Click
Bookings

✓ Click Open

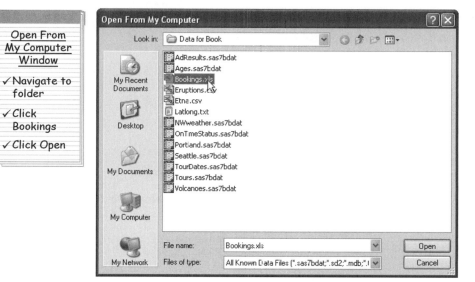

Click **Open** to open the Open Tables window.

All the worksheets belonging to the Microsoft Excel file are listed in this window with the $ suffix. If your Microsoft Excel file contains any named ranges, then they will also be listed, but will not have the $ suffix. Select the **Sheet1$** table. If you have more than one worksheet, you can select one or more worksheets to open at the same time.

Click **Open** and you will be presented with two options in the Open Data window. You can choose between opening the file as is, or converting the file to a SAS data set.

Choose to open the file as is by clicking the icon next to **Select this option if you want to view the file as is**.

When you open a Microsoft Excel file as is, SAS Enterprise Guide decides for you which rows and columns to read, and what formats to use for the columns. By default, SAS Enterprise Guide uses the first row as headings to label the columns.

The data from the Microsoft Excel file appear in the workspace, and a new icon is added to the Project Explorer for the Bookings file.

Dates and Times

SAS Enterprise Guide stores dates and times as numbers. Dates are the number of days since January 1, 1960, times are the number of seconds past midnight, and a datetime value is the number of seconds since midnight on January 1, 1960. Did you notice that the values for the Deposit_Date column now show a date and a time (you may need to widen your column to see the entire value)? That's because, by default, SAS Enterprise Guide 4 reads Excel dates as datetime values (earlier versions of SAS Enterprise Guide read Excel dates as date values). If a date, time, or datetime value does not have a display format associated with it, then SAS Enterprise Guide will simply display the number of days or seconds.

In many cases, it may be just fine to open a file as is, but if you open the file as a SAS data set, then you have more control over how SAS Enterprise Guide reads the data. To see the difference, open the Microsoft Excel file again, this time choosing to open it as a SAS data set. Select **File ▶ Open ▶ Data** from the menu bar, and then select **Local Computer**. Navigate to the folder that contains the **Bookings.xls** file, select it, and click **Open**. Select the **Sheet1$** table and click **Open**. This brings up the Open Data window.

Menu Bar

✓ Select File ▶ Open ▶ Data

Open Data From

✓ Click Local Computer

Open From My Computer Window

✓ Navigate to folder
✓ Click Bookings
✓ Click Open

Open Tables Window

✓ Select Sheet1$
✓ Click Open

Open Data Window

✓ Click SAS data set icon

Data Exists

✓ Click OK

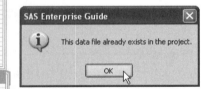

Open Data

Options for Opening File "Bookings.xls"
Select one of the following two ways of opening the selected file.

Select this option if you want to view the file as is.

For data files, the data formats will be automatically chosen for you. The data formats may not be correct if you want to perform analysis against the file opened in this way.

Select this option if you want to open the file as a SAS data set.

You may go through Import Data task multiple times, once for each file or sheet you selected, to specify data formats. The result will be one or more SAS data sets, suitable as data input for further analysis.

☐ Do not show this dialog again - always open file as is.

Cancel

This time, choose to open the file as a SAS data set by clicking the icon next to **Select this option if you want to open the file as a SAS data set**. Because you have already opened the Bookings Excel file in this project, SAS Enterprise Guide lets you know in case you mistakenly opened the same file twice. In this case it is exactly what you want to do.

SAS Enterprise Guide

ⓘ This data file already exists in the project.

OK

Click **OK** to open the Import Data window.

There are several options in the Import Data task that affect how files are read into SAS Enterprise Guide. To see how the options affect your file, you can make changes in the Import Data window, run the task, and then view the results, or you can preview the results in the Preview Window before running the task. The Preview Window can be very helpful, especially if the file you are reading is large and takes a long time to process.

Import Data Window

✓ Click Preview window box

Open the Preview Window by clicking the box next to **Preview window** in the lower-left corner of the Import Data window.

There are three parts to the Preview Window: the Code tab, the Results tab, and the Log tab. The Code and Log tabs are useful if you are familiar with the SAS programming language. The Code tab shows the actual SAS code that is being generated by the task, while the Log tab shows messages that result from running the task. The Results tab shows a sample of the results that the task would produce with the options selected. Click the **Results** tab to view the results. Notice that the column headings in the first row of the Excel file have become the column names. If your Excel file does not have column headings that you want to use as column names, then you can choose not to use them by unchecking **Specify line to use as column headings** in the Region to Import window.

	Office	CustomerID	Tour	Travelers	Deposit	Deposit_Date
1	Portland	SL28	SH43	10	425	05JUL2006:12:00:00 AM
2	Portland	DE27	PS27	6	75	11JUL2006:12:00:00 AM
3	Portland	SL34	FJ12	4	200	19JUL2006:12:00:00 AM
4	Portland	DI33	SH43	4	150	23JUL2006:12:00:00 AM
5	Portland	BU12	SH43	2	75	23JUL2006:12:00:00 AM
6	Portland	DE31	FJ12	3	175	25JUL2006:12:00:00 AM
7	Portland	WI48	FJ12	2	100	26JUL2006:12:00:00 AM
8	Portland	NG17	PS27	5	65	26JUL2006:12:00:00 AM
9	Portland	RA28	PS27	2	30	28JUL2006:12:00:00 AM
10	Portland	ME11	PS27	2	30	28JUL2006:12:00:00 AM
11	Portland	GI08	SH43	8	300	31JUL2006:12:00:00 AM
12	Portland	HI15	SH43	4	150	31JUL2006:12:00:00 AM
13	Portland	MA09	SH43	2	75	31JUL2006:12:00:00 AM

Preview Window — Refresh Results — Code / Results / Log

Preview
Window

✓ Click Results
tab

Note that the Preview Window appears on top of the Import Data window and that you may need to move it to the side, or close it to view the entire Import Data window.

Line Numbers
When SAS Enterprise Guide imports Microsoft Excel files, it determines which rows and columns in your worksheet contain data. If your worksheet has titles or other entries that are not part of the data, SAS Enterprise Guide will ignore those rows and columns. So, when you specify which lines to read from the Microsoft Excel file, start counting from the line at which the data start.

Import Data Window

✓ Click Column Options

Now click **Column Options** in the selection pane on the left of the Import Data window. On the Column Options page, you can make changes to how individual columns are read and displayed. Select the **Deposit** column. The Deposit column has been assigned a type of Numeric and has no display or read-in formats. A display format changes how the values of the column are displayed but does not change how the values are stored in the SAS data set.

Import Data Window

✓ Click Deposit column

✓ Click button with three dots

Add a display format to the Deposit column by clicking the button with the three dots next to **Display format**. (If you do not see the button with the three dots, click the white box next to **Display format** to make the button appear.)

Read-in Formats
Read-in formats tell SAS Enterprise Guide how to interpret data in the column. SAS Enterprise Guide will make a choice about how to read the data in a column, but you may not like the results. Use read-in formats to tell SAS Enterprise Guide exactly how to interpret the data. For example, SAS Enterprise Guide uses a datetime read-in format to read dates in Excel files, producing SAS datetime values as a result. If you want date values instead, you could change the read-in format to a date (ANYDTDTE*w*. works for Excel files) instead. If you do this, just make sure the display format is also a date type or the values will not be displayed properly.

This opens the Display format window. There are several categories of display formats for numeric data. Select the **Currency** category, and then select the **DOLLARw.d** format. Notice that when you select a format, an example appears at the bottom of the window that shows what the value will look like using the selected format.

Display format
Window

✓ Click
   Currency

✓ Select
   DOLLARw.d

✓ Click OK

Click **OK** to assign the format to the Deposit column.

Attributes of Formats

For numeric formats you can specify the **Overall width** and the number of **Decimal places** to display in the **Attributes** area of the Display format window. The Overall width tells SAS Enterprise Guide how many spaces to allow for displaying the numbers. The width includes any commas, periods, or decimal places that are displayed with the number. The Decimal places tells how many decimal places to display; it does not change the number of decimal places that are stored with the number.

Now, the DOLLAR6.0 format appears next to Display format for the Deposit column.

Click the **Refresh Results** button in the Preview Window to show what the Deposit column looks like with the DOLLAR6.0 display format.

Preview
Window

✓ Click Refresh
Results

	Office	CustomerID	Tour	Travelers	Deposit	Deposit_Date
1	Portland	SL28	SH43	10	$425	05JUL2006:12:00:00 AM
2	Portland	DE27	PS27	6	$75	11JUL2006:12:00:00 AM
3	Portland	SL34	FJ12	4	$200	19JUL2006:12:00:00 AM
4	Portland	DI33	SH43	4	$150	23JUL2006:12:00:00 AM
5	Portland	BU12	SH43	2	$75	23JUL2006:12:00:00 AM
6	Portland	DE31	FJ12	3	$175	25JUL2006:12:00:00 AM
7	Portland	WI48	FJ12	2	$100	26JUL2006:12:00:00 AM
8	Portland	NG17	PS27	5	$65	26JUL2006:12:00:00 AM
9	Portland	RA28	PS27	2	$30	28JUL2006:12:00:00 AM
10	Portland	ME11	PS27	2	$30	28JUL2006:12:00:00 AM
11	Portland	GI08	SH43	8	$300	31JUL2006:12:00:00 AM
12	Portland	HI15	SH43	4	$150	31JUL2006:12:00:00 AM
13	Portland	MA09	SH43	2	$75	31JUL2006:12:00:00 AM

In addition to setting display formats, you can use Column Options to exclude particular columns. Click the **Office** column, and then select **No** from the drop-down list next to **Include in output**.

Click the **Refresh Results** button in the Preview Window to show that the Office column no longer appears in the results.

If you click **Run** now, SAS Enterprise Guide will import your data, place the SAS data set in the SASUSER library, and give it an arbitrary name starting with the letters IMPW. To control the name given to the data set and to determine the storage location, click **Results** in the selection pane on the left in the Import Data window. This opens the Results page.

Import Data Window

✓ Click Results

✓ Click Browse

To set the name and location of the SAS data set, click **Browse**. This opens the Save As window. Make sure that you are in the SASUSER library (or an alternate library if your SASUSER library is read-only), and type the name **Bookings** in the box next to **File name**.

Save As Window

✓ Verify SASUSER

✓ Type Bookings

✓ Click Save

Click **Save** to return to the Import Data window.

Notice that the Save location for the data now says SASUSER.BOOKINGS. This means that the data set will be saved in the SASUSER library and will be given the name Bookings.

Import Data Window
✓ Click Run

Click **Run** to create the Bookings data set.

Notice that an icon for the Bookings SAS data set (labeled SASUSER.BOOKINGS) appears in the Project Explorer. The Bookings SAS data set is derived from the Bookings Microsoft Excel file via the Import Data task. If changes are made to the Microsoft Excel file from which this SAS data set was created, then you would need to rerun the Import Data task for the changes to be reflected in the SAS data set. An easy way to rerun the task (if no changes to the task are necessary) is to right-click the task icon in the Project Explorer or Project Designer and select **Run Import Data**.

Project Explorer

✓ Click Project icon

Completing the tutorial To complete the tutorial, add a note to the project with a project description. Click the **Project** icon in the Project Explorer to make sure the note is associated with the project instead of a particular item in the project. Then select **File ▶ New ▶ Note** from the menu bar. Enter a brief description of the project in the Note window that appears in the workspace.

Menu Bar

✓ Select File ▶ New ▶ Note

Note

✓ Type descriptive text

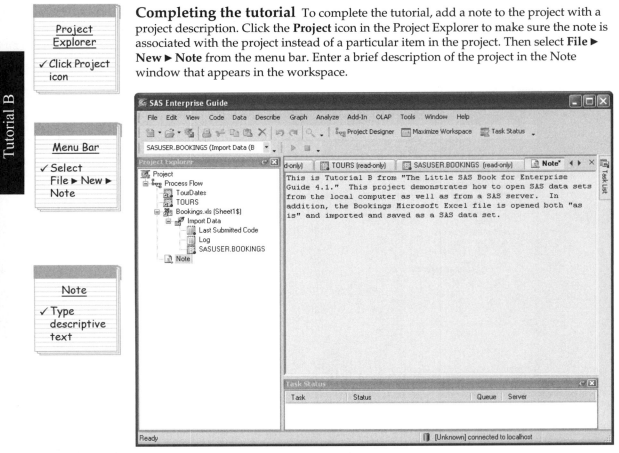

Menu Bar

✓ Save project

✓ Exit

Now save the project and exit SAS Enterprise Guide. Select **File ▶ Save Project** from the menu bar. Navigate to the location where you want to save the project, give the project the name **TutorialB**, and click **Save**. Select **File ▶ Exit** from the menu bar to close SAS Enterprise Guide.

Creating Reports

In this tutorial, you will create a simple report using the List Data task. Then using several of the options in the List Data task, you will make modifications to the report. Also, you will learn ways of formatting data that apply to most tasks. Here are the topics covered in this tutorial:

- Creating simple list reports

- Titles, footnotes, and labels

- Display formats

- User-defined formats

- Grouped reports

- Styles

Before beginning this tutorial This tutorial uses the Tours data set, which contains information about the volcano tours offered by the Fire and Ice Tours company. The Tours data set is created as part of Tutorial A. If you did not complete Tutorial A, see Appendix A for the data and instructions for downloading the Tours data set.

Starting SAS Enterprise Guide Start SAS Enterprise Guide by either double-clicking the **SAS Enterprise Guide 4** icon on your desktop, or selecting **SAS Enterprise Guide 4** from the Windows **Start** menu. Starting SAS Enterprise Guide brings up the SAS Enterprise Guide windows in the background, with the Welcome window in the foreground. The Welcome window allows you to choose between opening an existing project or starting a new project. Click **New Project**.

Desktop

✓Double-click SAS Enterprise Guide 4 icon

Welcome Window

✓Click New Project

Tutorial C

Welcome to SAS Enterprise Guide

Select one of these options to get started:

Open a project
- TutorialB.egp
- TutorialA.egp
- Volcanoes.egp
- SalesQ1.egp
- Flights.egp
- More projects ...

New
- New Project
- New SAS Program
- New Data

Assistance
- Tutorial: Getting Started with SAS Enterprise Guide

☐ Don't show this window again

This opens an empty SAS Enterprise Guide window.

Opening the Tours data set Open the Tours data set created in Tutorial A by selecting **File ▶ Open ▶ Data** from the menu bar, choosing **SAS Servers**, and navigating to the **SASUSER** library. If you are unsure about how to open the Tours data set, see Tutorial B. To make more room to see the data and the reports that you will be generating, close the Task Status window located at the bottom of the SAS Enterprise Guide window by clicking the × in the upper-right corner of the Task Status window. If you want to reopen the Task Status window later, select **View ▶ Task Status** from the menu bar.

Menu Bar

✓ Select File ▶ Open ▶ Data

✓ Choose SAS Servers

✓ Open Tours data set

Task Status Window

✓ Click X to close

Pushpins

Did you notice the symbol next to the × that looks like a pushpin? If you click the pushpin, SAS Enterprise Guide will reduce that window to a tab along the edge of the SAS Enterprise Guide application. Then, when you move the cursor over the tab, the window will expand. When you move the cursor out of the window, it will be reduced to a tab again. To unpin a window, click the sideways pushpin icon.

After you open the Tours data set and close the Task Status window, your screen should look like the following.

Creating a simple report　To produce a price list of all the tours offered by the Fire and Ice Tours company, use the List Data task. Select **Describe ▶ List Data** from the menu bar.

This opens the List Data window. Before doing anything else, you need to assign variables to task roles. For a price list, all the variables in the data set should be listed, so assign all the variables to the **List variables** role. You can drag each variable separately, or you can highlight all the variables, and then drag the group to the List variables role. The order of the variables under List variables will be the order that the variables will appear in the report. To change the order, click and drag the variables up or down the list, or highlight the variable and use the up or down arrow buttons under the **Task Roles** box.

List Data
Window

✓ Drag
variables to
List variables
role

✓ Click Run

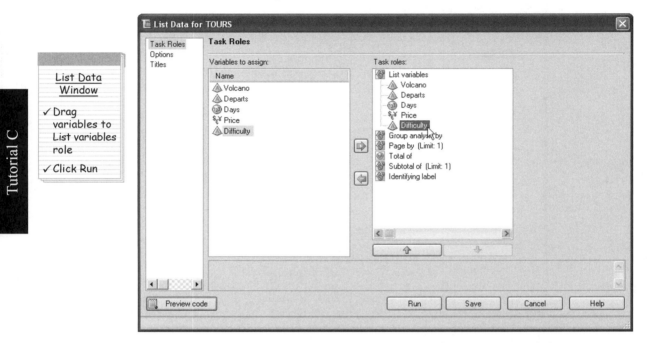

When you have all the variables under List variables in the proper order, click **Run**.

This produces a list of all the data in the Tours data set with some simple formatting. The report appears in the workspace of the SAS Enterprise Guide window and, by default, the report will be in HTML format.

§sas. | Enterprise Guide.

The Power to Know.

Report Listing

Row number	Volcano	Departs	Days	Price	Difficulty
1	Etna	Catania	7	$1,025	m
2	Fuji	Tokyo	2	$195	c
3	Kenya	Nairobi	6	$780	m
4	Kilauea	Hilo	1	$45	e
5	Kilimanjaro	Nairobi	9	$1,260	c
6	Krakatau	Jakarta	7	$850	e
7	Poas	San Jose	1	$50	e
8	Reventador	Quito	4	$525	m
9	St. Helens	Portland	2	$157	e
10	Vesuvius	Rome	6	$950	e

Generated by the SAS System (Local, XP_PRO) on 31MAR2006 at 11:59 AM

Don't like HTML?

HTML is the default type of output that SAS Enterprise Guide produces when you run a task that generates a report. If you don't like HTML, you can choose PDF, RTF, or SAS Report (see section 10.5 for details on this output type) instead—or all four at once. To choose the type of output, select **Tools ▶ Options** from the menu bar. Then select the **Results General** group of options and place a check mark next to the types of output you want to produce. Changes you make in the Options window affect all future SAS Enterprise Guide sessions. You can also change the output type for a particular task by right-clicking the task icon and selecting **Properties**. Then select the result format on the **Results** page of the Properties window.

Changing titles and footnotes The report contains all the information needed for the price list, but it could use some improvements. There are many parts of this simple listing that can be changed to meet specific needs. The first change to be made is to edit the title and footnote for the report. To change the titles and footnotes, reopen the List Data task by right-clicking the icon for the task in the Project Explorer or the Project Designer and selecting **Open**.

Click **Titles** in the list of options in the selection pane on the left of the List Data window. You can make changes to both the titles and the footnotes from this window. When you click **Report Titles** in the box labeled **Section**, the current title is displayed in the box on the right side of the window. SAS Enterprise Guide has default text it will use for your report for both titles and footnotes. To change the title for your report, uncheck the box to the left of **Use default text**. Now you can edit the default text that SAS Enterprise Guide supplied. Delete the default text and replace it with **Fire and Ice Tours** on one line, followed by **Price List** on the second line. This produces a two-line title with both lines centered at the top of the report.

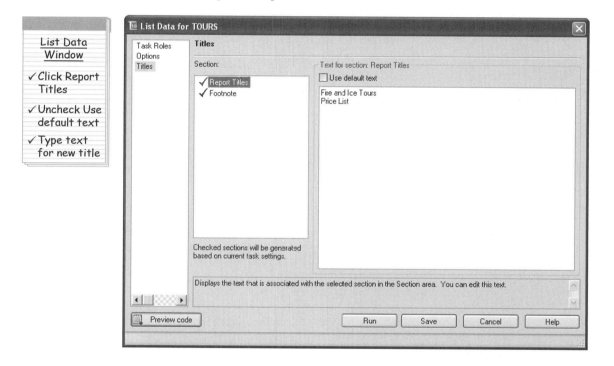

To make changes to the footnote, click **Footnote** in the box labeled **Section**.

List Data
Window

✓Click
Footnote

Why does the default footnote text look so odd?

If you take a close look at the default text for the footnote, you will notice that it does not look much like the footnote that appears at the bottom of your reports. The default text contains calls to SAS macros (starting with **%**) and macro variables (starting with **&**). These calls generate the actual text for the footnote, and the text that is generated depends on the date and time the report was produced, and the name and type of SAS server that generated the report. You can change the default footnote text by selecting **Tools ▶ Options** from the menu bar and selecting the **Tasks General** page. Enter the desired text in the **Default footnote text for task output** box. Then all tasks run after this change will have the new footnote text, even if you open a new project.

Change the footnote the same way you changed the title. Uncheck **Use default text**. Then because no footnote is necessary for this report, simply delete the text that SAS Enterprise Guide supplied.

List Data
Window

✓ Uncheck Use
default text
✓ Delete text
✓ Click Run

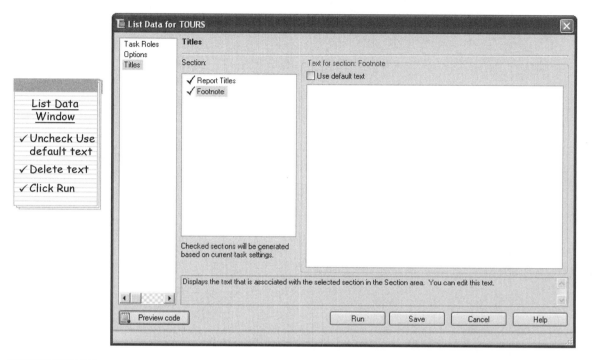

Click **Run** to produce a revised report with a new title and no footnote. When SAS Enterprise Guide asks if you want to replace the previous results, click **Yes**.

Replace
Results?

✓ Click Yes

Tutorial C

The following report will appear in the workspace. Note the new title and the lack of a footnote.

Ssas. | Enterprise Guide*

The Power to Know.

Fire and Ice Tours
Price List

Row number	Volcano	Departs	Days	Price	Difficulty
1	Etna	Catania	7	$1,025	m
2	Fuji	Tokyo	2	$195	c
3	Kenya	Nairobi	6	$780	m
4	Kilauea	Hilo	1	$45	e
5	Kilimanjaro	Nairobi	9	$1,260	c
6	Krakatau	Jakarta	7	$850	e
7	Poas	San Jose	1	$50	e
8	Reventador	Quito	4	$525	m
9	St. Helens	Portland	2	$157	e
10	Vesuvius	Rome	6	$950	e

Tutorial C

Project
Explorer

✓ Right-click
List Data
icon

✓ Select Open

Changing column labels and formatting values To make more changes to the report, open the List Data window again by right-clicking the **List Data** icon in the Project Explorer or Project Designer and selecting **Open**. Click **Options** in the selection pane on the left. By default, SAS Enterprise Guide will show the row number in the report and give it the label Row number. You can choose not to show the row numbers by unchecking **Print the row number**. For this report, keep the row numbers, but replace the label for the column heading with the word **Tour**.

List Data
Window

✓ Click Options

✓ Type **Tour**
in Column
heading box

List Data for TOURS

| Task Roles |
| Options |
| Titles |

Options

Rows to list

All rows

Heading direction
- ⦿ Default
- ○ Horizontal
- ○ Vertical

☑ Print the row number

Column heading: Tour

☑ Use variable labels as column headings

☐ Print number of rows

☐ Round values before summing

☑ Divide page into sections (no effect on HTML output)

Column width
- ⦿ Default
- ○ Full
- ○ Minimum
- ○ Uniform
- ○ Uniform by

☐ Split labels at:

Specify a label for the column that contains the row numbers. The default name of this column is Row number.

Preview code | Run | Save | Cancel | Help

Tutorial C

Now click **Task Roles** in the selection pane on the left. Each variable in the task has properties associated with it and you can make changes to the properties. Right-click the variable **Price** and select **Properties** from the pop-up menu.

This opens the Properties window for the variable Price.

There are six properties listed in the Properties window, two of which you can change in the window: the Label and the Format. Changes that you make in this window will only affect the results of the List Data task. The changes are not stored with the data. The Label is text that can be used for labeling the variable in the report. If the variable does not have a label, then SAS Enterprise Guide will use the variable's name as a label. Variable labels are useful when you want to use more than one word to describe a variable. Give the variable Price the label "Price USD" by typing **Price USD** in the box next to the word **Label**.

Properties
Window

✓ Type **Price USD**

✓ Click Change

Price Properties ☒

General

$ ¥ €   Price

Label: Price USD

Type: Currency

Length: 8

Format: DOLLAR10.   Change...

Informat:

Sorted: No

OK   Cancel

The current format for Price is the DOLLAR10. format. Click **Change** to change the format for Price. This opens the Formats window.

Tutorial C

Formats determine how values for the variable will be displayed. The format DOLLAR10. that was assigned to Price displays values with dollar signs and commas. The number at the end of the format name determines how many spaces to allow for the value, including any commas, decimal places, and dollar signs. If decimal places are to be displayed, then the number of decimals follows the period at the end of the format name. Because there is no number after the period in the DOLLAR10. format, no decimal places will be displayed. Change the number of decimal places displayed for Price to **2** in the box next to **Decimal places**. Notice that when you do this, an example of how values will be displayed using this format appears at the bottom of the Formats window.

Formats   [X]

Categories: Formats:

None	DOLLARw.d
Numeric	DOLLARXw.d
Currency	EURFRATSw.d
User Defined	EURFRBEFw.d
All	EURFRCHFw.d
	EURFRCZKw.d
	EURFRDEMw.d
	EURFRDKKw.d

Attributes

Overall width: |10| [↕]   Min: 2   Max: 32

Decimal places: |2| [↕]   Min: 0   Max: 9

Description

dollar sign, commas and decimal point

Example

Value: 12345.1

Output: $ 1 2 , 3 4 5 . 1 0

[OK]   [Cancel]

Click **OK** to close the Formats window.

(margin note:)

Tutorial C

Formats Window

✓ Change Decimal places to 2

✓ Click OK

Now Price has a label and will be formatted with the DOLLAR10.2 format.

Price Properties

General

$\$\,^¥_€$ Price

Label:	Price USD
Type:	Currency
Length:	8
Format:	DOLLAR10.2 Change...
Informat:	
Sorted:	No

OK   Cancel

Properties Window

✓Click OK

List Data Window

✓Click Run

Click **OK** to close the Properties window, and then click **Run** in the List Data window.

Select **Yes** when SAS Enterprise Guide asks if you want to replace the previous results.

Replace Results?

✓Click Yes

Tutorial C

The following report will appear in the workspace. Notice the column heading for the row number and the Price variable, and that the values for Price are now displayed in dollars and cents.

§sas. | Enterprise Guide

The Power to Know.

Fire and Ice Tours Price List

Tour	Volcano	Departs	Days	Price USD	Difficulty
1	Etna	Catania	7	$1,025.00	m
2	Fuji	Tokyo	2	$195.00	c
3	Kenya	Nairobi	6	$780.00	m
4	Kilauea	Hilo	1	$45.00	e
5	Kilimanjaro	Nairobi	9	$1,260.00	c
6	Krakatau	Jakarta	7	$850.00	e
7	Poas	San Jose	1	$50.00	e
8	Reventador	Quito	4	$525.00	m
9	St. Helens	Portland	2	$157.00	e
10	Vesuvius	Rome	6	$950.00	e

Defining your own formats Many different formats come with SAS Enterprise Guide, but sooner or later you will have a particular need for which there is no format defined. Fortunately, SAS Enterprise Guide provides a way for you to create your own formats. This type of format is called a user-defined format. For example, the variable **Difficulty** has coded values of c, e, and m. These single-letter values are too cryptic for a price list; it would be better to spell out the values: challenging, easy, and moderate. To create a user-defined format, select **Data ▶ Create Format** from the menu bar. This opens the Create Format window.

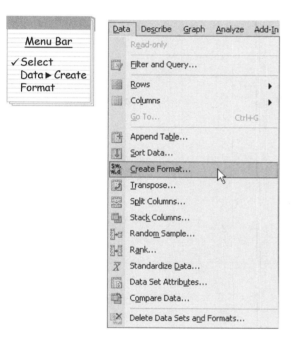

Menu Bar

✓ Select
Data ▶ Create
Format

Location for Storing Formats

Formats can be temporary or permanent. If they are temporary, they are stored in the WORK library and are automatically deleted when you exit SAS Enterprise Guide. If you have a temporary format in your project that you want to use, then you will need to rerun the Create Format task every time you open SAS Enterprise Guide. You can save a format permanently by choosing a library other than WORK. Then the format will not only be available for the project in which it was created, it will also be available for other projects. If you have access to more than one SAS server, store the format on the same server that is used for the task. To see which server is used for a task, place the cursor over the task icon in the Project Designer and the server name will be displayed in the pop-up window.

Tutorial C

Give the format a name by typing **Diff** in the box under **Format name**. Because this format will be used for a character variable, leave the **Format type** as **Character**.

Click **Define formats** in the selection pane on the left to set values and ranges for the format.

Format Names

Character format names must be 31 characters or fewer in length, while numeric format names must be 32 characters or fewer. For both format types, names must contain only letters, numerals, or underscores, and cannot start or end with a numeral.

There are instructions in this window telling you how to define your format.

Create Format

Options
Define formats

Define formats

How to define a format:

1. Select [New Label] to create a value Label.

2. Type the new label in the Label edit field.

3. Select [New Range] to enter values or ranges for the above label.

4. Enter each value or range as a separate item.

5. Repeat steps 1-4 for each value label.

An example format can be found in the Help.

Label | Ranges

New Label | Remove Label

Label definition
Label:

Type | Values

New Range | Remove Range

The selection pane enables you to choose different sets of options for the task.

Preview code

Run | Save | Cancel | Help

You must define a valid format.

First, click **New Label** and type **Easy** in the box under the word **Label**. As you type the label, the label appears in the Label and Ranges section of the window.

Create Format
Window

✓ Click New
Label

✓ Type **Easy**

Tutorial C

Next click **New Range**. In the box under **Values**, type the lowercase letter **e**, which is the value to be associated with the label Easy. When you enter text values, it is important that the case of the text matches the case of the actual value. Character formats are case-sensitive. As you type the value, it will appear in the Label and Ranges portion of the window, beside the label Easy.

Create Format Window

✓ Click New Range

✓ Type **e**

Multiple Ranges for a Label

You can enter more than one range for a label by clicking **New Range** again before adding another new label. For example, you might want the months SEP, OCT, and NOV to all be given the label Fall (or Spring if you are in the southern hemisphere). If you have a consecutive range of values that should all have the same label, then select **Range** from the **Type** drop-down list. For example, you might want the values 13 to 19 to all have the label Teenager. If your format is character and you use the Range type, then all values that fall alphabetically between the end points of the range will be included.

Now add labels for the other two values, m and c. Click **New Label** and type **Moderate** in the box under the word **Label**. Click **New Range** and in the box under **Values**, type the letter **m**. Next click **New Label** and type **Challenging** in the box under **Label**. Click **New Range** and type the letter **c** in the box under **Values**.

Tutorial C

Create Format Window

✓ Create labels for m and c ranges

✓ Click Run

When you have all the labels and ranges defined, click **Run**.

Click the **Project Designer** tab to view the Process Flow. An icon for the Create Format task appears in the Project Explorer and the Process Flow. If you need to make changes to the format, right-click the **Create Format** icon and select **Open**. Notice that the Create Format task is not connected to anything in the Process Flow, and nothing in the report changed.

Project
Explorer

✓ Right-click
List Data
icon

✓ Select Open

You created the format, but the format has not been associated with any variables yet. To associate the new format with the Difficulty variable, reopen the List Data window by right-clicking the **List Data** icon in the Project Explorer or Project Designer and selecting **Open**. Then right-click the **Difficulty** variable and select **Properties**.

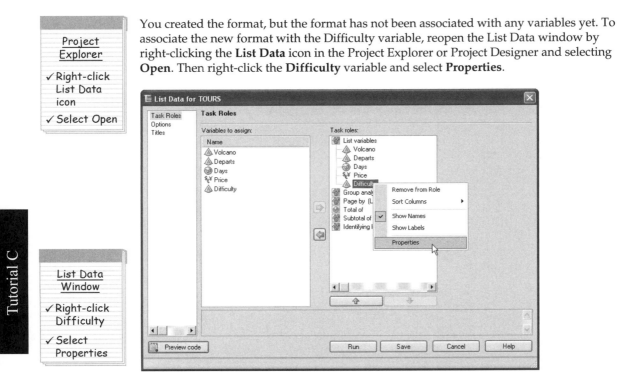

List Data
Window

✓ Right-click
Difficulty

✓ Select
Properties

This opens the Properties window for the variable Difficulty.

Properties
Window

✓ Click Change

Click **Change** to open the Formats window.

Formats Window

✓ Click User Defined

✓ Click $DIFF.

✓ Click OK

From the **Categories** list, select **User Defined**. Any formats defined in the current SAS Enterprise Guide session or any formats that have been saved in a permanent location appear in the list of formats. The format $DIFF. should be in your list and you may or may not have additional formats. The $ in the format name indicates that the format is for character values. Click the **$DIFF.** format.

Properties Window

✓ Click OK

List Data Window

✓ Click Run

Replace Results?

✓ Click Yes

Click **OK** to close the Formats window, and then click **OK** again in the Properties window to return to the List Data window. Click **Run** in the List Data window, and click **Yes** to replace the previous results.

The following report will appear in the workspace, showing the formatted values for the Difficulty variable.

Fire and Ice Tours
Price List

Tour	Volcano	Departs	Days	Price USD	Difficulty
1	Etna	Catania	7	$1,025.00	Moderate
2	Fuji	Tokyo	2	$195.00	Challenging
3	Kenya	Nairobi	6	$780.00	Moderate
4	Kilauea	Hilo	1	$45.00	Easy
5	Kilimanjaro	Nairobi	9	$1,260.00	Challenging
6	Krakatau	Jakarta	7	$850.00	Easy
7	Poas	San Jose	1	$50.00	Easy
8	Reventador	Quito	4	$525.00	Moderate
9	St. Helens	Portland	2	$157.00	Easy
10	Vesuvius	Rome	6	$950.00	Easy

Tutorial C

Creating a grouped report Now, instead of having the list of tours in alphabetical order, you will create a list with the tours grouped by difficulty. Right-click the **List Data** icon in the Project Explorer or Project Designer and select **Open** to reopen the List Data window. Now move **Difficulty** from the **List variables** role to the **Group analysis by** role.

Project Explorer

✓ Right-click List Data icon

✓ Select Open

List Data Window

✓ Move Difficulty to Group analysis by role

✓ Click Run

List Data for TOURS

Task Roles
Options
Titles

Task Roles

Variables to assign:

Name
⚠ Volcano
⚠ Departs
🕐 Days
$ Price
⚠ Difficulty

Task roles:

- List variables
  - ⚠ Volcano
  - ⚠ Departs
  - 🕐 Days
  - $ Price
- Group analysis by
  - ⚠ Difficulty
- Page by (Limit: 1)
- Total of
- Subtotal of (Limit: 1)
- Identifying label

Difficulty sort order:

Ascending

☑ Sort by variables

Preview code   Run   Save   Cancel   Help

Click **Run** and then click **Yes** to replace the previous results.

Replace Results?

✓ Click Yes

Tutorial C

This produces the following report where the tours are grouped by the three levels of difficulty.

§sas. | Enterprise Guide.

The Power to Know..

Fire and Ice Tours
Price List

Difficulty=Challenging

Tour	Volcano	Departs	Days	Price USD
1	Fuji	Tokyo	2	$195.00
2	Kilimanjaro	Nairobi	9	$1,260.00

Difficulty=Easy

Tour	Volcano	Departs	Days	Price USD
3	Kilauea	Hilo	1	$45.00
4	Krakatau	Jakarta	7	$850.00
5	Poas	San Jose	1	$50.00
6	St. Helens	Portland	2	$157.00
7	Vesuvius	Rome	6	$950.00

Difficulty=Moderate

Tour	Volcano	Departs	Days	Price USD
8	Etna	Catania	7	$1,025.00
9	Kenya	Nairobi	6	$780.00
10	Reventador	Quito	4	$525.00

Project
Explorer

✓ Right-click
List Data
icon

✓ Select Open

To make a more compact report, you can specify that you want to keep Difficulty as the Group analysis by variable, but also use it as the Identifying label. This still keeps the groupings, but will produce a report where all the tours are in one table. Right-click the **List Data** icon in the Project Explorer or Project Designer and select **Open** to reopen the List Data window. Drag **Difficulty** from the **Variables to assign** list on the left to the **Identifying label** role. Difficulty should now appear under both the Identifying label role and the Group analysis by role.

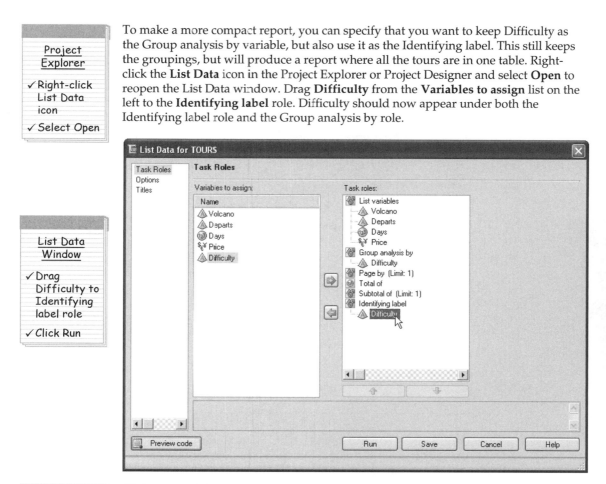

List Data
Window

✓ Drag
Difficulty to
Identifying
label role

✓ Click Run

Click **Run** and then click **Yes** to replace the previous results.

Replace
Results?

✓ Click Yes

Now the following report has the same information as the previous report, but all the information is in one table.

§sas. | Enterprise Guide.

The Power to Know.

Fire and Ice Tours
Price List

Difficulty	Volcano	Departs	Days	Price USD
Challenging	Fuji	Tokyo	2	$195.00
	Kilimanjaro	Nairobi	9	$1,260.00
Easy	Kilauea	Hilo	1	$45.00
	Krakatau	Jakarta	7	$850.00
	Poas	San Jose	1	$50.00
	St. Helens	Portland	2	$157.00
	Vesuvius	Rome	6	$950.00
Moderate	Etna	Catania	7	$1,025.00
	Kenya	Nairobi	6	$780.00
	Reventador	Quito	4	$525.00

Selecting a style for the report Every report that you produce in SAS Enterprise Guide has a style associated with it. All the reports that you have produced so far have been in HTML, and the default style for HTML results is EGDefault. The style of the report includes the color scheme, fonts, and the size and style of the font. The style can include an image, such as the one that appears at the top of the EGDefault style. This image includes the SAS logo and the SAS slogan "The Power to Know". You do not have to use the default style for your reports. SAS Enterprise Guide comes with many different styles for you to choose from, and if you can't find one that suits your needs, you can create your own.

To change the report style, right-click the **List Data** task icon in the Project Explorer or the Project Designer and select **Properties**.

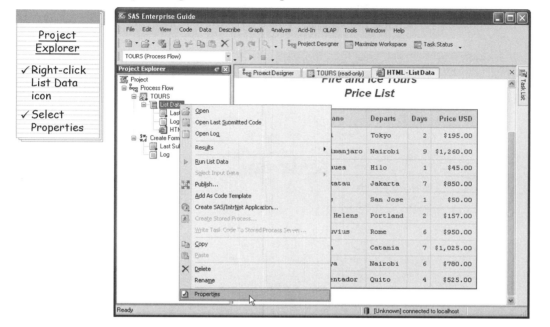

This opens the Properties window for the List Data task.

Click **Results** in the selection pane on the left to open the Results page.

In the Results page, check **Override the preferences set in Tools -> Options**. This allows you to choose the result formats for the task as well as the style associated with each result format. Make sure that the HTML result format is checked, and then select the **BarrettsBlue** style from the drop-down list next to **HTML**.

Click **OK**.

When you change the style in the Properties window, you won't see the new style until the next time you run the task. Since you don't need to make any changes to the task — you just want to see the report with the new style — you can re-run the task without opening it. Right-click the **List Data** icon in the Project Explorer or Project Designer and select **Run List Data**.

Project
Explorer

✓Right-click
List Data
icon

✓Select Run
List Data

When SAS Enterprise Guide asks if you want to replace previous results, click **Yes**.

Replace
Results?

✓Click Yes

Your report should look like the following, except that yours will be in shades of blue.

Fire and Ice Tours
Price List

Difficulty	Volcano	Departs	Days	Price USD
Challenging	Fuji	Tokyo	2	$195.00
	Kilimanjaro	Nairobi	9	$1,260.00
Easy	Kilauea	Hilo	1	$45.00
	Krakatau	Jakarta	7	$850.00
	Poas	San Jose	1	$50.00
	St. Helens	Portland	2	$157.00
	Vesuvius	Rome	6	$950.00
Moderate	Etna	Catania	7	$1,025.00
	Kenya	Nairobi	6	$780.00
	Reventador	Quito	4	$525.00

Changing the default style used for SAS Enterprise Guide

If you find a style that you want to use for all your SAS Enterprise Guide projects, you can set it to be the default. Select **Tools ▶ Options** from the menu bar. Click the **HTML** group of options, and select the desired style from the **Style** drop-down list. You can change the default styles for PDF, RTF, and SAS Report output types using this same method.

Completing the tutorial To complete the tutorial, add a note to the project with a project description. Click **Project** in the Project Explorer, and then select **File ▶ New ▶ Note** from the menu bar. Enter a brief description of the project in the Note window that appears in the workspace.

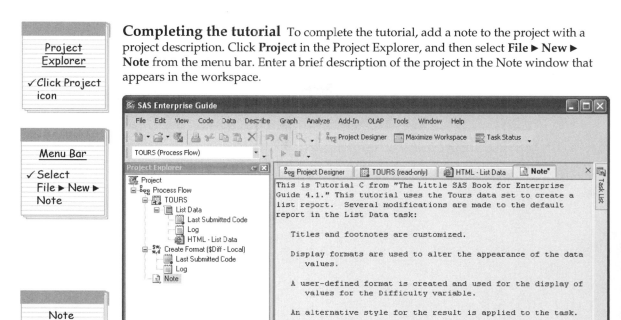

Now save the project and exit SAS Enterprise Guide. Select **File ▶ Save Project** from the menu bar. Navigate to the location where you want to save the project, give the project the name **TutorialC**, and click **Save**. Select **File ▶ Exit** from the menu bar to close SAS Enterprise Guide.

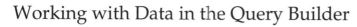

D▶ Working with Data in the Query Builder

Often the data sets you have are not exactly what you want. You may need to compute a new column based on existing columns, or you may need just part of the data set for your analysis. Using SAS Enterprise Guide, there are many ways in which you can manipulate your data. Here are the topics covered in this tutorial:

- Selecting columns

- Using the Expression Editor to create new columns

- Filtering rows

- Sorting data

Before beginning this tutorial This tutorial uses the Volcanoes SAS data table, which contains information about volcanoes around the world. The data and instructions for downloading the file can be found in Appendix A.

Starting SAS Enterprise Guide Start SAS Enterprise Guide by either double-clicking the **SAS Enterprise Guide 4** icon on your desktop, or selecting **SAS Enterprise Guide 4** from the Windows **Start** menu. Starting SAS Enterprise Guide brings up the SAS Enterprise Guide windows in the background, with the Welcome window in the foreground. The Welcome window allows you to choose between opening an existing project or starting a new project. Click **New Project**.

Desktop

✓ Double-click SAS Enterprise Guide 4 icon

Welcome Window

✓ Click New Project

Tutorial D

Welcome to SAS Enterprise Guide

Select one of these options to get started:

Open a project
- TutorialC.egp
- TutorialB.egp
- TutorialA.egp
- Volcanoes.egp
- SalesQ1.egp
- More projects ...

New
- New Project
- New SAS Program
- New Data

Assistance
- ? Tutorial: Getting Started with SAS Enterprise Guide

☐ Don't show this window again

This opens an empty SAS Enterprise Guide window. Because you may have opened, closed, or resized windows in a previous SAS Enterprise Guide session, your SAS Enterprise Guide window may look different. To reset all windows to their original state, select **Tools ▶ Options** from the menu bar and click **Reset Docking Windows**.

Opening the Volcanoes SAS data table

Open the Volcanoes SAS data table by selecting **File ▶ Open ▶ Data** from the menu bar. Choose **Local Computer**, and navigate to the location where you stored the Volcanoes file. If you are unsure about how to open the SAS data tables stored on your local computer, see Tutorial B. To make more room to see the data, close the Task Status window located at the bottom of the SAS Enterprise Guide window by clicking the × in the upper-right corner of the Task Status window.

Menu Bar
✓ Select File ▶ Open ▶ Data
✓ Choose Local Computer
✓ Open Volcanoes data table

SAS Enterprise Guide Window
✓ Close Task Status window

After you open the Volcanoes SAS data table and close the Task Status window, your screen should look like the following.

Opening the Query Builder The Query Builder is a powerful tool for data manipulation. In the Query Builder, you can filter and sort data, create new columns, and join tables. To open the Query Builder, make the Volcanoes data set active by clicking it in the Project Explorer, and then select **Data ▶ Filter and Query** from the menu bar. (You can also open the Query Builder by right-clicking the **Volcanoes** data icon in the Project Explorer or Project Designer and selecting **Filter and Query**.)

Project
Explorer

✓ Click
Volcanoes
data icon

Menu Bar

✓ Select
Data ▶ Filter
and Query

The Query Builder window has three tabs for different tasks: Select Data, Filter Data, and Sort Data. In addition, there are several buttons including Add Tables, Delete, Join, Computed Columns, and Parameters. So, you can see there is a lot going on in the Query Builder. The name of the active data table appears in the list on the left, along with all the columns in the data table. The Query Builder opens with the Select Data tab on top and no columns selected.

Selecting columns   To select columns for your query, click the column name in the box on the left and drag it over to the box on the right under the Select Data tab. For this query, select all the columns except Type. You can select them individually, or you can select the whole group at once by clicking Volcano, and then holding down the shift key and clicking Activity. Drag the selected columns to the Select Data tab.

Query Builder Window

✓ Click Volcano

✓ Drag to Select Data tab

✓ Repeat for Country, Region, Height, and Activity

✓ Click Preview

At this point, you could click **Run** to see the results of this simple query. However, the Query Builder has a Preview window that allows you to see the results, or a sample of the results, without having to exit the Query Builder. To open the Preview window, click **Preview** at the top of the Query Builder window.

Alternate Methods for Selecting Columns

In addition to clicking and dragging columns, you can double-click column names to select them. After you double-click it, the column name will appear on the Select Data tab. To select all columns from a data table, click and drag the table name to the Select Data tab.

In addition to showing a preview of the query results, the Preview window also has a tab for the code that the Query Builder generates as well as a tab for the SAS log for the query. The log contains notes about how the query ran as well as any warnings or errors. The code and log may be of particular interest to people familiar with SAS programming. Normally you do not need to concern yourself with the Code and Log tabs.

Preview Window
✓Click Results

Click the **Results** tab to see a preview of the query results. Notice that all the columns from the Volcanoes data table are in the result except the Type column.

You can choose to leave the Preview window open at this time, or you can close it by clicking the × in the top right corner of the window. To reopen the Preview window, simply click **Preview** again in the Query Builder window.

Tutorial D

Creating a new column Sometimes you want to create a new column based on values in an existing column. For example, the Height column in the Volcanoes data table contains the height of each volcano in meters. You can create a new column that uses the values in the Height column to compute a new column containing the height in feet.

To create a new column which contains the height in feet, click **Computed Columns**.

This opens the Computed Columns window where you can create new columns as well as edit, delete, or rename existing computed columns.

Computed
Columns Window

✓ **Click New**

✓ **Select Build Expression**

To create a new computed column, click **New** and choose **Build Expression** from the drop-down list. This opens the Advanced Expression Editor.

What if I choose Recode a Column?

When you create a new column by building an expression, then all values in the new column will be generated using that expression. But what if you want to take an existing column and change only some of the values, or treat a group of values differently from others? For example, the Activity column has some missing values. You could recode those missing values as "Unknown." Or, say you want to group the volcanoes according to height: short, medium, and tall? To do these types of operations, you would choose **Recode a Column**.

The empty box at the top of the Advanced Expression Editor is where the expression is displayed. If you know the expression you want to use, you can type it directly in the box. But, if you are unsure exactly what the expression should look like, SAS Enterprise Guide gives you some help. Under the box are several mathematical symbols you can add to the expression. Below the symbols are the Data and Functions tabs. The Data tab lists data tables and columns in your query, and the Functions tab lists all the functions available for use in your expression.

What are functions?

If you find you can't build the expression you want using the simple mathematical operators, then chances are SAS Enterprise Guide has a function that can help. Functions take a value and turn it into another related value. For example, the ABS function takes a number and returns the absolute value of that number. There are hundreds of functions available to you in several categories including: arithmetic, character, mathematical, date, and time.

On the left side of the Data tab, the box labeled Available variables shows all the sources of data available to you for this expression: both the table names and the columns contained in the tables. The items listed in the Variable values box always correspond to the highlighted item in the Available variables box. So, if the item highlighted is a data table, as shown here, all the columns will appear in the Variable values box. (Remember variables are the same thing as columns.) If you highlight a column name in the Available variables box, then all the values of the column will appear in the Variable values box.

To calculate the volcano's height in feet, you need to multiply the Height column by 3.25. Click **Height** in the **Variable values** box on the right, and then click **Add to Expression**. When you do this, the full name of the Height column is inserted into the Expression text box at the top of the window. The full name, Volcanoes.Height, includes the source for the column, which is the Volcanoes data table.

Advanced
Expression
Editor

✓ Click Height in Variable values box

✓ Click Add to Expression

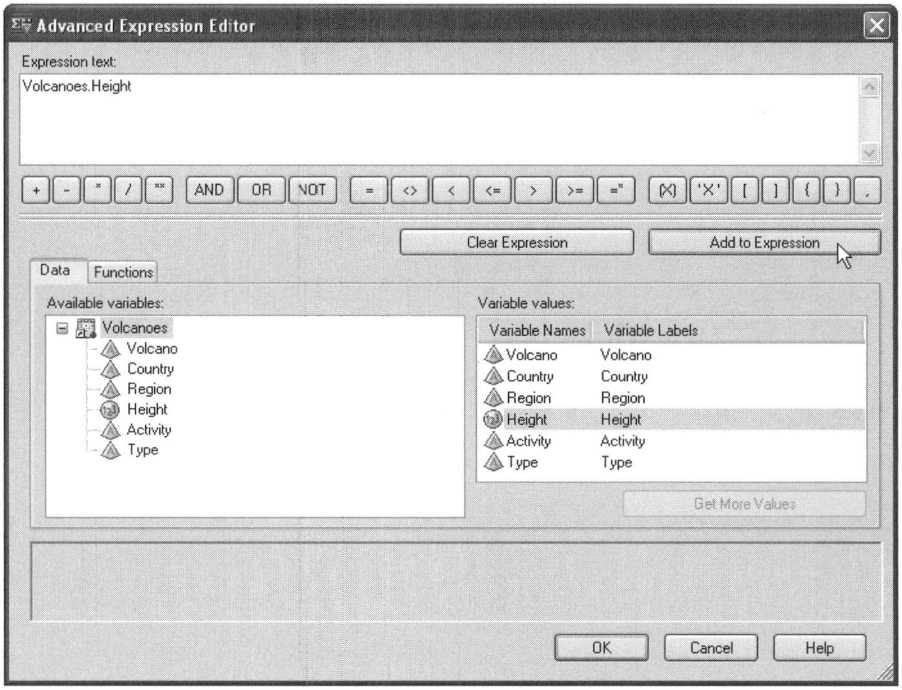

Now click the multiplication button 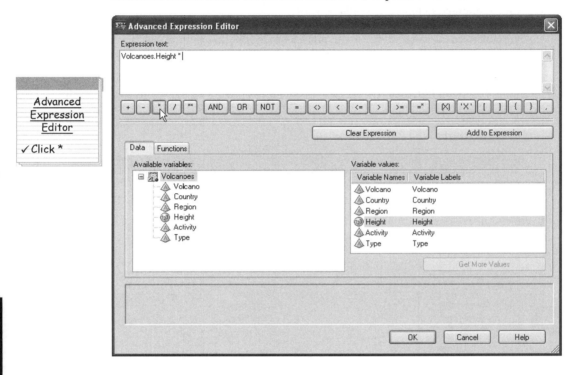 under the Expression text box. Notice that the asterisk is inserted after the column name in the Expression text box.

Advanced
Expression
Editor

✓ Click *

To complete the expression, type the number **3.25** in the Expression text box after the asterisk.

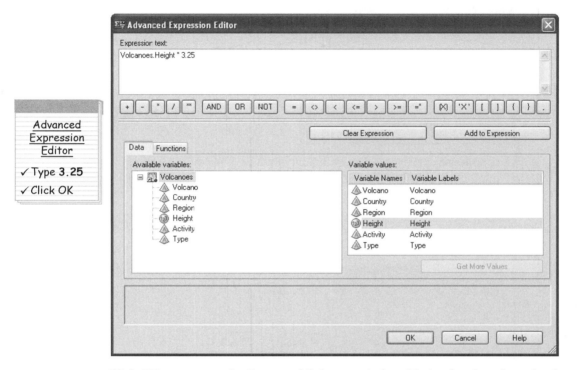

Advanced
Expression
Editor

✓ Type **3.25**

✓ Click OK

Click **OK** to return to the Computed Columns window. Notice that the column has been given the name Calculation1. You could leave this as is, but it is better to give the column a meaningful name.

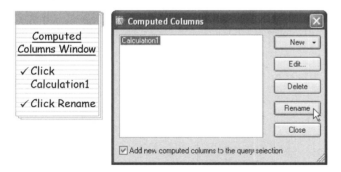

Computed
Columns Window

✓ Click
  Calculation1

✓ Click Rename

Click **Calculation1**, then click **Rename**.

Rename the column HeightInFeet.

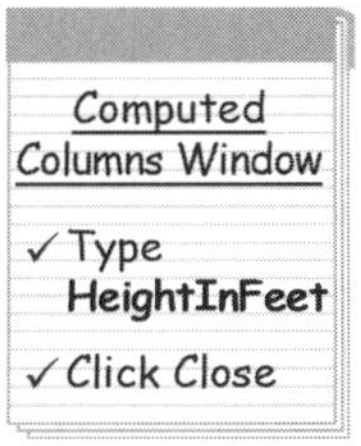

Computed Columns Window

✓ Type **HeightInFeet**

✓ Click Close

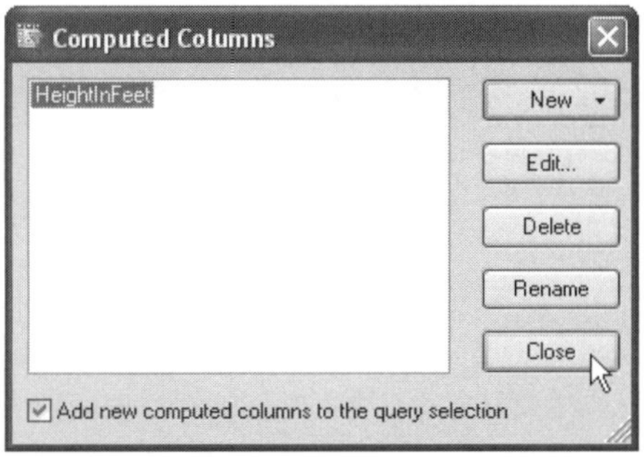

Click **Close** to return to the Query Builder window. Notice that the new column, HeightInFeet, appears in the list of columns in the Select Data tab as well as under Computed Columns in the list on the left.

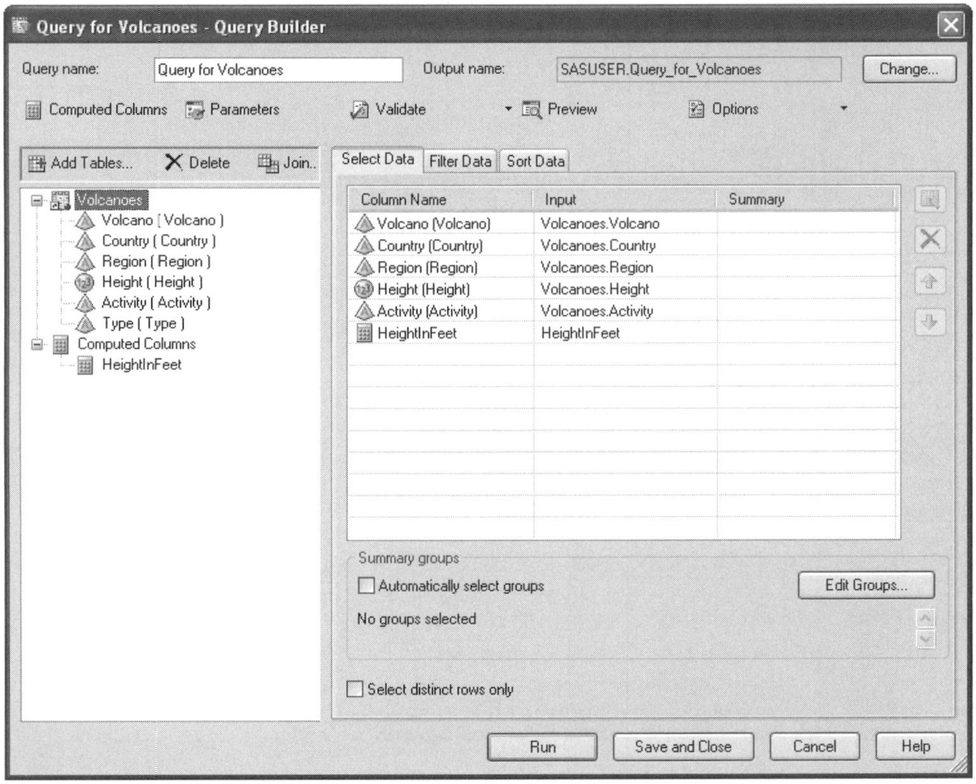

Click **Refresh Results** in the Preview window to preview the result of the query with the newly computed column.

VOLCANO	COUNTRY	REGION	HEIGHT	ACTIVITY	HEIGHTINFEET
Altar	Ecuador	SA	5321	Extinct	17293.25
Arthur's Seat	UK	Eu	251	Extinct	815.75
Barren Island	India	As	354	Active	1150.5
Elbrus	Russia	Eu	5633	Extinct	18307.25
Erebus		An	3794	Active	12330.5
Etna	Italy	Eu	3350	Active	10887.5
Fuji	Japan	As	3776	Active	12272

The values for HeightInFeet are correct, but they could use some formatting. It is not necessary to show fractions of feet, and it would be nice to have commas in the numbers to make them easier to read.

Preview Window

✓ Click Refresh Results

To change the display format of the HeightInFeet column, open the Properties window for the column. Click **HeightInFeet** in the list of column names in the Select Data tab.

Then, click the Properties icon on the right side of the Query Builder window. The HeightInFeet column currently has no format associated with it.

Click **Change**.

This brings up a window where you can select a format for the column. Select the **COMMAw.d** format from the **Numeric** group. The default width of 6 is fine for this column because the heights of all the volcanoes are at most 6 digits including the comma. Make sure that the number of decimal places is set to **0**.

Formats Window

✓ Click Numeric

✓ Click COMMAw.d

✓ Click OK

Click **OK** to return to the Properties window.

Now the format for the column, COMMA6.0, appears in the Format area of the Properties window.

Properties for HeightInFeet

Alias:	HeightInFeet
Label:	
Format:	COMMA6.0 [Change...]
Expression:	Volcanoes.Height * 3.25
	[Edit...]
Input column:	
Input table:	

[OK] [Cancel] [Help]

**Properties
Window**

✓ Click OK

Click **OK**, then click **Refresh Results** in the Preview window to see the result of setting the format for the HeightInFeet column.

Preview

[Refresh Results]

Code	Results	Log

VOLCANO	COUNTRY	REGION	HEIGHT	ACTIVITY	HEIGHTINFEET
Altar	Ecuador	SA	5321	Extinct	17,293
Arthur's Seat	UK	Eu	251	Extinct	816
Barren Island	India	As	354	Active	1,151
Elbrus	Russia	Eu	5633	Extinct	18,307
Erebus		An	3794	Active	12,331
Etna	Italy	Eu	3350	Active	10,888
Fuji	Japan	As	3776	Active	12,272

Preview Window

✓ Click Refresh
Results

Ordering and removing columns Now that you have the HeightInFeet column, you no longer need the Height column. To remove it from the query, first select it by clicking **Height** in the list of columns in the Select Data tab.

Then click the Delete button ⊠ on the right side of the Query Builder window. It is important to note that deleting the column from the query result does not delete the column from the original data table.

In the results, the columns will be listed in the order that they appear in the Query Builder. You can change the order in the Select Data tab. Click the new column

HeightInFeet and then click the up arrow icon on the right side of the Query Builder window until the column is listed just above the column Activity.

Click **Refresh Results** in the Preview window. Notice that HeightInFeet now appears before Activity and the Height column is no longer in the result.

VOLCANO	COUNTRY	REGION	HEIGHTINFEET	ACTIVITY
Altar	Ecuador	SA	17,293	Extinct
Arthur's Seat	UK	Eu	816	Extinct
Barren Island	India	As	1,151	Active
Elbrus	Russia	Eu	18,307	Extinct
Erebus		An	12,331	Active
Etna	Italy	Eu	10,888	Active
Fuji	Japan	As	12,373	Active

Tutorial D

Filtering data To filter, or create subsets of your data, use the Filter Data tab of the Query Builder. Click the **Filter Data** tab to bring it forward. To create a filter, drag the column that you want to use as the basis of your filter over to the Filter Data tab. For this example, use the HeightInFeet column to select only the volcanoes with heights over 12,000 feet.

Click the **HeightInFeet** column on the left side of the window and drag it over to the **Filter Data** tab.

As soon as you release the mouse button, the Edit Filter window will open. The column for the Edit Filter is automatically set to HeightInFeet, and the Operator is initially set to Equal to.

Because you want all volcanoes with a height over 12,000 feet, you need to select a different operator. Click the down arrow to the right of **Operator** to display the drop-down list of operators. Select the **Greater than** operator. Next, type the value **12000** in the box labeled **Value**. When you enter numeric values, do not enter any commas or dollar signs.

Edit Filter Window

✓ From Operator list, select Greater than

✓ In Value box, type **12000**

✓ Click OK

Edit Filter

Column: HeightInFeet

Operator: Greater than

Value: 12000

Filter definition

HeightInFeet > 12000

☐ Enclose values in quotes

☑ Use formatted dates

[OK]   [Cancel]   [Help]

Click **OK** to close the Edit Filter window and return to the Query Builder.

Tutorial D

Now the Filter Data tab shows the filter you created.

Click **Refresh Results** in the Preview window and see that now all the volcanoes listed are over 12,000 feet.

Preview Window

✓ Click Refresh Results

VOLCANO	COUNTRY	REGION	HEIGHTINFEET	ACTIVITY
Altar	Ecuador	SA	17,293	Extinct
Elbrus	Russia	Eu	18,307	Extinct
Erebus		An	12,331	Active
Fuji	Japan	As	12,272	Active
Illimani	Bolivia	SA	20,989	Extinct
Kenya	Kenya	Af	16,897	Extinct
Kilimanjaro	Tanzania	Af	19,450	

You can create more complicated filters by adding more conditions to your filter. Add the Activity column to the filter to create a data set having only volcanoes that are over 12,000 feet and are active.

> **Query Builder Window**
>
> ✓ Click Activity
>
> ✓ Drag to Filter Data tab

Query for Volcanoes - Query Builder

| Query name: | Query for Volcanoes | Output name: | SASUSER.Query_for_Volcanoes | Change... |

Computed Columns   Parameters   Validate   ▾   Preview   Options   ▾

Add Tables...   Delete   Join. | Select Data | Filter Data | Sort Data |

Filter the raw data

HeightInFeet > 12000

- Volcanoes
  - Volcano (Volcano)
  - Country (Country)
  - Region (Region)
  - Height (Height)
  - Activity (Activity)
  - Type (Type)
- Computed Columns
  - HeightInFeet

WHERE CALCULATED HeightInFeet > 12000

Combine Filters...

Filter the summarized data

(Optional) Drop a column here to filter the summarized data.

Combine Filters...

| Run | Save and Close | Cancel | Help |

Click the column **Activity** and drag it over to the **Filter Data** tab.

When you release the mouse button, the Edit Filter window will open. This time, there is no need to change the operator because you want all volcanoes where the column Activity equals Active. At this point, you could type the value **Active** (paying attention to the casing of the letters) in the **Value** box to complete the filter. However, SAS Enterprise Guide gives you the option of choosing from a list of values for the column. Choosing the value from a list has the advantage that you can't accidentally misspell the value or use lowercase where it should be uppercase. But use caution if your data sets are very large, as it may take a long time to generate the list of values.

Edit Filter Window

✓ Click down arrow next to Value box

Click the down arrow next the **Value** box to open a new window where you can view the values for the Activity column.

Values Tab

✓ Click Get Values

Click **Get Values** to load all possible values for Activity.

Values Tab

✓ Click Active

The Activity column has three values: Active, Extinct, and a null or missing value. Click **Active** in the list of values. The window will close, and the value will appear in the Value box of the Edit Filter window.

Edit Filter
Window

✓ Click OK

Click **OK** to complete the filter and return to the Query Builder.

AND or OR?

In this example, you want all rows that meet two conditions: volcanoes over 12,000 feet and active. Because the volcano must pass both conditions, you use the AND operator (the default). But suppose you are not such a thrill seeker, and you would rather just look at volcanoes that are either extinct or less than 8,000 feet. The volcano has to meet only one of the conditions to be included. For this type of filter, use the OR operator. To change the operator from AND to OR, click the **Combine Filters** button in the Filter Data tab to open the Filter Combination window. Then click the word **AND**, and choose **Change to OR**.

Notice that a new condition has been added to the filter in the Filter Data tab.

If you wanted to change either filter condition, you could simply double-click the condition to reopen the Edit Filter window, or highlight the filter in the Filter Data tab and click the Edit Filter icon [icon] on the right side of the window. Now click **Refresh Results** in the Preview window and notice that all the volcanoes listed are over 12,000 feet and are active.

Preview Window

✓ Click Refresh Results

Sorting the data rows There is one last change to make to this query. The data came sorted alphabetically by the name of the volcano. For this list, it would be better to sort the volcanoes by height, showing the tallest volcano at the top of the list. To sort the data, click the **Sort Data** tab.

Query Builder
Window

✓ Click Sort
Data tab

✓ Click
HeightInFeet

✓ Drag to Sort
Data tab

Click and drag the **HeightInFeet** column over to the **Sort Data** tab.

Initially, the sort direction for the column is set to Ascending. To change the sort direction so that the tallest volcano will be first, click **Ascending** and select **Descending** from the drop-down list.

Sort Data Tab

✓ In Sort
  Direction box,
  click
  Ascending

✓ Select
  Descending

Click **Refresh Results** in the Preview window and notice how the volcanoes are now sorted according to height, with the tallest volcano listed first.

Preview Window

✓ Click Refresh Results

Preview					☒
Refresh Results					

Code | **Results** | Log

VOLCANO	COUNTRY	REGION	HEIGHTINFEET	ACTIVITY
Sabancaya	Peru	SA	19,422	Active
Popocatepetl	Mexico	NA	17,635	Active
Kliuchevskoi	Russia	As	15,714	Active
Mauna Loa	USA	AF	13,553	Active
Erebus		An	12,331	Active
Fuji	Japan	As	12,272	Active

Query Builder Window

✓ Click Run

You have no more changes to make to this query, so click **Run** in the Query Builder window to run the query and close the window.

When you run the query, SAS Enterprise Guide will create a SAS data table by default. The new data table is given a name starting with Query, and is stored in a default location. The data are displayed in the workspace. This data table is now ready for any other tasks that you may want to perform.

If you want to make any changes to the query, right-click the query icon in the Project Explorer or Project Designer, and select **Open** to reopen the Query Builder.

Specifying the name and location for the results of a query

In this example, you are creating a SAS data table as a result of the query. If you want, you can create a report instead. Also, you may want to specify a meaningful name for your results, or store the results in a different location. You can change all these settings in the Result Options window. Open the Result Options window by clicking **Options** in the Query Builder window, and selecting **Options for This Query**.

Completing the tutorial To complete the tutorial, add a note documenting the project. Click **Project** in the Project Explorer, and then select **File ▶ New ▶ Note** from the menu bar. Type comments about the project into the Note window in the workspace.

Project Explorer

✓ Click Project icon

Menu Bar

✓ Select File ▶ New ▶ Note

Note

✓ Type descriptive text

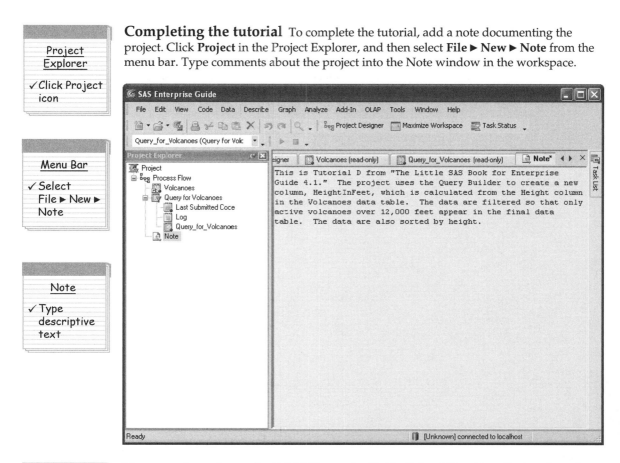

Menu Bar

✓ Save project

✓ Exit

Now save the project and exit SAS Enterprise Guide. Select **File ▶ Save Project** from the menu bar. Navigate to the location where you want to save the project, give the project the name **TutorialD**, and click **Save**. Then select **File ▶ Exit** from the menu bar to close SAS Enterprise Guide.

Tutorial D

Tutorial D

Joining Two Data Files Together

Often the data you need for a particular analysis are in more than one table. To perform the analysis, you need to join tables together. In this tutorial, you will be joining together two data tables, and then manipulating the data after the join. Here are the topics covered in this tutorial:

- Joining two tables together

- Filtering data after the join

- Modifying the type of join

Before beginning this tutorial This tutorial uses the Volcanoes SAS data table, which contains information about volcanoes around the world. This tutorial also uses the Tours data table, which contains information about the volcano tours offered by the Fire and Ice Tours company. The data and instructions for downloading the data tables can be found in Appendix A.

The Fire and Ice Tours company wants to produce a list of tours for all volcanoes in Europe. The problem is that the Tours data set does not contain information about the region of the volcano. The region of the volcano is contained in the Volcanoes file. So, for the company to produce the desired list, the Volcanoes data and the Tours data must be joined together.

Starting SAS Enterprise Guide Start SAS Enterprise Guide by either double-clicking the **SAS Enterprise Guide 4** icon on your desktop, or selecting **SAS Enterprise Guide 4** from the Windows Start menu. Starting SAS Enterprise Guide brings up the SAS Enterprise Guide windows in the background, with the Welcome window in the foreground. The Welcome window allows you to choose between opening an existing project or starting a new project. Click **New Project**.

Desktop

✓ Double-click SAS Enterprise Guide 4 icon

Welcome Window

✓ Click New Project

This opens an empty SAS Enterprise Guide window. Because you may have opened, closed, or resized windows in a previous SAS Enterprise Guide session, your SAS Enterprise Guide window may look different. To reset all windows to their original state, select **Tools ▶ Options** from the menu bar and click **Reset Docking Windows**.

Opening the two data files to be joined Open the Volcanoes and Tours data tables by selecting **File ▶ Open ▶ Data** from the menu bar, choosing **Local Computer**, and navigating to the location where you saved the data for this book. You can select both tables at once by clicking one table, holding the ctrl key down and then clicking the other table. Click **Open**. (If you created the Tours data table in Tutorial A and saved it in the SASUSER library, you may prefer to open your version instead by selecting **File ▶ Open ▶ Data** from the menu bar, and clicking **SAS Servers**.) If you are unsure about how to open SAS data tables, see Tutorial B.

Menu Bar

✓ Select File ▶
 Open ▶ Data

✓ Click Local
 Computer

✓ Open
 Volcanoes
 and Tours

Tutorial E

After opening both files, your SAS Enterprise Guide window should look like the following.

Here is what the Tours data table looks like. The Tours data contain information about the tour: the name of the volcano, the city where the tour departs, the number of days the tour lasts, the price, and a difficulty rating for the tour. The region of the volcano is not part of the Tours data set, so it would not be possible, using this data set alone, to produce a list of volcano tours in Europe.

	Volcano	Departs	Days	Price	Difficulty
1	Etna	Catania	7	$1,025	m
2	Fuji	Tokyo	2	$195	c
3	Kenya	Nairobi	6	$780	m
4	Kilauea	Hilo	1	$45	e
5	Kilimanjaro	Nairobi	9	$1,260	c
6	Krakatau	Jakarta	7	$850	e
7	Poas	San Jose	1	$50	e
8	Reventador	Quito	4	$525	m
9	St. Helens	Portland	2	$157	e
10	Vesuvius	Rome	6	$950	e

Here is a partial listing of the Volcanoes file. These data include the country and region of the volcano, as well as the height, activity, and type of volcano. While the two data tables contain different information, they do have one column in common, the name of the volcano. To join data tables together in a meaningful way, they must have at least one column that appears in both data tables. The common column does not have to have the same name in both data tables, but it must contain the same information and have the same possible values.

	Volcano	Country	Region	Height	Activity	Type
1	Altar	Ecuador	SA	5321	Extinct	Stratovolcano
2	Arthur's Seat	UK	Eu	251	Extinct	
3	Barren Island	India	As	354	Active	Stratovolcano
4	Elbrus	Russia	Eu	5633	Extinct	Stratovolcano
5	Erebus		An	3794	Active	Stratovolcano
6	Etna	Italy	Eu	3350	Active	Stratovolcano
7	Fuji	Japan	As	3776	Active	Stratovolcano
8	Garibaldi	Canada	NA	2678		Stratovolcano
9	Grimsvotn	Iceland	Eu	1725	Active	Caldera
10	Illimani	Bolivia	SA	6458	Extinct	Stratovolcano
11	Kenya	Kenya	Af	5199	Extinct	
12	Kilauea	USA	AP	1222	Active	Shield

Tabs: Project Designer | Tours (read-only) | **Volcanoes (read-only)**

Joining tables You join tables using the Query Builder. In the Query Builder, in addition to joining tables, you can filter and sort data, and create new columns. To open the Query Builder, make the Volcanoes data set active by clicking it in the Project Explorer or Project Designer, and then select **Data ▶ Filter and Query** from the menu bar. Or, you can right-click the **Volcanoes** data icon and select **Filter and Query**.

Project Explorer

✓ Click Volcanoes data icon

Menu Bar

✓ Select Data ▶ Filter and Query

Data menu:

- Read-only
- Filter and Query...
- Rows ▶
- Columns ▶
- Go To...   Ctrl+G
- Append Table...
- Sort Data...
- Create Format...
- Transpose...
- Split Columns...
- Stack Columns...
- Random Sample...
- Rank...
- Standardize Data...
- Data Set Attributes...
- Compare Data...
- Delete Data Sets and Formats...

Tutorial E

The Query Builder window has three tabs for different tasks: Select Data, Filter Data, and Sort Data. In addition, in the box on the left side of the Query Builder, you can choose from these tasks: Add Tables, Delete, and Join tables. The name of the active data set appears in the list on the left, along with all the columns in the data set.

Even though both the Tours and the Volcanoes data tables are in the project, only the Volcanoes table is in the current query. In order to join the two tables together, you must add the Tours table to the query. Click **Add Tables**.

SAS Enterprise Guide will ask you where to find the data you want to add.

**Open Data
Window**

✓ Click Project

Both data tables are open in your project, so click **Project**. This opens the Add From Project window.

Add From Project

Name	Type	Source	Container	Date Modified
Tours	Input Data		Process Flow	3/7/2006 7:39:40 PM
Volcanoes	Input Data		Process Flow	3/7/2006 7:40:29 PM

OK   Cancel

**Add From
Project Window**

✓ Select Tours

✓ Click OK

Add the Tours table to the query by clicking **Tours**, and then clicking **OK**.

When you add data tables to the query, SAS Enterprise Guide checks to see if the data tables have a matching column. If there is a matching column, SAS Enterprise Guide will automatically use that column for the join. Because the Volcanoes data table and the Tours data table both have a column named Volcano, SAS Enterprise Guide will use it to find matching rows.

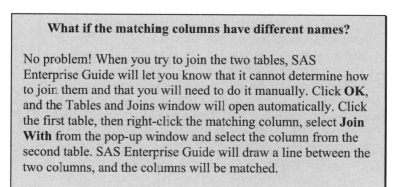

It's not obvious from the Query Builder window that SAS Enterprise Guide has selected matching columns for the join. To see what the join looks like, click **Join** to open the Tables and Joins window.

What if the matching columns have different names?

No problem! When you try to join the two tables, SAS Enterprise Guide will let you know that it cannot determine how to join them and that you will need to do it manually. Click **OK**, and the Tables and Joins window will open automatically. Click the first table, then right-click the matching column, select **Join With** from the pop-up window and select the column from the second table. SAS Enterprise Guide will draw a line between the two columns, and the columns will be matched.

In the Tables and Joins window, both tables are visible along with the columns in the tables. Notice the line drawn between the Volcano column in the Volcanoes table and the Volcano column in the Tours table. This shows how the tables will be joined. Also, there is a diagram on the line which shows the type of join. In this case only rows found in both tables will be included in the resulting table.

Tables and
Joins Window

✓ Click Close

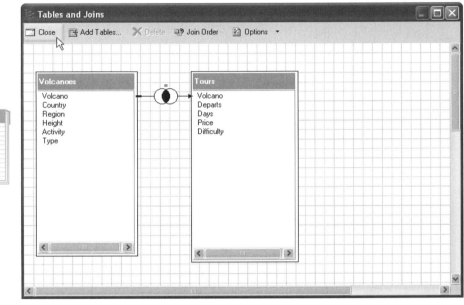

Click **Close** to close the Tables and Joins window and return to the Query Builder.

Tables with More Than One Matching Column

It is possible to join data tables that have more than one matching column. For example, you may have year and month columns in both data tables, and you want to match the tables based on the values of both columns. SAS Enterprise Guide does not handle this type of join automatically, but it is easy to do it yourself. SAS Enterprise Guide will match the first pair of columns for you. To match the second pair, open the Tables and Joins window by clicking **Join** in the Query Builder window. Create another join by clicking the first table, then right-clicking the column name, choosing **Join With** in the pop-up window, and selecting the column from the second table.

Before you can run the query, you must select the columns you want in the result. To select columns, click the column in the box on the left and drag it over to the Select Data tab. For this query, select the **Volcano**, **Country**, **Region**, **Height**, and **Activity** columns from the Volcanoes table. Then select the **Departs**, **Days**, and **Price** columns from the Tours table.

Query Builder Window

✓ Drag columns to Select Data tab

✓ Click Preview

To get an idea of what the results of the join will look like, click the **Preview** button near the top of the Query Builder window. Then click the **Results** tab in the Preview window.

Preview Window

✓ Click Results tab

When you preview the results of a query, usually you will not see the complete result. The Preview window is designed to show you what to expect from your join without having to complete the entire join. With these small data tables, it wouldn't take long to perform the join, so the Preview window does not save you much time. But if you have very large data tables, it can take a long time for SAS Enterprise Guide to complete the join, so the Preview window allows you to make sure the query is correct before starting the join.

Notice that the volcanoes from the Volcanoes data table have been matched with the corresponding row from the Tours data table.

VOLCANO	COUNTRY	REGION	HEIGHT	ACTIVITY	DEPARTS	DAYS	PRICE
Etna	Italy	Eu	3350	Active	Catania	7	$1,025
Fuji	Japan	As	3776	Active	Tokyo	2	$195
Kenya	Kenya	Af	5199	Extinct	Nairobi	6	$780
Kilauea	USA	AP	1222	Active	Hilo	1	$45

What if one table has repeated values of the common column?

In this example, each table has only one entry for each volcano, so there is a one-to-one match between the tables. But suppose the Tours table had two tours for one volcano. Then the values for the columns in the Volcanoes data table will be repeated for these two tours for the same volcano.

Click **Run** in the Query Builder window to run the query and see the complete result. Notice that only the rows that appear in both data tables are part of the result. This is the default type of join for SAS Enterprise Guide. Because all the volcanoes in the Tours data table also appear in the Volcanoes data table, all the tours are represented here. However, some volcanoes do not have matching tours, and so they are not included in the result.

	Volcano	Country	Region	Height	Activity	Departs	Days	Price
1	Etna	Italy	Eu	3350	Active	Catania	7	$1,025
2	Fuji	Japan	As	3776	Active	Tokyo	2	$195
3	Kenya	Kenya	Af	5199	Extinct	Nairobi	6	$780
4	Kilauea	USA	AP	1222	Active	Hilo	1	$45
5	Kilimanjaro	Tanzania	Af	5895		Nairobi	9	$1,260
6	Krakatau	Indonesia	As	813	Active	Jakarta	7	$850
7	Poas	Costa Rica	NA	2708	Active	San Jose	1	$50
8	Reventador	Ecuador	SA	3562	Active	Quito	4	$525
9	St. Helens	USA	NA	2549	Active	Portland	2	$157
10	Vesuvius	Italy	Eu	1281	Active	Rome	6	$950

Click the **Project Designer** tab to view the Process Flow for the project. It is not obvious from the Project Explorer that the query uses both the Tours and the Volcanoes tables, but in the Process Flow it is easy to see that both tables contribute to the query. By default, results of queries are given an arbitrary name starting with the letters QUERY and are stored in a default location.

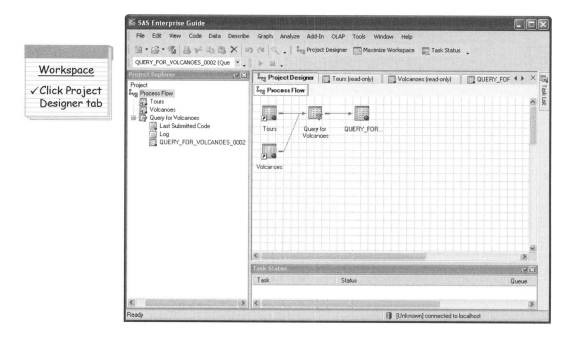

Filtering the data Now that the Tours data table and the Volcanoes data table have been joined together, it is possible to create a data table of tours for volcanoes in Europe. To do this, you create a filter as part of the same query that you used to join the data tables.

Right-click the query icon in the Project Explorer or Project Designer and select **Open** to reopen the query. The Query Builder window opens with the Select Data tab on top. Click **Filter Data** to open the Filter Data tab. The Region column in the Volcanoes data table gives the general location of the volcano: North America, South America, Europe, Asia, Australia Pacific, Africa, or Antarctica.

Project
Explorer

✓ Right-click
Query icon

✓ Select Open

Query Builder
Window

✓ Click Filter
Data tab

✓ Drag Region

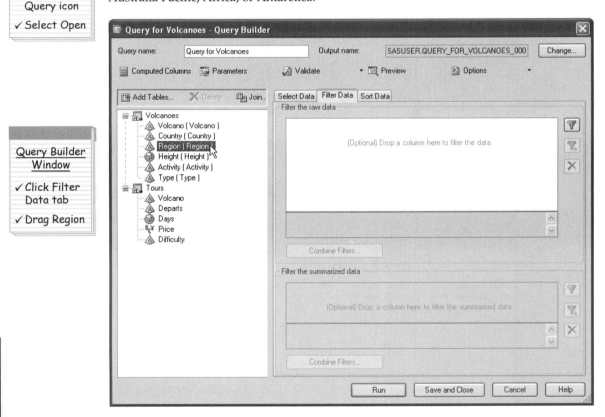

To create a filter based on the Region column, click **Region** in the list on the left, and drag it to the box under the **Filter Data** tab.

Tutorial E

This automatically opens the Edit Filter window with Region from the Volcanoes data table listed as the Column.

Edit Filter

Column:	Volcanoes.Region
Operator:	Equal to
Value:	

Filter definition

Volcanoes.Region = "

☑ Enclose values in quotes
☑ Use formatted dates

OK   Cancel   Help

Click the down arrow next to the **Value** box to open a window where you can display all possible values for Region.

Values	Columns	Parameters
Value		Formatted Value

Get Values

Click **Get Values**.

Values	Columns	Parameters
Value	Formatted Value
Af	Af
An	An
AP	AP
As	As
Eu	Eu
NA	NA
SA	SA

More Values

The values for Region are coded, and the code for Europe is Eu. Click the value **Eu** in the list of column values.

When you do this, the window will close and Eu will appear in the box next to Value in the Edit Filter window.

Edit Filter Window

✓Click OK

Click **OK** to complete the filter condition and return to the Query Builder.

Choosing an Operator

In this example, you want all the volcanoes whose region equals Eu, so you use the Equal to operator. The Equal to operator is the default operator, so you didn't need to change it. But you can change it if you want. To choose a different operator, click the down arrow in the **Operator** box, and choose from the list. For example, if you wanted all volcanoes in North and South America, you would use the **In a list of values** operator. The **In a list of values** operator selects all rows in a table whose values for the column are contained in the specified list.

Now the filter appears in the Filter Data tab of the Query Builder window.

Click **Run** to see the results of this change to the query.

When SAS Enterprise Guide asks if you would like to replace the results from the previous run, click **Yes**.

Look at the resulting data table and note that only the tours of volcanoes in Europe appear in the data table.

	Volcano	Country	Region	Height	Activity	Departs	Days	Price
1	Etna	Italy	Eu	3350	Active	Catania	7	$1,025
2	Vesuvius	Italy	Eu	1281	Active	Rome	6	$950

Modifying the type of join Suppose the Fire and Ice Tours company wants to expand the number of tours that it offers in Europe. It wants to include in the list all the volcanoes in Europe, not just volcanoes that currently have tours. In SAS Enterprise Guide the default action of a join is to include only the rows that appear in both tables. To change this default action, you need to modify the join.

Right-click the query icon in the Project Explorer or Project Designer and select **Open** to reopen the query.

> **Project Explorer**
>
> ✓ Right-click Query icon
>
> ✓ Select Open

Query for Volcanoes - Query Builder

Query name: `Query for Volcanoes`   Output name: `SASUSER.QUERY_FOR_VOLCANOES_000`   Change...

Computed Columns   Parameters   Validate   ▾   Preview   Options   ▾

Add Tables...   ✕ Delete   Join | Select Data | Filter Data | Sort Data

Volcanoes
- Volcano (Volcano)
- Country (Country)
- Region (Region)
- Height (Height)
- Activity (Activity)
- Type (Type)

Tours
- Volcano
- Departs
- Days
- Price
- Difficulty

Column Name	Input	Summary
Volcano (Volcano)	Volcanoes.Volcano	
Country (Country)	Volcanoes.Country	
Region (Region)	Volcanoes.Region	
Height (Height)	Volcanoes.Height	
Activity (Activity)	Volcanoes.Activity	
Departs	Tours.Departs	
Days	Tours.Days	
Price	Tours.Price	

Summary groups

☐ Automatically select groups   Edit Groups...

No groups selected

☐ Select distinct rows only

Run   Save and Close   Cancel   Help

> **Query Builder Window**
>
> ✓ Click Join

Click **Join** to open the Tables and Joins window.

In the Tables and Joins window, notice the diagram with the equals sign (=) above it on the line connecting the two tables. Right-click this join indicator to display a list of options. Then select **Modify Join** from the pop-up list.

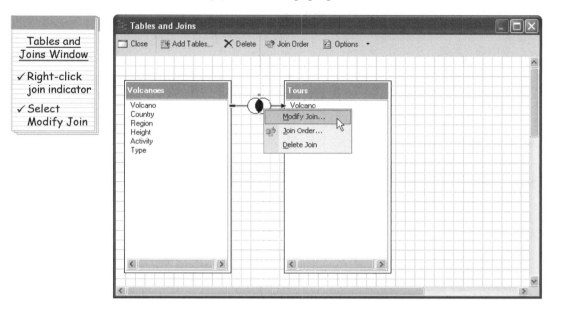

This opens the Modify Join window. There are four types of joins: matching rows only (the default), all rows from the left table, all rows from the right table, and all rows from both tables. Each type of join has its own diagram using overlapping circles. For the Matching rows only type of join, only the intersection of the two circles is filled with black.

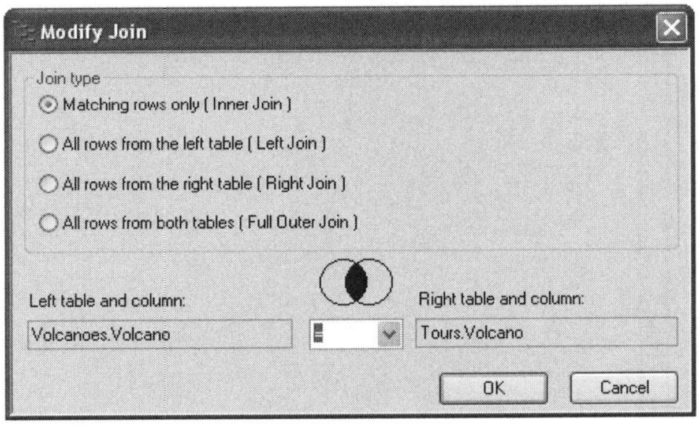

For this join, you want all the rows from each data table, even if there is no match. So, click the button next to **All rows from both tables.**

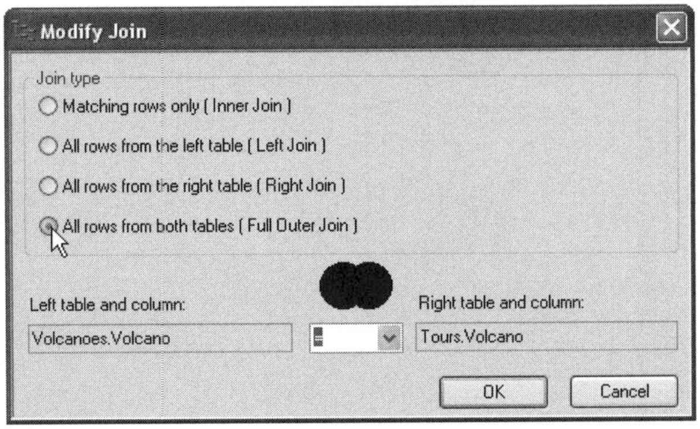

Notice that the join symbol has changed so that now both circles are completely filled. Click **OK**.

Modify Join
Window

✓ Select All
rows from
both

✓ Click OK

Tutorial E

The join indicator in the Tables and Joins window has changed to reflect the type of join you just selected.

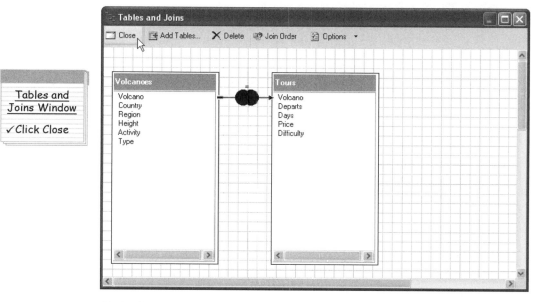

Tables and Joins Window

✓ Click **Close**

Click **Close** to return to the Query Builder window.

Query Builder Window

✓ Click **Run**

Click **Run** to see the results.

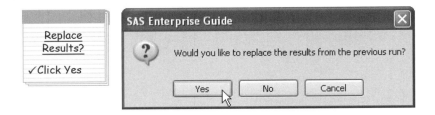

Replace
Results?

✓ Click Yes

Click **Yes**, indicating you would like to replace the previous results.

Look at the resulting data table in the workspace. Now the data include all the volcanoes in Europe, even if they don't have tours. Notice that all the columns from the Tours data table (Departs, Days, and Price) have missing values for the volcanoes for which there are no tours. Because all the volcanoes in the Tours data table also appear in the Volcanoes data table, all the columns from the Volcanoes data table have values.

	Volcano	Country	Region	Height	Activity	Departs	Days	Price
1	Arthur's Seat	UK	Eu	251	Extinct		.	.
2	Elbrus	Russia	Eu	5633	Extinct		.	.
3	Etna	Italy	Eu	3350	Active	Catania	7	$1,025
4	Grimsvotn	Iceland	Eu	1725	Active		.	.
5	Puy de Dome	France	Eu	1464	Extinct		.	.
6	Santorini	Greece	Eu	367	Active		.	.
7	Vesuvius	Italy	Eu	1281	Active	Rome	6	$950

Tutorial E

Completing the tutorial To complete the tutorial, add a note describing the project. Click **Project** in the Project Explorer. Then select **File ▶ New ▶ Note** from the menu bar. Enter a brief description of the project in the Note window in the workspace.

Project
Explorer

✓Click Project
icon

Menu Bar

✓Select
File ▶ New ▶
Note

Note

✓Type
descriptive
text

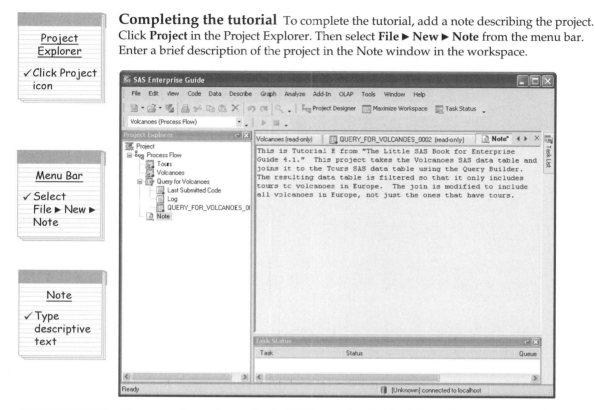

Menu Bar

✓Save project

✓Exit

Now save the project and exit SAS Enterprise Guide. Select **File ▶ Save Project** from the menu bar. Navigate to the location where you want to save the project, give the project the name **TutorialE**, and click **Save**. Then select **File ▶ Exit** from the menu bar to close SAS Enterprise Guide.

Tutorial E

REFERENCE SECTION

CHAPTER 1

SAS Enterprise Guide Basics

1.1 ▶ SAS Enterprise Guide Windows

SAS Enterprise Guide has many windows. You can customize the appearance of SAS Enterprise Guide—closing some windows, opening others, and rearranging them all—until it looks just the way you want. Then SAS Enterprise Guide will save those changes so the next time you open it, everything will be just where you left it.

Here is SAS Enterprise Guide with its windows in their default positions.

Docking windows Some of the windows in SAS Enterprise Guide are docking windows. Docking windows appear around the edges of the application. You can undock a window by clicking its title bar and dragging it. To dock it, drag it to an edge of the application until it changes shape, and then release it. Some docking windows are open by default while others are closed. If a docking window is closed, you can open it using the **View** menu. Here are the basic docking windows:

 Project Explorer The Project Explorer displays the items in a project in a hierarchical tree diagram. This window is open by default.

 Task Status The Task Status window displays notes about any tasks that are currently running either locally or on a remote server. This window is open by default.

Task List The Task List window is also open by default, but it is minimized and appears as a tab on the right side. To expand the Task List window, move your cursor over the Task List tab. This window lists all available tasks. You can view tasks sorted by category or in alphabetical order by clicking the tabs at the top of the window. To open a task, select it from the menu bar, or click its name in the Task List window.

 Server List The Server List window lists available SAS servers, and the files and SAS data libraries on those servers. This window is closed by default.

 Binder List The Binder List window lists available binders and their contents, and is closed by default. See section 2.2 for more information about binders.

 SAS Folders The SAS Folders window lists any stored processes available to you, and is closed by default.

 What is The What is window displays information describing menus and tools, and is closed by default. See section 1.14 for more information about using the What is window.

 Project Log The Project Log window displays a single log for your entire project, and is closed by default.

Pinning windows You can minimize docking windows by clicking the pushpin icon in the upper-right corner. SAS Enterprise Guide will reduce that window to a tab along the edge of the SAS Enterprise Guide application. Then, when you move the cursor over the tab, the window will expand. When you move the cursor out of the window, it will be reduced to a tab again. To unpin a window, click the sideways pushpin icon .

Workspace The workspace is not itself a window, but it is very important. This is where the Project Designer and document windows appear. The workspace is always there and cannot be closed. However, you can open and close individual items inside the workspace.

Project Designer The Project Designer displays the items in a project and their relationship using a process flow diagram. You can display only one project at a time in the Project Designer, but you can create as many process flow diagrams as you wish inside a single project. You can turn the Project Designer into a docking window by right-clicking its tab and selecting **Dockable** from the pop-up menu. To reverse this, right-click the Project Designer's title bar and uncheck **Dockable**.

Document windows The document windows display your data, results, code, logs, and notes. There is a different type of icon for every kind of document. This icon represents a SAS data table.

Restoring windows Once you have rearranged your windows, you may decide you want them back where they started. To restore them to their original locations, just select **Tools ▶ Options** from the menu bar. Then, in the General page of the Options window, click **Reset Docking Windows**.

1.2 Projects

In SAS Enterprise Guide, all the work you do is organized into projects. A project is a collection of related data, tasks, results, code, logs, and notes. Projects help you by keeping track of everything, even if your data are scattered in many directories or on more than one computer. That way, when you come back to an old project six months or a year later, you won't be left wondering which data sets you used or what reports you ran.

You can have as many projects as you like, and you can use a data set over and over again in different projects, so there is a lot of flexibility. However, you can have only one project open at a time. Also, if you share a project file with someone else, that person must have access to your data files and any other items you reference.

To create a new project, select **File ▶ New ▶ Project** from the menu bar. To open an existing project, select **File ▶ Open ▶ Project** and navigate to your project.

Project Explorer and Project Designer The Project Explorer displays projects in a hierarchical tree diagram, while the Project Designer displays projects using a process flow diagram. In either window, the items in your project are represented by icons, and connected to show the relationship between items. Here are examples of a Project Explorer and a Project Designer showing the same project. This project contains several types of items: data, tasks, results, code, logs, and a note.

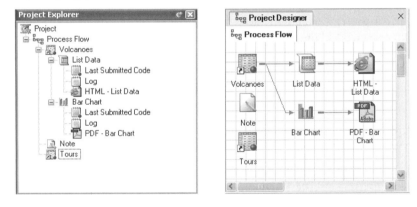

Data Data files in a project may be SAS data tables, raw data files, or files from other databases or applications, such as Microsoft Excel spreadsheets. Projects contain pointers to data files, not the actual data. If you delete a project, your data files will still exist.

Tasks Tasks are specific analyses or reports that you run, such as Analysis of Variance or Bar Chart. Every time you run a task, SAS Enterprise Guide adds an icon representing that task.

Results Results are the reports or graphs produced by tasks you run. Results are represented by icons labeled with the type of output (HTML, PDF, RTF, SAS Report, or text) and the name of the task.

Notes Notes are optional text files you can use to document your work, or record comments or instructions for later use. To create a note, select **File ▶ New ▶ Note** from the menu bar. A text window will open, allowing you to type whatever you wish.

Showing properties and opening items You can display the properties for any item by right-clicking its icon in the Project Explorer or Project Designer and selecting **Properties** from the pop-up menu. You can open any item by double-clicking its icon, or by right-clicking its icon and selecting **Open** from the pop-up menu.

Code and log files Code files are SAS programs, either ones that SAS Enterprise Guide writes when you run a task, or ones that you have written. Log files are text files written by SAS that contain details about how a particular task ran. When you run a task, code and log icons are automatically added to the Project Explorer, but not to the Project Designer. To display a code file, double-click the icon for **Last Submitted Code** in the Project Explorer or right-click the icon and select **Open** from the pop-up menu. To display a log file, double-click the log icon in the Project Explorer or right-click the log icon and select **Open** from the pop-up menu. If you want the code and log to appear automatically in the Project Designer, select **Tools ▶ Options** from the menu bar. In the selection pane on the left, click **Project Views** and then check the boxes next to **Show generated code items** and **Show SAS output log**.

Renaming and deleting items You can rename most items by right-clicking the item and selecting **Rename** from the pop-up menu. You can delete an item in a project by right-clicking and selecting **Delete**. Note that if you delete data from a project, only the pointer to that data is deleted, not the actual data file.

Saving a project To save a project, select **File ▶ Save** *project-name* or **File ▶ Save** *project-name* **As** from the menu bar. Each project is saved as a single file and has a file extension of .egp. You can save results, code, and logs as separate files by right-clicking and selecting **Export** from the pop-up menu.

1.3 ▶ Managing Process Flows

In SAS Enterprise Guide, you can have only one project open at a time. However, you can have multiple process flows within a single project. So, if you have a complex project, you may want to divide it into several process flows.

Adding new process flows To add a new process flow to a project, select **File ▶ New ▶ Process Flow** from the menu bar, or right-click the current process flow and select **New ▶ Process Flow** from the pop-up menu.

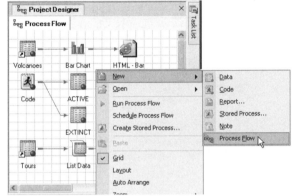

Note that no matter how many process flows you create in the Project Designer, the Project Explorer always shows your entire project in a single tree diagram.

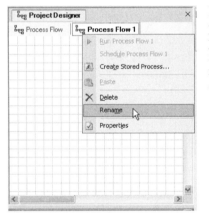

Renaming process flows When you open a new process flow, it is named Process Flow *n*. To give your process flows more descriptive names, right-click the tab for each process flow and select **Rename** from the pop-up menu. Then type the new name in the Rename window and click **OK**.

Moving and copying items To move items from one process flow to another, hold down the control button, and click the items you want to move. Then right-click, and select **Move to ▶** *process-flow-name* from the pop-up menu. In this example, three items are being moved.

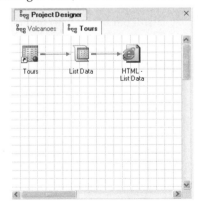

Copying items is similar to moving items except that you cannot copy results. Select the items to be copied using control-click. Then right-click the items and select **Copy** from the pop-up menu, and right-click the target process flow and select **Paste**.

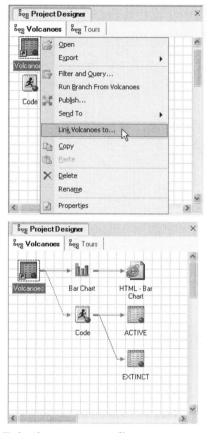

Linking items You can add links between items to show relationships that may not be clear, or to force items to run in a particular order. For example, if you create a format that is used by a task, you might want to add a link indicating that the task follows the format. To add a link, right-click the initial item and select **Link** *item-name* **to** from the pop-up menu. A Link window will open showing all the other items to which you can link. Select the item to which you want to link, and click **OK**.

In this process flow, the Volcanoes data table has been linked to a code icon to show that this code uses the Volcanoes data table. Notice that links you add use a dashed line instead of a solid line.

Printing process flows You can print a copy of your process flow. To control page size and orientation, right-click the process flow and select **Page setup**. To preview a printout, right-click and select **Print preview**. To print the process flow, right-click and select **Print**. Here is the Print preview window for the Volcanoes process flow.

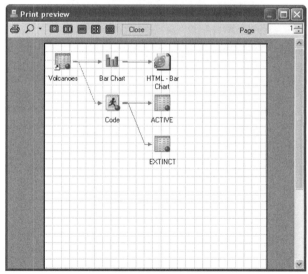

1.4 Maximizing and Splitting the Workspace

The workspace is where you see the Project Designer and the document windows (data, results, code, logs, and notes). By default, you see these items one at a time, but you can enlarge and divide the workspace so you can see two or more items side by side.

Maximizing the workspace To make the workspace as large as possible, select **View ▶ Maximize Workspace** from the menu bar or click the **Maximize Workspace** button on the toolbar

When you maximize the workspace, the Project Explorer and Task Status windows become tabs pinned to the edges of the SAS Enterprise Guide application. You can temporarily expand those windows by moving the cursor over the tab. When you move the cursor away, the window will be reduced to a tab again.

Splitting the workspace You can display the Project Designer and document windows side by side or one above the other. First, open all the items you wish to view. Then, in the workspace, right-click the tab for one item and select either **New Horizontal Tab Group** or **New Vertical Tab Group**. This splits the workspace in two. Repeat this until all the documents you wish to see are visible.

This example shows the workspace split into three vertical sections. The first section displays the Project Designer, the second the Volcanoes data set, and the last the result of a List Data task.

Unsplitting and restoring the workspace To move documents from one section of the workspace to another, right-click a tab and select **Move Previous** or **Move Next** from the pop-up menu. The item you move will appear on top of the other items in that section. To completely unsplit the workspace simply move the items until they are all in a single section.

To return the workspace to its normal size, either select **View ▶ Maximize Workspace** from the menu bar or click the **Maximize Workspace** button on the toolbar. You can unsplit the workspace and restore it to normal size at the same time by selecting **Tools ▶ Options** from the menu bar and clicking the **Reset Docking Windows** button.

1.5 ▶ Running and Rerunning Tasks

Running tasks is, of course, what SAS Enterprise Guide is all about. Regardless of which task you choose to run, the basic steps are the same: select the data, open the task and select settings, and then run the task.

Setting the active data table SAS Enterprise Guide will run a task using the data table that is currently active. The name of the active data table appears in the Active Data box on the left side of the toolbar. To change to one of the other data tables in your project, click the down arrow in the Active Data box and select another data table from the pull-down list, or just click the data table icon in the Project Explorer or Project Designer. This example shows the Tours data table being selected.

Opening a task
To open a task, select it using menus or click its name in the Task List window. The window for that task will open. In this case, the List Data task is being selected from the Task List window.

Running a task In the task window, you assign variables to task roles and then select options. When you are satisfied with all the settings, click the **Run** button.

If you decide you want to stop a task while it's running, click the **Stop** button on the bottom line of the toolbar, or select **Code ▶ Stop** from the menu bar.

Rerunning a task

To make changes to a task and run it again, first reopen the task by right-clicking the task icon in the Project Explorer or Project Designer, and selecting **Open** from the pop-up menu. You can also reopen the task by double-clicking the task icon. Once the task window is open, you can make changes. Then click the **Run** button to rerun the task.

If the data have been updated and you want to rerun a task without making any changes to the task settings, you can right-click the task icon and select **Run** *task-name* to run just that one task, or select **Run Branch From** *task-name* to run that task and any items that are downstream in the process flow.

1.6 SAS Data Tables

SAS Enterprise Guide can read and write many kinds of data files (see Chapter 2 for more on this topic), but for most purposes, you will want to have your data in a special form called a SAS data table. When you open a SAS data table, it is displayed in the workspace in a Data Grid. The following Data Grid shows the Tours data table. A new tour has been added for Lassen.

Data Table
(also called a Data Set)

Columns
(also called Variables)

Rows
(also called Observations)

	Volcano	Departs	Days	Price	Difficulty
1	Etna	Catania	7	$1,025	m
2	Fuji	Tokyo	2	$195	c
3	Kenya	Nairobi	6	$780	m
4	Kilauea	Hilo	1	$45	e
5	Kilimanjaro	Nairobi	9	$1,260	c
6	Krakatau	Jakarta	7	$850	e
7	Lassen	Sacramento	3	.	
8	Poas	San Jose	1	$50	e
9	Reventador	Quito	4	$525	m
10	St. Helens	Portland	2	$157	e
11	Vesuvius	Rome	6	$950	e

Terminology   In SAS Enterprise Guide, rows are also called observations, columns are also called variables, and data tables are also called data sets. SAS Enterprise Guide uses all these terms. Some tasks refer to columns and others to variables, depending on the context.

Data types and data groups   In SAS Enterprise Guide, there are two basic types of data: numeric and character. Numeric data are divided into four data groups: numeric, currency, time, and date. For each of these, SAS Enterprise Guide has special tools: informats for reading that type of data, functions for manipulating that type of data, and formats for displaying that type of data. SAS Enterprise Guide uses a different icon to identify each kind of data in Data Grids and tasks.

 Character data may contain numerals, letters, or special characters (such as $ or !) and can be up to 32,767 characters long. Character data are represented by a red pyramid with the letter A on it.

 Currency data are numeric values for money and are represented by a picture of the dollar, euro, and yen symbols.

Date data are numeric values equal to the number of days since January 1, 1960. The table below lists four dates, and their corresponding SAS date and formatted values:

Date	SAS date value	MMDDYY10. formatted value
January 1, 1959	-365	01/01/1959
January 1, 1960	0	01/01/1960
January 1, 1961	366	01/01/1961
January 1, 2007	17176	01/01/2007

You will rarely see unformatted SAS date values in SAS Enterprise Guide. However, because dates are numeric, you can use them in arithmetic expressions to find, for example, the number of days between two dates. Datetime values are included in this data group, and are the number of seconds since January 1, 1960. Date data are represented by a picture of a calendar.

 Time data are numeric values equal to the number of seconds since midnight. Time data are represented by a picture of a clock.

 Other numeric data that are not dates, times, or currency are simply called numeric. They may contain numerals, decimal places (.), plus signs (+), minus signs (-), and E for scientific notation. Numeric data are represented by a blue ball with the numbers 1, 2, and 3 on it.

Numeric versus character If the values of a column contain letters or special characters, they must be character data. However, if the values contain only numerals, then they may be either numeric or character. You should base your decision on how you will use the data. Sometimes data that consist solely of numerals make more sense as character data than as numeric. Zip codes, for example, are made up of numerals, but it just doesn't make sense to add, subtract, multiply, or divide zip codes. Such numbers work better as character data.

Column names Column names in SAS Enterprise Guide may be up to 32 characters in length, and can begin with or contain any character, including blanks.

Using SAS Enterprise Guide data in Base SAS Any data created in SAS Enterprise Guide can be used in Base SAS, but the default rules for naming variables are different in Base SAS because Base SAS uses the VALIDVARNAME=V7 system option, while SAS Enterprise Guide uses VALIDVARNAME=ANY. For the sake of compatibility, you may want to follow these rules when naming columns: choose column names that are 32 characters or fewer in length, start with a letter or underscore, and contain only letters, numerals, and underscores.

Missing data Sometimes despite your best efforts, your data may be incomplete. The value of a particular column may be missing for some rows. In those cases, missing character data are represented by blanks, and missing numeric data are represented by a single period (.). In the preceding Data Grid, the value of Price is missing for the tour of Lassen, and its place is marked by a period. The value of Difficulty is missing for the same tour and is left blank.

Documentation stored in SAS data tables In addition to your actual data, SAS data tables contain information about the data table, such as its name, the date that you created it, and the version of SAS you used to create it. SAS also stores information about each column in the data table, including its name, type, and length. This information is sometimes called the descriptor portion of the data table, and it makes SAS data tables self-documenting. This information is what you see in the Properties windows for data tables and columns, which are described in more detail in the next two sections.

1.7 ► Properties of Data Tables

Someday you might be given a SAS Enterprise Guide project that was created by someone else. If you want to figure out what it does, the first thing you would probably do is read any notes. The next thing you would probably do is check the properties of the data tables.

Opening the Properties window You can display information about a data table by right-clicking its icon in the Project Explorer or Project Designer and selecting **Properties** from the pop-up menu. In the following window, Properties is being selected for the Volcanoes data table.

General page

When the table Properties window opens, it displays the General page. The General page lists basic information about the table: its name, when it was created and last modified, the number of rows and columns, and whether it is indexed or compressed.

Properties for Volcanoes

General
Columns
Advanced
Summary

General

Volcanoes

File properties

| File name: | C:\EG Data\Volcanoes.sas7bdat | Change... |

Last modified: Friday, July 22, 2005 4:21 PM

Label:

Created: Friday, February 04, 2005 11:33 AM

Data set properties

Columns:	6	Indexed:	No
Rows:	32	Compressed:	No
Data set type:	Not applicable		

Label that identifies the data set. Specified by the LABEL= option.

More (F1)...

OK   Cancel

Properties for Volcanoes

General
Columns
Advanced
Summary

Columns

Name	Type	Length	Format	Informat	Label
Volcano	Character	15	$15.0	$15.0	Volcano
Country	Character	13	$13.0	$13.0	Country
Region	Character	8	$8.0	$12.0	Region
Height	Numeric	8	F6.0	F12.0	Height
Activity	Character	10	$10.0	$10.0	Activity
Type	Character	15	$15.0	$15.0	Type

The selection pane enables you to select a category of options to view.

More (F1)...

OK   Cancel

Columns page If you click **Columns** in the selection pane on the left, the Columns page will open. Here, SAS Enterprise Guide displays information about each column: its name, type, length, format, informat, and label. You cannot change the properties of columns in the Properties window for a data table. To make changes, use the Properties window for an individual column as described in the next section.

1.8 Properties of Columns

The column Properties window displays properties for an individual column. If you open the column Properties window from a Data Grid, you can make changes to those properties.

Setting the update mode If the words **read-only** appear after the name of the data table at the top of the Data Grid, then the table is in read-only mode and you will not be able to make changes. To switch to update mode, select **Data ► Read-only** from the menu bar. This toggles the data table from read-only to update mode.

Opening the Properties window To open the column Properties window, right-click the header of a column and select **Properties** from the pop-up menu. In the preceding Data Grid, Properties is being selected for the column Height.

General page The Properties window has several pages. If there is no selection pane on the left, then the data table is in read-only mode and you need to switch to update mode.

The General page displays basic information for the column: its name, label, type, group, and length. You can change any of these properties. In this example, the column name has been changed to **HeightMeters**, and the label to **Height in Meters**. This column is **numeric** and has a length of **8**.

Informats page Click **Informats** in the selection pane on the left to open the Informats page. Informats (also called input formats or read-in formats) tell SAS Enterprise Guide how to interpret input data. If you edit the data table, SAS Enterprise Guide will use informats to interpret any values you type. There are different informats for character, numeric, date, time, and currency data. In this example, the column uses the default numeric informat, *w.d*, with a width of **12** and no decimal places. This informat can be written as 12.0. See the next section for a table of commonly used informats.

Formats page Click **Formats** in the selection pane on the left to open the Formats page. Formats (also called display formats) tell SAS Enterprise Guide how data should look in Data Grids or reports. There are different formats for character, numeric, date, time, and currency data. In this example, the format **COMMA*w.d*** with a width of **6** and no decimal places has been selected. This format can be written as COMMA6.0. See section 1.10 for a table of commonly used formats.

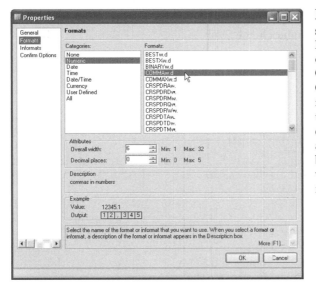

Results Here is the Data Grid showing the new name, HeightMeters, and format with commas.

	Volcano	Country	Region	HeightMeters	Activity	Type
1	Altar	Ecuador	SA	5,321	Extinct	Stratovolcano
2	Arthur's Seat	UK	Eu	251	Extinct	
3	Barren Island	India	As	354	Active	Stratovolcano
4	Elbrus	Russia	Eu	5,633	Extinct	Stratovolcano
5	Erebus		An	3,794	Active	Stratovolcano

1.9 Selected Informats

SAS informats (also called input formats or read-in formats) tell SAS Enterprise Guide how to interpret input data. You can specify informats in the column Properties window of a Data Grid, or in the Column Options page when reading data. Here are a few of the many informats available in SAS Enterprise Guide.

Informat	Definition	Width range	Default width
Character			
$w.	Reads character data—trims leading blanks	1–32,767	none
$UPCASEw.	Converts character data to uppercase	1–32,767	8
Date, Time, and Datetime[1]			
ANYDTDTEw.	Reads dates in any form—when dates are ambiguous, uses the DATESTYLE system option to determine	5–32	9
DATEw.	Reads dates in the form: *ddmonyy* or *ddmonyyyy*	7–32	7
DATETIMEw.	Reads datetime values in the form: *ddmonyy hh:mm:ss.ss*	13–40	18
DDMMYYw.	Reads dates in the form: *ddmmyy* or *ddmmyyyy*	6–32	6
JULIANw.	Reads Julian dates in the form: *yyddd* or *yyyyddd*	5–32	5
MMDDYYw.	Reads dates in the form: *mmddyy* or *mmddyyyy*	6–32	6
TIMEw.	Reads time in the form: *hh:mm:ss.ss* (hours:minutes:seconds—24-hour clock)	5–32	8
Numeric			
w.d	Reads standard numeric data	1–32	none
COMMAw.d	Removes embedded commas and $, converts left parentheses to minus sign	1–32	1
PERCENTw.	Converts percentages to numbers	1–32	6

---

[1] SAS date values are the number of days since January 1, 1960. Time values are the number of seconds past midnight, and datetime values are the number of seconds past midnight on January 1, 1960.

The examples below show input data and resulting data values for each informat. The results shown are unformatted data values. See sections 3.1 and 3.2 for more information about assigning display formats.

Informat	Input data	Results	Input data	Results
Character				
$10.	Lassen	Lassen	St. Helens	St. Helens
$UPCASE10.	Lassen	LASSEN	St. Helens	ST. HELENS
Date, Time, and Datetime				
ANYDTDTE10.	01jan1961	366	31.01.1961	396
	1961001	366	01/31/61	396
DATE9.	1jan1961	366	31 jan 61	396
DATETIME14.	1jan1960 10:30	37800	1jan1961 10:30	31660200
DDMMYY10.	01.01.1961	366	31/01/61	396
JULIAN7.	1961001	366	61031	396
MMDDYY10.	01-01-1961	366	01/31/61	396
TIME8.	10:30	37800	10:30:15	37815
Numeric				
5.1	1234	123.4	-12.3	-12.3
COMMA10.0	$1,000,001	1000001	(1,234)	-1234
PERCENT5.	5%	0.05	(20%)	-0.2

1.10 Selected Standard Formats

SAS formats (also called display formats) tell SAS Enterprise Guide how to display or print data. You can apply formats in the column Properties window of a Data Grid, in the Properties window within a task, or in a query. Here are a few of the many formats available in SAS Enterprise Guide.

Format	Definition	Width range	Default width
Character			
$UPCASE*w*.	Converts character data to uppercase	1–32767	Length of variable or 8
$*w*.	Writes standard character data—default for character data	1–32767	Length of variable or 1
Date, Time, and Datetime[1]			
DATE*w*.	Writes SAS date values in form *ddmonyy* or *ddmonyyyy*	5–9	7
DATETIME*w.d*	Writes SAS datetime values in form *ddmmmyy:hh:mm:ss.ss*	7–40	16
DTDATE*w*.	Writes SAS datetime values in form *ddmonyy* or *ddmonyyyy*	5–9	7
EURDFDD*w*.	Writes SAS date values in form *dd.mm.yy* or *dd.mm.yyyy*	2–10	8
JULIAN*w*.	Writes SAS date values in Julian date form *yyddd* or *yyyyddd*	5–7	5
MMDDYY*w*.	Writes SAS date values in form *mm/dd/yy* or *mm/dd/yyyy*—default for dates	2–10	8
TIME*w.d*	Writes SAS time values in form *hh:mm:ss.ss*—default for times	2–20	8
WEEKDATE*w*.	Writes SAS date values in form *day-of-week, month-name dd, yy* or *yyyy*	3–37	29
WORDDATE*w*.	Writes SAS date values in form *month-name dd, yyyy*	3–32	18
Numeric			
BEST*w*.	SAS System chooses best format—default format for numeric data	1–32	12
COMMA*w.d*	Writes numbers with commas	2–32	6
DOLLAR*w.d*	Writes numbers with a leading $ and commas separating every three digits—default for currency	2–32	6
E*w*.	Writes numbers in scientific notation	7–32	12
EUROX*w.d*	Writes numbers with a leading € and periods separating every three digits	2–32	6
PERCENT*w.d*	Writes numeric data as percentages	4–32	6
w.d	Writes standard numeric data	1–32	none

[1] SAS date values are the number of days since January 1, 1960. Time values are the number of seconds past midnight, and datetime values are the number of seconds past midnight on January 1, 1960.

The examples below show unformatted data values and formatted results for each display format.

Format	Data value	Results	Data value	Results
Character				
$UPCASE10.	Lassen	LASSEN	St. Helens	ST. HELENS
$10.	Lassen	Lassen	St. Helens	St. Helens
Date, Time, and Datetime				
DATE9.	366	01JAN1961	396	31JAN1961
DATETIME16.	37800	01JAN60:10:30	2629800	31JAN60:10:30
DTDATE9.	37800	01JAN1960	2629800	31JAN1960
EURDFDD10.	366	01.01.1961	396	31.01.1961
JULIAN7.	366	1961001	396	1961031
MMDDYY10.	366	01/01/1961	396	01/31/1961
TIME8.	37800	10:30:00	37815	10:30:15
WEEKDATE15.	366	Sun, Jan 1, 61	396	Tue, Jan 31, 61
WORDDATE12.	366	Jan 1, 1961	396	Jan 31, 1961
Numeric				
BEST10.	1000001	1000001	-12.34	-12.34
BEST6.	1000001	1E6	100001	100001
COMMA12.2	1000001	1,000,001.00	-12.34	-12.34
DOLLAR13.2	1000001	$1,000,001.00	-12.34	$-12.34
E10.	1000001	1.000E+06	-12.34	-1.234E+01
EUROX13.2	1000001	€1.000.001,00	-12.34	€-12,34
PERCENT9.2	0.05	5.00%	-1.20	(120.00%)
10.2	1000001	1000001.00	-12.34	-12.34

1.11 Scheduling Projects to Run at Specific Times

Sometimes you may want to create a project now, but run it later. For example, if you have data that are updated on a regular basis, you might want to automatically rerun the project once a week using the new data. Or, if your data files are very large, you might want to run your projects at night so that SAS Enterprise Guide is not using valuable resources during work hours.

Scheduling a project To schedule a project, select **Tools ▶ Schedule Project** from the menu bar. This opens the Schedule window with the Task page displayed. When you schedule a project, SAS Enterprise Guide creates a script that is saved in a file on your computer. The name and path of this script is displayed in the **Run** box. The **Start in** box displays the folder in which the script will run. Your computer and user name are displayed in the **Run as** box.

If you will not be logged on at the time the project runs, then make sure the box next to **Run only if logged on** is unchecked, and click the **Set password** button to open the Set Password window. Enter the password for your user name (the same password you use when you log on to your computer), and click **OK**.

Setting the run frequency To tell SAS Enterprise Guide when to run the project, click the **Schedule** tab of the Schedule window. Click the **New** button. Then select the frequency to run the project from the drop-down list under **Schedule Task**. You can schedule your project to run just once at a specified time as shown here, or you can schedule your project to run on a regular basis.

Setting the date and time To set the time the project will start running, click the up and down arrows on the **Start time** box, or simply click the time and type a new value. To choose a date other than today, click the down arrow in the **Run on** box and select a date from the pop-up calendar.

Other settings If you click the **Settings** tab, you will see other options, including the maximum length of time a project will be allowed to run and whether it will run if your computer has gone into sleep mode.

When you are satisfied with all the settings, click **OK** to schedule the project.

Running the project The project will not run if it is open or if the computer is turned off at the time the project is scheduled to run. However, if you have a different project open, the scheduled project will still run.

Viewing the results To see the results of your scheduled run, open the project after it has completed running. If you are not sure whether a project ran, you can confirm this by opening the Properties window for that project. To open the Properties window for a project, select **File ▶ Properties** from the menu bar. The **Last modified** field shows the date and time that the project last ran.

1.12   Viewing and Editing SAS Code Generated by a Task

If you are a SAS programmer, you'll probably want to see the SAS code generated by SAS Enterprise Guide. Sometimes, you may also want to edit the SAS code generated by SAS Enterprise Guide. There is more than one way to do this. You can insert your own custom code into the SAS program written by a task, or you can save the code generated by a task in a separate file which allows you to edit any part of the program.

Viewing code generated by a task
Many task windows have a **Preview code** button in the lower-left corner. If you click this button, SAS Enterprise Guide will open a Code Preview window displaying the code that SAS Enterprise Guide has written for that task.

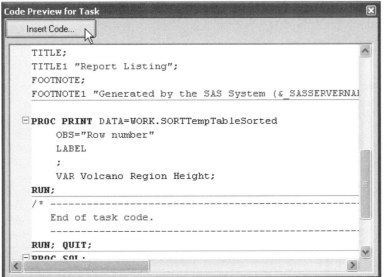

Inserting code in a task Here is a Code Preview window for a List Data task. You can see that it uses PROC PRINT. If you want to add code to the task, click the **Insert Code** button. This opens a User Code window.

You cannot edit the existing code generated by a task, but the User Code window allows you to add code at specific points in the program. In the User Code window, double-click **<double-click to insert code>** at the point where you wish to add your own custom code. An Enter User Code window will open. Type the custom code you wish to add. When you are done, click **OK**. Your new code will appear in the User Code window. Click **OK** in the User Code window. When you run the task, SAS Enterprise Guide will run the code you inserted, in addition to the code generated by the task.

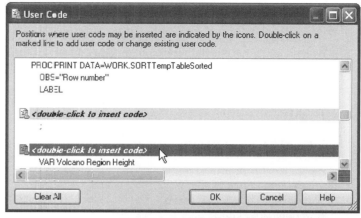

Editing code generated by a task If you

want to be able to edit the entire program generated by a task, or code from tasks that do not have a Preview code button, you can make a copy of the generated code, and then edit it. To do this, run the task, and then right-click the task icon in the Project Explorer or Project Designer, and select **Add As Code Template**. SAS Enterprise Guide will open a code window in the workspace containing the code generated by the task.

You can edit this code in any way you wish. Because this code is a copy of the code generated by the task, any changes you make here will not affect the task, nor will any changes you make to the task be reflected in this code. When you have made all the changes you wish to the code and are ready to run it, select **Code ▶ Run** *program-name* **On** *server-name* from the menu bar. To choose a different server, select **Code ▶ Select Server**.

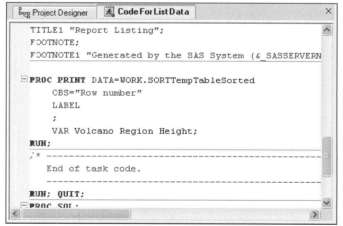

Code created in this way is embedded in your project, and is not saved as a separate file. For more information on embedding code, see the next section.

1.13 Writing and Running Custom SAS Code

You can accomplish a lot using tasks in SAS Enterprise Guide, but sometimes you may need to do something for which there is no predefined task. At those times, you can open a SAS program that was written outside SAS Enterprise Guide or you can write a new one.

Writing a new SAS program To create a new SAS program, open a new Code window by selecting **File ▶ New ▶ Code** from the menu bar. An empty Code window will open in the workspace. The code editor in SAS Enterprise Guide is syntax-sensitive, which means that SAS keywords are displayed in blue, comments are green, quoted strings are pink, and so forth.

```
* Add new price and new tour to Tours data table;
Data NewData;
    INPUT Volcano :$12. Departs :$12. Days
        Price Difficulty $;
    DATALINES;
    Etna . . 1175 .
    Lassen Scramento 3 250 m
    ;
DATA NewToursData;
    UPDATE 'C:\EG DATA\Tours' NewData;
    BY Volcano;
PROC PRINT DATA = NewToursData;
    TITLE1 'Updated Tours Price List';
RUN;
```

Opening an existing SAS program If you have existing SAS programs that you want to include in your project, you can open them by selecting **File ▶ Open ▶ Code** from the menu bar. Navigate to the existing SAS program and click **Open**. This opens a Code window in the workspace, where you can edit the program.

Saving code in a file Any new programs you write are automatically embedded in your project. This means that the program's code does not exist in a file outside the project. To save the SAS code outside the project, right-click the code icon in the Project Explorer or Project Designer and select **Save Code As** from the pop-up menu. You can also save code from the Properties window. To view the properties of code, right-click the code icon in the Project Explorer or Project Designer and select **Properties** from the pop-up menu. Then in the General page, click **Save As**. If you save the code in a file, then the program is not embedded, and any changes you make to the code in SAS Enterprise Guide will be saved in the file rather than as part of your project.

The icon for code saved in a file includes a little arrow indicating that the project contains a shortcut to the code rather than the actual code.

Embedding code in a project

When you open a SAS program that has been saved in a separate file, it is not automatically embedded in your project. If you want to embed the program in your project, then open the Properties window for the code and click the **Embed** button. After you embed the code, any changes you make to the code in SAS Enterprise Guide will be saved as part of your project rather than in the file. The icon for embedded code looks like this.

Properties for Code

General
Results
Parameters
Summary

General

Label:
NewTours.sas

Code will run on server:
Local

Last Execution Time:
0 seconds

File path:
NewTours

Location: My Computer

[Embed]   [Save As...]

Embeds the code in the SAS Enterprise Guide project so that any changes that you make to the code in SAS Enterprise Guide are not applied to the original code file. This option is available only for existing code files that you have inserte More (F1)...

[OK] [Cancel]

Running your code and viewing the SAS log When you are ready to run your code, select **Code ► Run** *program-name* **On** *server-name*. To choose a different server use **Code ► Select Server**. When you run code in SAS Enterprise Guide, if there is an error, the default action is to open a SAS log window in the workspace. If there are no errors, then the SAS log will not open automatically. To open the SAS log, double-click the icon for the log in the Project Explorer. Here is a portion of the SAS log generated by the SAS program at the beginning of this section.

Project Designer | **Log (Code (Process Flow))**

```
22          DATA NewToursData;
23              UPDATE 'C:\EG DATA\Tours' NewData;
24              BY Volcano;

NOTE: There were 10 observations read from the data set C:\EG DATA\Tours.
NOTE: There were 2 observations read from the data set WORK.NEWDATA.
NOTE: The data set WORK.NEWTOURSDATA has 11 observations and 5 variables.
NOTE: DATA statement used (Total process time):
      real time           0.01 seconds
      cpu time            0.01 seconds

25          PROC PRINT DATA = NewToursData;

26              TITLE1 'Updated Tours Price List';
27          RUN;
```

1.14 Using SAS Enterprise Guide Help

In SAS Enterprise Guide, help is never far away. You can find help via the Help menu, of course, but you can also find help inside many windows.

What is window To open the What is window, select **View ▶ What is** from the menu bar. Then point the cursor at a menu item or tool, and the What is window will describe that menu item or tool.

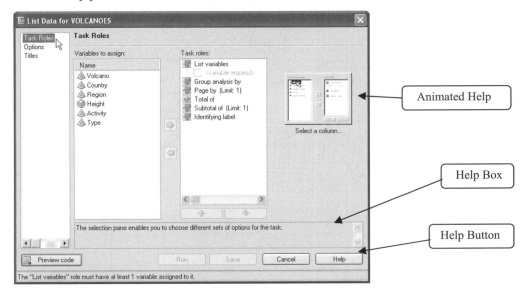

Context-sensitive help The List Data window provides a good example of the context-sensitive help provided inside task windows.

There are three main types of context-sensitive help:

- Animated help demonstrates how to assign variables to task roles.

- The Help box near the bottom of the window displays textual help. As you move your cursor around the window, the text automatically changes to describe what the cursor is pointing to.

- The Help button in the right corner gives you more extensive help. When you click it, the SAS Enterprise Guide Help window opens.

SAS Enterprise Guide Help If you click the **Help** button in a task window, SAS Enterprise Guide will open the Help window and display information about the current task. You can also open the Help window by selecting **Help ▶ SAS Enterprise Guide Help** from the menu bar, but then it's up to you to find the right section of help for your needs.

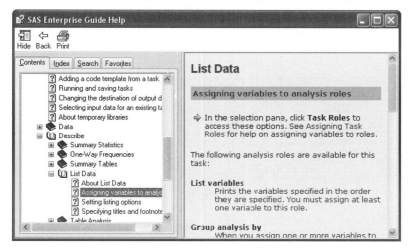

The Help window has two main panes: the Navigation pane on the left, and the Topic pane on the right. In the Navigation pane, you can choose from four tabs.

- The Contents tab shows an expandable table of contents for the SAS Enterprise Guide documentation.

- The Index tab allows you to browse the index for both SAS Enterprise Guide and SAS syntax help. If you type a keyword or part of a keyword, you will jump to that part of the index.

- The Search tab finds every occurrence of the words you type, in both the SAS Enterprise Guide and SAS syntax help.

- The Favorites tab allows you to make a list of your favorite help topics so that you can find them more easily in the future.

1.15 Using the Options Window

The Options window allows you to change many default behaviors in SAS Enterprise Guide. To open the Options window, select **Tools ▶ Options** from the menu bar.

Data General options To open the Data > Data General page, click **Data General** in the selection pane on the left.

Options	
General	**Data > Data General**
Project Views	
Results	☑ Use cell value to determine column type
Results General	☑ Display columns in alphabetical order
Viewer	☑ Use labels for column names
HTML	☐ Display log for errors that occur while modifying data
RTF	☐ Use data tables in unprotected (read/write) mode
PDF	☐ Automatically open data when added to project
SAS Report	☑ Always prompt when closing a project with temporary data references
Graph	☐ Always obtain the total record count for DBMS tables
Stored Process	
Data	Default Action for Opening Data Files
Data General	○ Open file as is ⊙ Always prompt to open file as SAS data set
Performance	
Query	Default Dimensions for New Data Grid
OLAP Cube	Default number of columns: 6 Default number of rows: 12
Query	
Data	SAS Formats/Informats Cache
Table and Graph	Clear cache No formats/informats information is currently cached.
Tasks	
Tasks General	
Custom Code	
Output Library	
SAS Programs	
Security	
Administration	Automatically displays the contents of data tables in a data grid when they are added to a project.
Repository and Server	
Transfer Mode	
E-mail Settings	More (F1)...
Reset All	OK Cancel

If you have large data tables, columns might be easier to find if they are arranged in alphabetical order. To list columns alphabetically in task windows, check the box in front of **Display columns in alphabetical order**.

By default, the Data Grid uses column names, not labels, for column headers. To change this, check the box in front of **Use labels for column names**.

If you have large data tables on remote servers, you may be able to improve performance by unchecking **Automatically open data when added to project**.

Tasks General options To open the Tasks > Tasks General page, click **Tasks General** in the selection pane on the left.

At the top of this page, you can type a new default title and footnote, or set them to blank.

Near the bottom of the page is another useful option. Some tasks in SAS Enterprise Guide include in the results the name of the SAS procedure used by that task. In these results, you will see titles like "The FREQ Procedure," or "The ANOVA Procedure." You can eliminate these titles by unchecking the box for **Include SAS procedure titles in results**.

Restoring the default windows To restore windows to their default layout, click **General** in the selection pane on the left. Then click the **Reset Docking Windows** button.

Changing the default output type or style To change the default output type, click **Results General** in the selection pane on the left, and check the type of output you want. To change the default output style, click **HTML, RTF, PDF,** or **SAS Report** in the selection pane on the left. Then select the output style you want. See Tutorial C or section 10.2 for more information about changing output styles. Section 4.13 discusses changing the output type for queries, and section 9.6 discusses changing the output type for graphs.

Saving and resetting options Click **OK** to close the Options window and save the changes you have made. Once you set options, they stay in effect for future SAS Enterprise Guide sessions. If at a later time, you decide you want to restore everything in the Options window to the default settings, simply click the **Reset All** button in the lower left corner.

CHAPTER 2

Bringing Data into a Project

2.1 Sources of Data

Before you can analyze your data, before you can run a report, before you can do anything with your data, SAS Enterprise Guide must be able to read your data. Your data might be in a data warehouse on a mainframe, or on a piece of paper sitting on your desk. Whatever form your data take, there is a way to get your data into SAS Enterprise Guide.

This section gives a general overview of the most common types of data. Details about how to read different types of data are covered in the rest of this chapter.

 Existing SAS data tables You may have SAS data tables (also called SAS data sets) that were created by you or by someone else, and your data tables may have been created in SAS or in another project in SAS Enterprise Guide. Regardless of how your SAS data tables were created, you can easily open them in SAS Enterprise Guide.

 New data tables If your data set is small or if you've collected the data yourself, then you may find the easiest way to get your data into SAS Enterprise Guide is to type them directly into a Data Grid. To do this, just open an empty Data Grid like the one below, set the properties for the columns, and type in your data. SAS Enterprise Guide makes a SAS data table from the data you type into a Data Grid.

⚙ Project Designer	📄 **MyNewData**					
	△ A	△ B	△ C	△ D	△ E	△ F
1						
2						
3						
4						
5						
6						
7						
8						
9						
10						
11						
12						

 Raw data files Raw data files are files that contain no special formatting. They are sometimes called text, ASCII, sequential, or flat files; and can be viewed using a simple text editor, such as Microsoft Notepad. SAS data tables and Microsoft Excel files are not raw data files. If you open a spreadsheet or SAS data table in Microsoft Notepad, you'll see lots of strange characters that Microsoft Notepad simply can't interpret.

SAS Enterprise Guide can read just about any type of raw data file including delimited data files and fixed-width data files. In delimited data files, a delimiter separates the data values. CSV (comma-separated values) files use commas as delimiters. Other files may use a different delimiter such as a tab, semicolon, or space. Fixed-width data files are similar to delimited data files, but instead of having a delimiter separating the data values, the data values are lined up in tidy vertical columns.

Other software files SAS Enterprise Guide can read files produced by many other types of software. When you install SAS Enterprise Guide, you get everything you need to read most PC data files. You do not need to install any additional software to read files in these formats:

- dBASE Files
- HTML Files
- IBM Lotus 1-2-3 Files
- Microsoft Access Files
- Microsoft Excel Files
- Microsoft Exchange Files
- Paradox Files

However, if you have large PC data files, you may be able to improve performance by using SAS/ACCESS software. To read files this way, you must have SAS/ACCESS (either SAS/ACCESS Interface to PC Files or SAS/ACCESS Interface to ODBC, depending on the type of data files you are reading), and it must be installed on the same server where SAS is installed. Then you simply define a SAS data library, specifying the appropriate SAS/ACCESS engine, so that SAS Enterprise Guide knows where to look for the data and how to read them.

SAS Enterprise Guide can read many other kinds of database files, including Oracle and DB2. To read these other database files, you must have the corresponding SAS/ACCESS product (such as SAS/ACCESS Interface to Oracle or SAS/ACCESS Interface to DB2) installed on the same server where SAS is installed. Then you define a SAS data library using the corresponding SAS/ACCESS engine so that SAS Enterprise Guide knows where the data are and how to read them.

2.2 Locations for Data

Before you can read a data file, you must tell SAS Enterprise Guide where to find it. For any particular file, there may be several ways for you to do this. But, regardless of which method you use to locate a file, you always start by selecting **File ▶ Open ▶ Data** from the menu bar. Then in

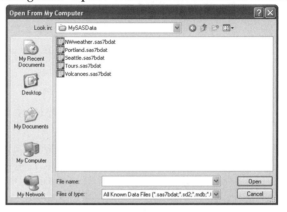

the Open Data From window, select either **Local Computer** or **SAS Servers**. If you select **Local Computer**, then the Open From My Computer window opens. If you select **SAS Servers**, the Open From SAS Servers window opens.

Open From My Computer

window In this window, you can navigate to any drive or directory on your local computer to find the file you want. This example shows a Windows directory named MySASData that contains five SAS data tables. Most SAS data tables have a file extension sas7bdat.

Open From SAS Servers

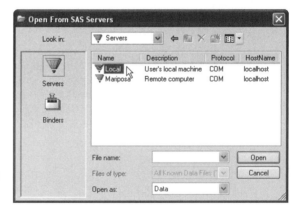

window SAS servers are networked computers on which SAS is installed (which may include your local computer). In this example, there are two SAS servers: Local and a computer named Mariposa. To show files on a server, double-click its name. Once you have selected a server, you can choose to display either files or libraries on that server.

Libraries A SAS data library is a set of SAS files residing in a particular location. Instead of referring to the location by its full path, you identify it by a short name, called a libref. If you double-click the word **Libraries**, SAS Enterprise Guide will list all the SAS data libraries that have been defined. Double-click a library name to display its contents.

Here are some libraries you are likely to see:

WORK is a special library for temporary data tables. The WORK library is erased when you exit SAS Enterprise Guide.

SASUSER is the default for output data tables and is permanent on most systems, so your data tables will not be erased by SAS Enterprise Guide. However, on OS/390 and some UNIX systems, SASUSER may be temporary. In some environments, SASUSER may be read-only. If you have more than one SAS server, then you may have a SASUSER library on each server.

EGTASK is another special library. If a library with this name has been defined on your system, then SAS Enterprise Guide will use it as the default for output data sets instead of SASUSER.

There are several ways to define new libraries. These include using the SAS Enterprise Guide Explorer (discussed in section 2.3), using the Assign Library task (discussed in section 2.4), or submitting a LIBNAME statement from a Code window.

Files If you double-click **Files** in the Open From SAS Servers window, SAS Enterprise Guide will list the folders or directories on that SAS server. From here, you can navigate through the server's directory system to find the file you want.

Binders If you see a binder icon in the Open From SAS Servers window, then you can also use binders to organize your data. Binders are virtual folders that can contain SAS Enterprise Guide projects, code files, SAS data files, and other data files. Binders are created using the SAS Enterprise Guide Explorer.

Binders are available only if you are using the SAS Enterprise Guide repository. Repositories store information about your environment including your servers and libraries. The SAS Enterprise Guide repository is more commonly used for stand-alone installations of SAS Enterprise Guide in which both SAS and SAS Enterprise Guide are installed on a single computer. Installations using the SAS Business Intelligence Server are more likely to use the SAS metadata repository. Binders are not available with the SAS metadata repository.

2.3 Creating SAS Data Libraries with SAS Enterprise Guide Explorer

A SAS data library is a set of SAS files stored in a particular location. You use SAS data libraries to tell SAS Enterprise Guide where to find existing SAS data tables, and where to save new ones. This section describes how to create SAS data libraries using the SAS Enterprise Guide Explorer. Note that the SAS Enterprise Guide Explorer is different from the Project Explorer window. The Project Explorer window displays your project in a hierarchical tree diagram; the SAS Enterprise Guide Explorer is an administrative tool. To open the SAS Enterprise Guide Explorer, select **Tools ▶ SAS Enterprise Guide Explorer** from the menu bar.

If you have administrator privileges, then you can use the SAS Enterprise Guide Explorer to define new SAS data libraries. An easy way to tell if you have administrator privileges is by looking at the SAS Enterprise Guide Explorer window. If you see the words **Admin Mode** in the lower right corner, then you have administrator privileges. If you do not have administrator privileges, you cannot use SAS Enterprise Guide Explorer to create libraries, but you can still create libraries using other methods including the Assign Library task described in the next section.

Any library definitions you create in SAS Enterprise Guide Explorer will be stored on the SAS server you select. So, they will always be available for your use (unless you delete them). They will also be available to anyone else who connects to that SAS server.

The preceding window shows how the SAS Enterprise Guide Explorer window looks when used with the SAS Enterprise Guide repository. If you are using the SAS metadata repository instead, then the window will offer somewhat different options, but the basic process for defining a library is the same.

Creating New Libraries To create a new library select **File ▶ New ▶ Library** from the menu bar inside SAS Enterprise Guide Explorer. The Library Wizard will open. Simply follow the directions in each window of the wizard.

In the first window, type a name for your new library and an optional description. The library name cannot be longer than eight characters, must start with a letter or an underscore, and can contain only letters, numerals, and underscores. This name is called a libref, and is like a nickname for your library. In this example, a library named FAITDATA is being created. Click **Next** when you are done.

In the second window (not shown), you can check the **Assign at Server Startup** option. If you leave it unchecked, the library will be assigned at first use. Click **Next** when you are done.

In the third window, select the server or servers on which the library will be used. Click **Next** when you are done.

In the fourth window, specify the SAS data engine for your library. The SAS data engine determines the kind of data that will reside in this library. To see a pull-down list of all the available engines, click the down arrow on the **Engine** box. For ordinary SAS data tables, use the **BASE** engine. In the box labeled **Path**, type the path for your library, or click the **Browse** button to navigate to the location for this library. Click **Next** when you are done.

In the fifth window, you can specify options for your library. In the sixth window, you can test your new library by clicking the **Start Test** button. The seventh window summarizes the details about your new library. Click **Finish** to create your library and close the Library wizard.

Your new library will be listed under its server in the SAS Enterprise Guide Explorer window.

2.4 Creating SAS Data Libraries with the Assign Library Task

If you do not have administrator privileges, then you cannot use the SAS Enterprise Guide Explorer to define new SAS data libraries. However, there are many other ways you can access your data. You can open data by browsing your computer's file directories and avoid specifying a SAS data library at all. (SAS Enterprise Guide will automatically define a library for you.) If you're a programmer, you can submit a LIBNAME statement from a code window. In addition, you can define a SAS data library using the Assign Library task as described in this section.

If you define a SAS data library using the SAS Enterprise Guide Explorer, then that library will be stored on a SAS server, and (unless you delete it) it will always be available to everyone who uses that server. If you define a SAS data library using the Assign Library task, then that library definition will be stored as part of your project, it will not be accessible to other people, and you will need to reassign the library every time you want to use it in a new SAS Enterprise Guide session. However, when you use the Assign Library task, an icon will be added to your project so you can easily rerun the task to reassign the library whenever you need it.

To open the Assign Library task, select **Tools ▶ Assign Library** from the menu bar. Simply follow the directions in each window of the Library wizard.

In the first window, type a name for your new library and an optional description. The library name cannot be longer than eight characters, must start with a letter or underscore, and can contain only letters, numerals, or underscores. This name is called a libref, and it is like a nickname for your library. In this example, a library named FAITDATA is being created. Click **Next** when you are done.

In the second window, select the server for the library. Click **Next** when you are done.

In the third window, specify the SAS data engine for your library. The SAS data engine determines the kind of data that will reside in this library. To see a pull-down list of all the available engines, click the down arrow on the **Engine** box. For ordinary SAS data tables, use the BASE engine. In the box labeled **Path**, type the path for your library, or click the **Browse** button to navigate to the location for this library. Click **Next** when you are done.

In the fourth window, you can specify options for your library. In the fifth window, you can test your new library by clicking the **Start Test** button. The sixth window summarizes the details about your new library. Click **Finish** to create your library and close the Library wizard. An Assign Library icon will be added to your project.

When you open SAS Enterprise Guide in the future, this library will not automatically be assigned. Before you can use the library (and any data accessed via this library), you must rerun the Assign Library task. You can run the Assign Library task by right-clicking its icon in the Project Explorer or Project Designer and selecting **Run Assign Library** from the pop-up menu.

You can also run the Assign Library task by rerunning your entire process flow. Right-click the process flow in the Project Explorer or Project Designer and select **Run Process Flow** from the pop-up menu. Just be sure that the Assign Library icon appears before any tasks using that library since projects run from top left to bottom right. For this reason, you may want to move the Assign Library icon to the upper left corner of your process flow.

2.5 Opening SAS Data Tables

You may have SAS data tables that were created by you or by someone else, and they may have been created using Base SAS or SAS Enterprise Guide. Regardless of how a SAS data table was created, you can easily open it in SAS Enterprise Guide.

Input data Here is a SAS data table created in Base SAS and displayed using the Viewtable window (in the Microsoft Windows operating environment). The Viewtable window in Base SAS is similar to the Data Grid in SAS Enterprise Guide. This data table is named Volcanoes, and contains six columns: the name of the volcano, its country, region, height in meters, activity (Active or Extinct), and the type of volcano.

Opening a SAS data table To open a SAS data table in SAS Enterprise Guide, select **File ▶ Open ▶ Data** from the menu bar. In the Open Data From window, select **Local Computer** (or **SAS Servers**). Then in the Open From My Computer window (or the Open From SAS Servers window), navigate to the location of the SAS data table. Once you have found the data table you want, click **Open**. SAS Enterprise Guide will immediately add the SAS data table to your project and display it in a Data Grid.

Results Here is the Volcanoes data table displayed in a Data Grid in SAS Enterprise Guide. The data table opens in read-only mode, but because the data are in a SAS data table, you can change to update mode if you wish to edit the data.

2.6 Editing Values in SAS Data Tables

In SAS Enterprise Guide, you see a lot of data tables displayed in Data Grids, but Data Grids aren't just for looking at data. If you need to add new rows or columns, fix errors, or update values, you can do that in a Data Grid, too.

Copying a SAS data table When you edit a SAS data table in a Data Grid, any changes you make are permanent, even if you don't save the project. So, unless you are absolutely sure about the changes you make, you should make a copy of the data table before editing. To make a copy, right-click the data icon in the Project Explorer or Project Designer window and select **Export ▶ Export** *table-name* from the pop-up menu. Choose a location for the new data table and give it a name. Or, you can click the data table icon to make it active, and select **File ▶ Export** *table-name* from the menu bar. When you export a data table, it does not appear in your project, so after you export the data table, you must open it in your project.

Setting the update mode Unless you are creating a new SAS data table, any data tables you open in SAS Enterprise Guide will initially be set to read-only mode. This prevents you from accidentally changing the data. To edit SAS data tables, you must change to update mode. Click the data table icon in the Project Explorer or Project Designer to make it active, and select **Data ▶ Read-only** from the menu bar. This toggles the data table from read-only to update mode.

Displaying the informat and format Any data you enter must match the informat associated with that column, which is not necessarily the same as the display format. If you are not sure which informat a column has, you can find out by displaying the column properties. Right-click the column name in the Data Grid, and select **Properties** from the pop-up menu.

In the Properties window, click **Informats** in the selection pane on the left to display the Informats page. (If **Formats** and **Informats** do not appear in the selection pane on the left, then your data table is in read-only mode. Change to update mode as described above.) In this Informats page, you can see that the column Price has an informat of *w.d*, a width of 12, and no decimal places. This informat can be written as 12.0, and it tells SAS Enterprise Guide that any new data for Price should be entered as plain numbers with 12 numerals or fewer, and without dollar signs, commas, or decimal places. See section 1.9 for a list of commonly used informats.

Click **Formats** in the selection pane on the left to display the Formats page. This Formats page shows that the column Price has a format of DOLLAR*w.d*, a width of 10, and no decimal places. This format can be written as DOLLAR10.0, and it tells SAS Enterprise Guide to add a dollar sign and commas whenever Price is displayed. See section 1.10 for a list of commonly used formats.

Editing values To change a value in a Data Grid, simply click the cell and start typing. Any value you enter must match the informat (not the format) for that column. You can copy and paste data from other data cells. In this Data Grid, a new value has been entered for Price. Notice that the number 1175 has been typed without a dollar sign or comma so it fits the 12.0 informat.

After you enter the new value, SAS Enterprise Guide will read the value using the informat, and then display it using the format. Notice the new price for Etna is displayed using the DOLLAR10.0 format.

2.7 Inserting Rows in SAS Data Tables

When you add rows to a data table, all the same caveats apply as when editing data tables. You'll probably want to save a copy of your table before making changes. You must switch to update mode. Any data you enter must match the informat assigned to that column. For a discussion of these topics, see the previous section.

Here is a copy of the Tours data table in update mode.

	Volcano	Departs	Days	Price	Difficulty
1	Etna	Catania	7	$1,175	m
2	Fuji	Tokyo	2	$195	c
3	Kenya	Nairobi	6	$780	m
4	Kilauea	Hilo	1	$45	e
5	Kilimanjaro	Nairobi	9	$1,260	c
6	Krakatau	Jakarta	7	$850	e
7	Poas	San Jose	1	$50	e
8	Reventador	Quito	4	$525	m
9	St. Helens	Portland	2	$157	e
10	Vesuvius	Rome	6	$950	e

	Volcano	Departs	Days	Price	Difficulty
1	Etna	Catania	7	$1,175	m
2	Fuji	Tokyo	2	$195	c
3	Kenya	Nairobi	6	$780	m
4	Kilauea	Hilo	1	$45	e
5	Kilimanjaro	Nairobi	9	$1,260	c
6	Krakatau	Jakarta	7	$850	e
7					

Cut
Copy
Paste
Hide
Show
Hold
Free
Delete rows
Insert rows...
Append a row
Height...

Inserting rows To add rows to a data table, right-click the table in the place where you want to add rows, and select **Insert rows** from the pop-up menu. An Insert Rows window will open. Choose **Above** or **Below**, enter the number of rows you wish, and click **OK**.

Insert Rows

Insert the new rows
○ Above   ● Below
Number of rows: [2]

[Ok] [Cancel]

Once the new empty rows are inserted, just click a cell and start typing the new data. Any data you enter must match the informat (not the format) associated with that column. If you are not sure what the informat and format are, then display the column properties as described in the previous section. After you enter new data, SAS Enterprise Guide will read the data value using the informat, and then display it using the format.

	Volcano	Departs	Days	Price	Difficulty
1	Etna	Catania	7	$1,175	m
2	Fuji	Tokyo	2	$195	c
3	Kenya	Nairobi	6	$780	m
4	Kilauea	Hilo	1	$45	e
5	Kilimanjaro	Nairobi	9	$1,260	c
6	Krakatau	Jakarta	7	$850	e
7				.	.
8				.	.
9	Poas	San Jose	1	$50	e
10	Reventador	Quito	4	$525	m
11	St. Helens	Portland	2	$157	e
12	Vesuvius	Rome	6	$950	e

In this example, a new tour is being added. The columns Volcano, Departs, and Difficulty use the basic character informat ($w.). The columns Days and Price use the basic numeric informat (w.d). The formats all match the informats except for the column Price. Price must be typed as a plain number (using informat w.d), but is displayed with a dollar sign (using format DOLLARw.d).

	Volcano	Departs	Days	Price	Difficulty
1	Etna	Catania	7	$1,175	m
2	Fuji	Tokyo	2	$195	c
3	Kenya	Nairobi	6	$780	m
4	Kilauea	Hilo	1	$45	e
5	Kilimanjaro	Nairobi	9	$1,260	c
6	Krakatau	Jakarta	7	$850	e
7	Lassen	Sacramento	3	250	
8					
9	Poas	San Jose	1	$50	e
10	Reventador	Quito	4	$525	m
11	St. Helens	Portland	2	$157	e
12	Vesuvius	Rome	6	$950	e

	Volcano	Departs	Days	Price	Difficulty
1	Etna	Catania	7	$1,175	m
2	Fuji	Tokyo	2	$195	c
3	Kenya	Nairobi	6	$780	m
4	Kilauea	Hilo	1	$45	e
5	Kilimanjaro	Nairobi	9	$1,260	c
6	Krakatau	Jakarta	7	$350	e
7	Lassen	Sacramento	3	$250	m
8					
9		ose	1	$50	e
10			4	$525	m
11		nd	2	$157	e
12			6	$350	e

Pop-up menu:
- Cut
- Copy
- Paste
- Hide
- Show
- Hold
- Free
- Delete rows
- Insert rows...
- Append a row
- Height...

Deleting rows If you want to delete rows, just click the number of the row you want to delete, or use shift-click to select more than one row. Then right-click the highlighted rows and select **Delete rows** from the pop-up menu. SAS Enterprise Guide will ask you to confirm that you do want to delete rows.

Enterprise Guide

? Delete rows?

Yes   No

Here is the final data table with the new row for a tour of Lassen.

	Volcano	Departs	Days	Price	Difficulty
1	Etna	Catania	7	$1,175	m
2	Fuji	Tokyo	2	$195	c
3	Kenya	Nairobi	6	$780	m
4	Kilauea	Hilo	1	$45	e
5	Kilimanjaro	Nairobi	9	$1,260	c
6	Krakatau	Jakarta	7	$850	e
7	Lassen	Sacramento	3	$250	m
8	Poas	San Jose	1	$50	e
9	Reventador	Quito	4	$525	m
10	St. Helens	Portland	2	$157	e
11	Vesuvius	Rome	6	$950	e

2.8 Inserting Columns in SAS Data Tables

When you insert a column in a SAS data table, the change is permanent whether you save your project or not. So, as with other editing tasks, you may want to save a copy of the table before inserting a column. Also, you can insert columns only while your table is in update mode. See section 2.6 for details about saving a copy of a data table, and changing to update mode.

Here is a copy of the Tours data table with the row that was added in the previous section.

	Volcano	Departs	Days	Price	Difficulty
1	Etna	Catania	7	$1,175	m
2	Fuji	Tokyo	2	$195	c
3	Kenya	Nairobi	6	$780	m
4	Kilauea	Hilo	1	$45	e
5	Kilimanjaro	Nairobi	9	$1,260	c
6	Krakatau	Jakarta	7	$850	e
7	Lassen	Sacramento	3	$250	m
8	Poas	San Jose	1	$50	e
9	Reventador	Quito	4	$525	m
10	St. Helens	Portland	2	$157	e
11	Vesuvius	Rome	6	$950	e

Inserting a column To add a column to a data table, right-click the column heading next to the place where you want to add a column, and select **Insert Column** from the pop-up menu. The Insert window will open.

In the General page of the Insert window, indicate whether you want the new column to be inserted to the left or the right. Then type a name and optional label for the column, and select the data type and group. Data types and groups are described in more detail in section 1.6. In this case, the column will be named NextDate, and will have a label of Date of Next Tour. Its type will be Numeric and it will be in the Date group.

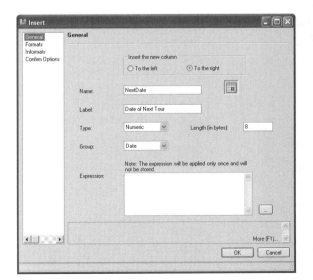

Click **Informats** in the selection pane on the left to open the Informats page. For the NextDate column, SAS Enterprise Guide has chosen the default informat for date columns, MMDDYY*w.d*, with a width of 10 and no decimal places. This informat can be written as MMDDYY10.0, and an example of what a data value looks like with this informat appears near the bottom of the window. If you want a different informat, you can specify it in this window. See section 1.9 for a list of commonly used informats. For the NextDate column, the default informat is fine.

Next click **Formats** in the selection pane on the left to open the Formats page. The default format for date columns is MMDDYY*w.d* with a width of 10 and no decimal places. This format can be written as MMDDYY10.0. You can choose a different format if you wish. The informat and format do not have to be the same. If, for example, you want to type dates in month-day-year form, but display them as Julian dates, you can do that. See section 1.10 for a list of commonly used formats. For the NextDate column, the default format is fine. When you are satisfied, click **OK** to insert the new column and return to the data table.

Now you can type data into the new column.

	Volcano	Departs	NextDate	Days	Price	Difficulty
1	Etna	Catania	08/05/2006	7	$1,175	m
2	Fuji	Tokyo	09/12/2006	2	$195	c
3	Kenya	Nairobi	05/31/2006	6	$780	m
4	Kilauea	Hilo	07/08/2006	1	$45	e
5	Kilmanjaro	Nairobi	06/09/2006	9	$1,260	c
6	Krakatau	Jakarta	07/19/06	7	$850	e
7	Lassen	Sacramento		3	$250	m
8	Poas	San Jose		1	$50	e
9	Reventador	Quito		4	$525	m
10	St. Helens	Portland		2	$157	e
11	Vesuvius	Rome		6	$950	e

2.9 Sorting Data Tables

There is little need for you to sort data in SAS Enterprise Guide. If a task requires data to be sorted, it will usually sort the data automatically. However, there may be times when you want to sort the data yourself. If you have a large data table, for example, you may want to store the data in sorted order. With the data presorted, SAS Enterprise Guide will not have to sort the data and your tasks will run more quickly. At other times, you may want to sort data to make it easier to find values in a Data Grid, or to eliminate duplicate rows.

There are two ways to sort data in SAS Enterprise Guide: the Sort task or a query. The Sort task gives you more control over how the data are sorted, whereas a query has other functions in addition to sorting. This section discusses the Sort task; sorting data using a query is covered in section 4.2.

Here is the Volcanoes data table. Notice that the rows are sorted by the name of the volcano. To change the sort order, click the data table icon in the Project Explorer or Project Designer to make it active, and select **Data ▶ Sort Data** from the menu bar. The Sort Data window will open.

	Volcano	Country	Region	Height	Activity	Type
1	Altar	Ecuador	SA	5321	Extinct	Stratovolcano
2	Arthur's Seat	UK	Eu	251	Extinct	
3	Barren Island	India	As	354	Active	Stratovolcano
4	Elbrus	Russia	Eu	5633	Extinct	Stratovolcano
5	Erebus		An	3794	Active	Stratovolcano
6	Etna	Italy	Eu	3350	Active	Stratovolcano
7	Fuji	Japan	As	3776	Active	Stratovolcano
8	Garibaldi	Canada	NA	2678		Stratovolcano
9	Grimsvotn	Iceland	Eu	1725	Active	Caldera
10	Illimani	Bolivia	SA	6458	Extinct	Stratovolcano

Project Designer / *Volcanoes (read-only)*

Assigning task roles Drag the columns you want to sort by to the **Sort by** role. If there is more than one **Sort by** column, SAS Enterprise Guide will sort rows by the first column, then by the second column within values of the first column, and so on. When you assign a column to the

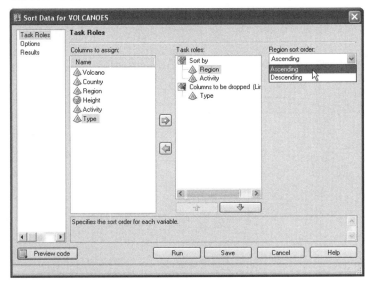

Sort by role, a box labeled **sort order** will appear on the right. If you click the down arrow, you can choose to have the data sorted in ascending (the default) or descending order. If you want to exclude columns from the output, drag those columns to the **Columns to be dropped** role. In this example, the Volcanoes data table will be sorted first by Region, then by Activity. The Type column will be dropped.

Sorting options To open the Options page, click **Options** in the selection pane on the left. In the Options page, you can select the collating sequence for the sort (such as ASCII, EBCDIC, or Server default). The collating sequence determines the sort order, including whether letters come before numerals or numerals before letters.

You can also choose options for duplicate records. You can keep all records (the default), keep only the first record for each combination of values of the Sort by columns, or keep only one of each record that is entirely duplicated. Duplicate records must be consecutive to be eliminated, so if you choose the last option, it is a good idea to sort by all the columns in the data table. For the Volcanoes data table, the default options are fine.

Results The Sort task creates a new SAS data table and displays it in a Data Grid. Notice that this table is sorted first by Region, and then by Activity within Region. The Region AP comes before Af because uppercase letters come before lowercase letters in the ASCII collating sequence (the default for Windows computers). Missing values are always lowest in the sort order. The first of the African volcanoes is Kilimanjaro with a missing value for Activity, followed by Nyamuragira and Nyiragongo which are active, and then Kenya which is Extinct. The Type column, which was dropped, is not part of the table. SAS Enterprise Guide stores the table with a default name in a default location. To save the data with a different name or location, use the Results page in the Sort Data task.

	Volcano	Country	Region	Height	Activity
1	Kilauea	USA	AP	1222	Active
2	Mauna Loa	USA	AP	4170	Active
3	Ruapehu	NZ	AP	2797	Active
4	Warning	Australia	AP	1125	Extinct
5	Kilimanjaro	Tanzania	Af	5895	
6	Nyamuragira	DRCongo	Af	3058	Active
7	Nyiragongo	DRCongo	Af	3470	Active
8	Kenya	Kenya	Af	5199	Extinct
9	Erebus		An	3794	Active
10	Barren Island	India	As	354	Active

2.10 Creating New Data Tables

The Data Grid allows you to browse and edit existing SAS data tables, but you can also create an empty Data Grid, and then type your data into it. To create an empty Data Grid, select **File ▶ New ▶ Data** from the menu bar. This opens the New Data wizard.

Name and location In the first window of the New Data wizard, type a name for your new data table in the **Name** box. This is a name that you make up. The name must follow the rules for standard SAS names (32 characters or fewer, start with a letter or underscore, and contain only letters, numerals, and underscores). Next choose a location where the new data table will be stored. This location must be a SAS data library. If a suitable library is not listed, then cancel the New Data wizard and define a new library before starting over (see sections 2.3 and 2.4). In this example, the name Seattle has been typed in the Name box and the FAITDATA library has been selected. When you are satisfied, click **Next**.

Column properties In the second window of the New Data wizard, you specify the properties for each column in your new data table. Columns start out with letters for names. To display the properties of a particular column, click its name in the list of columns on the left. To change a column property, click its value under **Column Properties** on the right. You can type a name for the column and an optional label. Then specify the data type and group by clicking the down arrows for those values. In the Seattle data table, the fourth column is named FlightPrice, and has a label of Flight Price USD, a data type of Numeric, and a data group of Currency.

To change a display format (or read-in format), click its value under Column Properties. A box with three dots will appear ⊡. Click the three dots to open a Formats window for that column. In the Seattle data table, the column Price uses the default numeric informat (*w.d*), but its format should be DOLLAR*w.d* with an overall width of 10 and two decimal places. See sections 1.9 and 1.10 for tables of commonly used informats and formats. When you are satisfied with the display format (or read-in format), click **OK**.

In the second window of the New Data wizard, you can add more columns by clicking **New**. You can delete columns by clicking the letter for that column and then clicking the delete button ☒. When you are satisfied with your columns and their properties, click **Finish** to close the wizard and create the new data table.

Formats

Categories:	Formats:
None	DOLLARw.d
Numeric	DOLLARXw.d
Date	EURFRATSw.d
Time	EURFRBEFw.d
Date/Time	EURFRCHFw.d
Currency	EURFRCZKw.d
User Defined	EURFRDEMw.d
All	EURFRDKKw.d

Attributes
Overall width: 10   Min: 2   Max: 32
Decimal places: 2   Min: 0   Max: 9

Description
dollar sign, commas and decimal point

Example
Value: 12345.1
Output: $ 1 2 , 3 4 5 . 1 0

OK   Cancel

Entering data Once you have created the data table, you can begin typing your data. To move the cursor, click a field, or use the **Tab** and arrow keys. You can copy and paste values. If you need more columns or rows, right-click a column or row and select **Insert** from the pop-up menu. If you have extra columns or rows, you can delete them by right-clicking the extra columns or rows and selecting **Delete** from the pop-up menu.

Project Designer   Seattle

	Origin	Destination	FlightNo	FlightPrice	E	F
1	Seattle	Catania	BA48	702		
2						
3						
4						
5						
6						
7						
8						
9						
10						
11						
12						

Here is the Seattle table with the column attributes defined, data entered, and extra rows and columns deleted.

Project Designer   Seattle

	Origin	Destination	FlightNo	FlightPrice
1	Seattle	Catania	BA48	$702.00
2	Seattle	Hilo	HA21	$577.00
3	Seattle	Jakarta	AA119	$1,715.00
4	Seattle	Nairobi	KLM6034	$1,661.00
5	Seattle	Quito	CA1086	$733.00
6	Seattle	Rome	USA6	$496.00
7	Seattle	San Jose	CA1100	$380.00
8	Seattle	Tokyo	UA875	$621.00

2.11 Using Microsoft Excel Spreadsheets As Is

When you read a Microsoft Excel spreadsheet in SAS Enterprise Guide, you have to choose whether to open the spreadsheet as is or as a SAS data set. If you open the spreadsheets as is, then:

- You can run tasks using the data.
- You cannot edit the data.
- If that spreadsheet changes, SAS Enterprise Guide will automatically read the updated version the next time it accesses the data (such as when you run a task or open a Data Grid).

Input data This example shows a Microsoft Excel spreadsheet named Bookings.xls which contains six columns: the office that booked the tour, followed by the customer's identification number, the identification number of the tour, the number of travelers, the money deposited, and the date the deposit was made. Notice that the first row contains the column names.

Opening a Microsoft Excel file To open a Microsoft Excel file, select **File ▶ Open ▶ Data** from the menu bar. In the Open Data From window, select **Local Computer** (or **SAS Servers**). Then in the Open From My Computer window (or the Open From SAS Servers window), navigate to the location of the file. Once you have found the file you want, click **Open**.

Open Tables window In the Open Tables window, check the sheet (or sheets) you want SAS Enterprise Guide to read, and click **Open**. The dollar sign in the sheet name indicates that SAS Enterprise Guide will read the entire sheet. If you have named ranges in a sheet, they will be listed without a dollar sign.

Open Data window

In the Open Data window, you may choose to open the spreadsheet as is or as a SAS data set. To open the file as is, click the **view the file as is** icon.

Open Data

Options for Opening File "Bookings.xls"

Select one of the following two ways of opening the selected file.

Select this option if you want to view the file as is.

For data files, the data formats will be automatically chosen for you. The data formats may not be correct if you want to perform analysis against the file opened in this way.

Select this option if you want to open the file as a SAS data set.

You may go through Import Data task multiple times, once for each file or sheet you selected, to specify data formats. The result will be one or more SAS data sets, suitable as data input for further analysis.

☐ Do not show this dialog again - always open file as is.

Cancel

Results The data will appear in a Data Grid. Because the table is as is, you cannot edit the file from inside SAS Enterprise Guide. However, if someone edits the file in Microsoft Excel, SAS Enterprise Guide will automatically read the updated version every time it accesses the data.

	Office	CustomerID	Tour	Travelers	Deposit	Deposit_Date
1	Portland	SL28	SH43	10	425	7/5/2006 12:00:00 AM
2	Portland	DE27	PS27	6	75	7/11/2006 12:00:00 AM
3	Portland	SL34	FJ12	4	200	7/19/2006 12:00:00 AM
4	Portland	DI33	SH43	4	150	7/23/2006 12:00:00 AM
5	Portland	BU12	SH43	2	75	7/23/2006 12:00:00 AM
6	Portland	DE31	FJ12	3	175	7/25/2006 12:00:00 AM
7	Portland	WI48	FJ12	2	100	7/26/2006 12:00:00 AM
8	Portland	NG17	PS27	5	65	7/26/2006 12:00:00 AM
9	Portland	RA28	PS27	2	30	7/28/2006 12:00:00 AM
10	Portland	ME11	PS27	2	30	7/28/2006 12:00:00 AM
11	Portland	GI08	SH43	8	300	7/31/2006 12:00:00 AM
12	Portland	HI15	SH43	4	150	7/31/2006 12:00:00 AM
13	Portland	MA09	SH43	2	75	7/31/2006 12:00:00 AM

Notice that SAS Enterprise Guide used the first row of the spreadsheet as column headings. This is the default behavior. If you do not want SAS Enterprise Guide to use the first row as column headings, then select **Tools ▶ Options** from the menu bar. In the selection pane on the left under **Data**, click **Performance**. In the Data > Performance page, uncheck **Use first row as column names**.

By default, SAS Enterprise Guide 4.1 reads dates in Excel spreadsheets as datetime values (the number of seconds since midnight January 1, 1960). You cannot change the way dates are read or displayed when you open a spreadsheet as is. However, you can change the way dates are read and displayed when you open a spreadsheet as a SAS data set as described in the next section.

2.12 Opening Microsoft Excel Spreadsheets as SAS Data Sets

When you open a Microsoft Excel spreadsheet as a SAS data set, SAS Enterprise Guide copies the data in the spreadsheet into a SAS data set. As a result:

- You can run tasks using the data (and the tasks will run more quickly because it's faster to read a SAS data set than a Microsoft Excel spreadsheet).
- You can edit the data, but any changes you make will not be applied to the original Microsoft Excel spreadsheet.
- If the original spreadsheet changes, SAS Enterprise Guide will not automatically read the updated version. To get the updated version, you must import the spreadsheet again.

Input data This example shows a Microsoft Excel spreadsheet named Bookings.xls, which contains six columns: the office that booked the tour, followed by the customer's identification number, the identification number of the tour, the number of travelers, the money deposited, and the date the deposit was made. Notice that the first row contains the column names.

Opening a Microsoft Excel file To open a Microsoft Excel file, select **File ▶ Open ▶ Data** from the menu bar. In the Open Data From window, select **Local Computer** (or **SAS Servers**). Then in the Open From My Computer window (or the Open From SAS Servers window), navigate to the location of the file. Once you have found the file you want, click **Open**.

Open Tables window In the Open Tables window, check the sheet (or sheets) you want SAS Enterprise Guide to read and click **Open**.

Open Data window To open the file as a SAS data set, click the **SAS data set** icon.

Region to import The Import Data window has several parts. In the Region to import page, you tell SAS Enterprise Guide which rows to import and which row (if any) to use as column headings. For the Bookings data, use the first row as column headings and import the entire file.

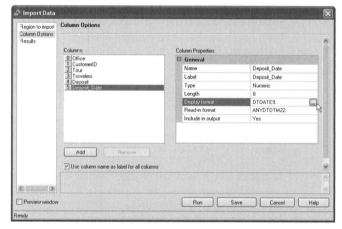

Column Options In the Column Options page, you can change column properties. By default, dates from Excel files, such as Deposit_Date, are read as datetime values (the number of seconds since midnight January 1, 1960). If you change the display format to **DTDATE9.**, then only the date portion of the datetime value will be displayed, but the value will still be stored as datetime. If you want to change Deposit_Date to a SAS date value (the number of days since January 1, 1960), then change its read-in format to the date read-in format ANYDTDTE*w*., and give it a date display format such as DATE9.

Preview window To see how your data will look once SAS Enterprise Guide imports the file, check the **Preview window** box in the lower-left corner of the Import Data window. Then, in the Preview Window, click the **Results** tab. If you make a change, click **Refresh Results**.

Results The data set will appear in a Data Grid. Because the data are now in a SAS data set, you can change to update mode if you wish. Any changes you make will not be applied to the original Microsoft Excel spreadsheet. SAS Enterprise Guide gives the data set a name starting with the letters IMPW and stores it in a default location. To choose a different name or location, use the Results page in the Import Data window.

	Office	CustomerID	Tour	Travelers	Deposit	Deposit_Date
1	Portland	SL28	SH43	10	425	05JUL2006
2	Portland	DE27	PS27	6	75	11JUL2006
3	Portland	SL34	FJ12	4	200	19JUL2006
4	Portland	DI33	SH43	4	150	23JUL2006
5	Portland	BU12	SH43	2	75	23JUL2006
6	Portland	DE31	FJ12	3	175	25JUL2006
7	Portland	WI48	FJ12	2	100	26JUL2006
8	Portland	NG17	PS27	5	65	26JUL2006
9	Portland	RA28	PS27	2	30	28JUL2006
10	Portland	ME11	PS27	2	30	28JUL2006
11	Portland	GI08	SH43	8	300	31JUL2006
12	Portland	HI15	SH43	4	150	31JUL2006
13	Portland	MA09	SH43	2	75	31JUL2006

2.13 Reading Delimited Raw Data

Delimited raw data files have a special character separating the data values. That character is often a comma (as in CSV or comma-separated values files), but it can also be a tab, semicolon, space, or some other character.

Input data This example uses data from a file named Eruptions.csv. There are four variables: the name of each volcano, followed by the date an eruption started, the date that eruption ended, and the Volcanic Explosivity Index (VEI). Notice that this file has commas between the data values, and the first line contains the column names.

```
Volcano, StartDate, EndDate, VEI
Barren Island, 12/20/1795, 12/21/1795, 2
Barren Island, 12/20/1994, 06/05/1995, 2
Erebus, 12/12/1912, . , 2
Erebus, 01/03/1972, . , 1
Etna, 02/06/1610, 08/15/1610, 2
Etna, 06/04/1787, 08/11/1787, 4
Etna, 01/30/1865, 06/28/1865, 2
Etna, 12/16/2005, 12/22/2005, 1
```

Opening a delimited data file To open a delimited data file, select **File ▶ Open ▶ Data** from the menu bar. In the Open Data From window, select **Local Computer** (or **SAS Servers**). Then in the Open From My Computer window (or the Open From SAS Servers window), navigate to the location of the file. Once you have found the file you want, click **Open**.

In the Open Data window, you can choose to open a raw data file as is or as a SAS data set. If you open the file as is, then SAS Enterprise Guide displays the file in a simple text editor. You can look at the data, and you can edit the data, but you cannot use a raw data file for any task when it is opened as is. Therefore, you will generally want to open a raw data file as a SAS data set. To do this, click the SAS data set icon in the Open Data window.

Import Data window The Import Data window has several parts. In the Region to import page, you tell SAS Enterprise Guide which rows to import and which row (if any) to use as column headings. For the Eruptions.csv file, use the first line as column headings and import the entire file.

Preview window To see how your data will look once SAS Enterprise Guide imports the file, check the **Preview window** box in the lower-left corner of the Import Data window. Then, in the Preview Window, click the **Results** tab. If you make a change, click **Refresh Results**.

Text Format In the Text Format page, you tell SAS Enterprise Guide whether your file is delimited or fixed width. If your file is delimited, you must specify whether the delimiter is a comma, semicolon, tab, space, or some other character. The Eruptions.csv file uses commas as delimiters.

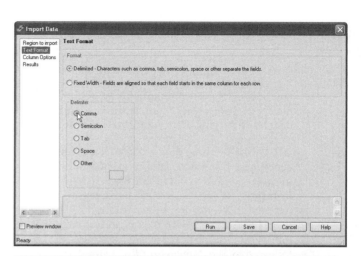

Column Options In the Column Options page, you can change column properties. If the file does not include column headings, you'll probably want to type them here. To change properties, click a column name in the **Columns** box on the left, and type the new properties in the **Column Properties** box on the right. For the Eruptions.csv file, you don't need to make any changes in the Column Options page. Once you are satisfied with the options in the Import Data window, click **Run** and SAS Enterprise Guide will create the new data set.

Results The data set will appear in a Data Grid. The data set opens in read-only mode, but because the data are now in a SAS data set, you can change to update mode to edit the data. SAS Enterprise Guide gives the data set a name starting with the letters IMPW and stores it in a default location. To choose a different name or location, use the Results page in the Import Data window.

	Volcano	StartDate	EndDate	VEI
1	Barren Island	12/20/1795	12/21/1795	2
2	Barren Island	12/20/1994	06/05/1995	2
3	Erebus	12/12/1912	.	2
4	Erebus	01/03/1972		1
5	Etna	02/06/1610	08/15/1610	2
6	Etna	06/04/1787	08/11/1787	4
7	Etna	01/20/1865	06/20/1865	2

Project Designer   SASUSER.IMPW_0001 (read-only)

2.14 Reading Formatted Data

Without special effort on your part, SAS Enterprise Guide can read data in many different formats. For example, if you have the value $100, SAS Enterprise Guide will generally interpret that value as numeric, disregarding the fact that dollar signs are characters, not numerals. But, if you have data in a more unusual format such as Julian dates, then SAS Enterprise Guide may not correctly interpret them. Fortunately, you can tell SAS Enterprise Guide how to read your data by specifying an input format (also called informats and read-in formats).

Input data These data are from a text file containing information about recent eruptions of the volcano Etna in Italy. This file is like the Eruptions.csv file, except that the dates are in day-month-year order, instead of month-day-year. The file is named Etna.csv and contains four variables: the name of each volcano,

```
Volcano, StartDate, EndDate, VEI
Etna, 17/07/2001, 09/08/2001, 3
Etna, . , 30/10/2002, 1
Etna, 26/10/2002, 28/01/2003, 2
Etna, 08/03/2003, 09/11/2003, 1
```

followed by the date an eruption started, the date that eruption ended, and the Volcanic Explosivity Index (VEI). Notice that one value for StartDate is a period, indicating a missing value, and the dates have the day first, followed by month and year.

Opening the data file To open the data file, select **File ▶ Open ▶ Data** from the menu bar. In the Open Data From window, select **Local Computer** (or **SAS Servers**). Then in the Open From My Computer window (or the Open From SAS Servers window), navigate to the location

of the file. Once you have found the file you want, click **Open**. To specify an input format, you must open the file as a SAS data set (not as is). Then import the file as you would normally. For the Etna data, you need to tell SAS Enterprise Guide that the first line contains column headings, and to treat commas as delimiters. (See section 2.13 for more information about reading a delimited file.) If you click **Run**, then SAS Enterprise Guide will read the file using default input formats. For Etna.csv, the result looks odd. Notice that SAS Enterprise Guide was not able to read the dates correctly. That's because the default informat for dates is MMDDYYw.d, but numbers over 12 cannot be valid months.

Column Options To fix the data, first reopen the Import Data task by right-clicking it in the Project Explorer or Project Designer, and selecting **Open** from the pop-up menu. Click **Column Options** in the selection pane on the left.

Then click the variable name **StartDate**. You can see that SAS Enterprise Guide assigned StartDate an input format of MMDDYY10. To change this, click the words **Read-in format**. A box with three dots will appear [...]. To change the input format, click the box. The Read-in format window will open.

Read-in format window In this window, you choose the data category (in this case, Date), the informat (DDMMYY*w.d* for day, followed by month and year), the width (10), and decimal places (0). This informat can be written as DDMMYY10.0. See section 1.9 for a list of commonly used informats. When you are satisfied with the informat, click **OK**.

Column Options

Notice that StartDate now has a read-in format of DDMMYY10.0 and a display format of MMDDYY10. At this point, you can change the properties of other columns. For the Etna data, the column EndDate needs the same changes as StartDate. Once you are satisfied with all the column properties, click **Run**.

Results The new data will appear in a Data Grid. Notice that the dates have now been read correctly. They are displayed in MMDDYY. format (the default). You could change that by reopening the Import Data task and choosing a different display format in the Column Options page.

	Volcano	StartDate	EndDate	VEI
1	Etna	07/17/2001	08/09/2001	3
2	Etna	.	10/30/2002	1
3	Etna	10/26/2002	01/28/2003	2
4	Etna	03/08/2003	11/09/2003	1

SASUSER.IMPW_0002 (read-only) / Project Designer

the Column Options page. See section 1.10 for a list of commonly used formats.

2.15 Reading Fixed-Width Raw Data

Fixed-width raw data files are similar to delimited raw data files, but instead of having a delimiter separating data values, the data values are lined up in tidy vertical columns.

Input data These data are a sample from a file named LatLong.txt, which contains three variables: the name of each volcano, followed by its latitude and longitude. Notice that the column names appear in the first row, and the data values are vertically aligned.

Volcano	Latitude	Longitude
Altar	-1.67	-78.42
Barren Island	12.28	93.52
Elbrus	43.33	42.45
Erebus	-77.53	167.17
Etna	37.73	15.00
Fuji	35.35	138.73

Opening a fixed-width data file To open the data file, select **File ▶ Open ▶ Data** from the menu bar. In the Open Data From window, select **Local Computer** (or **SAS Servers**). Then in the Open From My Computer window (or the Open From SAS Servers window), navigate to the location of the file. Once you have found the file you want, click **Open**.

In the Open Data window, you can choose to open a raw data file as is or as a SAS data set. If you open the file as is, then SAS Enterprise Guide displays the file in a simple text editor. You can look at the data, and you can edit the data, but you cannot use a raw data file for any task when it is opened as is. Therefore, you will generally want to open a raw data file as a SAS data set. To do this, click the SAS data set icon in the Open Data window.

Region to import The Import Data window has several parts. In the Region to import page, you tell SAS Enterprise Guide which rows to import. If your file contains column headings, then check the box next to **Specify line to use as column headings**, and enter the line number in the box on the right. The Latlong.txt file has column headings in line 1.

Preview window To see how your data will look once SAS Enterprise Guide imports them, check the **Preview window** box in the lower-left corner of the Import Data window. Then, in the Preview Window, click the **Results** tab. If you make a change, click **Refresh Results**.

Text Format In the Text
Format page, select the **Fixed
Width** button. A box will appear
displaying the data file. Click the
ruler above the data to tell SAS
Enterprise Guide where each
variable begins. For the Latlong
data, the volcano name starts at 1,
latitude starts at 14, and longitude
starts at 23.

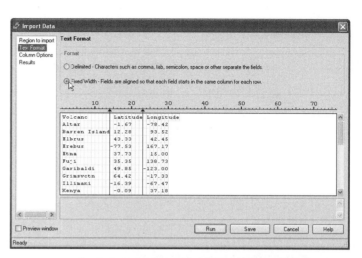

Column Options In the
Column Options page, you can
change column properties. To do
this, click a column name in the
Columns box on the left, and type
the new properties in the **Column
Properties** box on the right. For
the LatLong.txt data, all three
columns are initially set to
character. This is fine for Volcano,
but not for Latitude and
Longitude. For Latitude, click the
column name, and change the
type to numeric. Make the same
change for Longitude. Once you
are satisfied with the settings in
the
Import Data window, click **Run**.

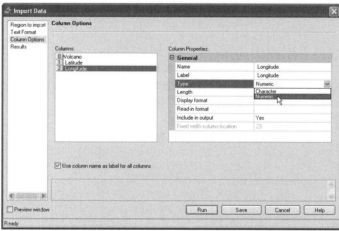

Results The data set will appear in a Data
Grid. The data set opens in read-only mode, but
because the data are now in a SAS data set, you
can change to update mode to edit the data. SAS
Enterprise Guide gives the data set a name
starting with the letters IMPW and stores it in a
default location. To choose a different name or
location, use the Results page in the Import Data
window.

	Volcano	Latitude	Longitude
1	Altar	-1.67	-78.42
2	Barren Island	12.28	93.52
3	Elbrus	43.33	42.45
4	Erebus	-77.53	167.17
5	Etna	37.73	15
6	Fuji	35.35	138.73
7	Garibaldi	49.85	-123

SASUSER.IMPW_0003 (read-only)

2.16 Exporting Data

After you have read your data into SAS Enterprise Guide and worked with it, you may want to write it out in some other form. Exporting data is easy in SAS Enterprise Guide.

Types of files that SAS Enterprise Guide can create include:

- Comma-Separated Values (CSV) Files
- dBASE Files
- HTML Files
- IBM Lotus 1-2-3 Files
- Microsoft Access Files
- Microsoft Excel Files
- Paradox Files
- SAS Data Tables
- Space-Delimited Text Files
- Tab-Delimited Text Files

Here is a Data Grid showing the Tours data table, which will be exported to a Microsoft Excel file.

To export a data table from SAS Enterprise Guide, click the icon for the desired data table in the Project Explorer or Project Designer to make it active, and select **File ▶ Export** from the menu bar. Then select either **Export** or **Export As A Step In Project**. If you simply export the data table, then the newly exported file will not appear in the Project Explorer or Project Designer. If you select **Export As A Step In Project**, then an Export File task icon will be added to your project. That way, if you rerun your project, your data table will be automatically re-exported.

Export wizard If you select **Export As A Step In Project**, the Export wizard will open. In the first window, select the data table you wish to export, and click **Next**.

In the second Export window, select the type of file you want to create, and click **Next**.

In the third Export window (not shown), indicate whether you want to use labels for column names, and click **Next.**

In the fourth Export window, choose either **Local Computer** or **SAS Servers**, and then click the **Edit** button to navigate to the location where you want the table to be saved. You can export a SAS data table to your local computer only if SAS is installed on your local computer. If SAS is not installed on your local computer, you can either export your data as a SAS data table to a server where SAS is installed, or save your data as another type of file. When you are satisfied, click **Next.**

In the fifth Export window, confirm your settings by clicking **Finish**.

An Export File task icon will appear in the Project Explorer and Project Designer, along with an icon for the newly exported data.

Results Here is how the Tours data look after being exported to a Microsoft Excel spreadsheet and opened in Microsoft Excel.

Sending data If your goal is to put your data into a Microsoft Excel spreadsheet, a Microsoft Word RTF table, or an e-mail attachment, then you can use a quicker method. Right-click the data set icon in the Project Explorer or Project Designer and select **Send To** from the pop-up menu. Then choose either **E-Mail Recipient**, **Microsoft Word**, or **Microsoft Excel**. SAS Enterprise Guide will immediately open that application and convert the data set to an e-mail attachment, RTF table, or spreadsheet.

CHAPTER 3

Changing the Way Data Values Are Displayed

3.1   Applying Standard Formats in a Data Grid

When you open a Data Grid, SAS Enterprise Guide decides how the data should be displayed—how many decimal places to print, for example, and whether to use a dollar or percent sign. Most of the time this is fine, but sometimes you may want to change the way a column looks. You can do this by telling SAS Enterprise Guide to use a different display format.

Here is a Data Grid showing the Eruptions data table. The columns StartDate and EndDate use the default format for dates, MMDDYY10.0 (month followed by day and year), but SAS Enterprise Guide offers many other date formats. See section 1.10 for a list of commonly used formats.

Setting the update mode If the data table is not already open, then open it by double-clicking the data icon in the Project Explorer or Project Designer. Before you can change a display format, your data table must be in update mode. If the data table is in read-only mode, then select **Data ▶ Read-only** from the menu bar to toggle from read-only to update.

Opening the Properties window In the Data Grid, right-click the name of the column you want to modify, and select **Properties** from the pop-up menu. This opens the Properties window for that column.

The Properties window has several pages. In the General page, check that the column has the correct type: either numeric or character. Sometimes when you import a data file, formatted values such as times and dates may be read as character data, instead of numeric. If the type is wrong, you can change it here. Then click **Formats** in the selection pane on the left to open the Formats page.

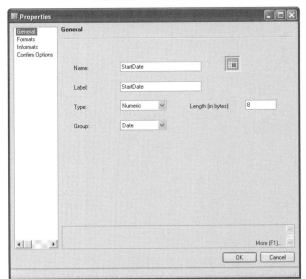

Selecting formats In the Formats page, choose the category of formats you want to see, and then click the name of the format you want to use. In the area labeled **Attributes**, specify the overall width (the longest number of characters that will be displayed for this column), and, for numeric columns, the number of decimal places. In this example, the category Date has been selected, along with the format WEEKDATE*w.d*, an overall width of 17, and no decimal places. This format can be written as WEEKDATE17.0. The area labeled **Example** shows a sample of how this format will look. When you are satisfied with the format, click **OK**.

Results Here is the Eruptions data table. Notice how different the values of StartDate look. When you make changes in a Data Grid, they are immediately saved with the data set, and will be applied in any tasks you run using that data table. However, formats affect only the way data are displayed—not the actual data values. That means you can easily select a different format or change the format back to what it was.

3.2 ▶ Applying Standard Formats in a Task

Every time you run a task that produces a report, SAS Enterprise Guide decides how the data should be displayed. That's good, but sometimes the way that SAS Enterprise Guide displays data may not be exactly what you want. You can apply a format in a Data Grid, but then the format will be saved with the data table. To avoid that, you can apply the format directly in a task.

🔲 Project Designer	🔲 **Eruptions (read-only)**		
⚠ **Volcano**	🔳 **StartDate**	🔳 **EndDate**	🔘 **VEI**
1 Barren Island	12/20/1795	12/21/1795	2
2 Barren Island	12/20/1994	06/05/1995	2
3 Erebus	12/12/1912	.	2
4 Erebus	01/03/1972	.	1
5 Etna	02/06/1610	08/15/1610	2
6 Etna	06/04/1787	08/11/1787	4
7 Etna	01/30/1865	06/28/1865	2
8 Etna	06/17/1994	07/17/2001	3
9 Fuji	12/16/1707	02/24/1708	5
10 Grimsvotn	10/31/1603	11/01/1603	2

Here is the Eruptions data set. The previous section showed how to apply the format WEEKDATE*w.d* to the variable StartDate in a Data Grid. This example uses the List Data task to show how you can apply the same format in a task.

In the Project Explorer or Project Designer, click the data set icon to make it active. Then select **Describe ▶ List Data** from the menu bar. The List Data window will open, displaying the Task Roles page.

Opening the Properties window To open a Properties window for a variable, right-click the name of the variable you want to modify (in either the **Variables to assign** area or the **Task roles** area), and select **Properties** from the pop-up menu. In this example, the variables Volcano, StartDate, and VEI have been assigned to the **List variables** role, and **Properties** is being selected for StartDate.

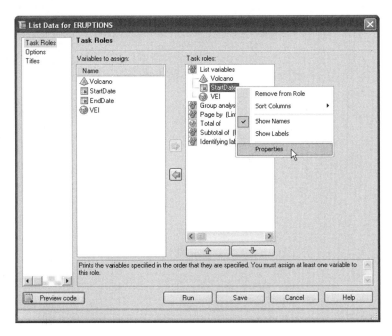

Here is the Properties window for the variable StartDate. You cannot change a variable from numeric to character (or vice versa) using the Properties window inside a task. To make that change, use the Properties window inside a Data Grid, as described in the preceding section.

Click **Change** to open the Formats window.

Selecting formats In the Formats window, choose the category of formats you want to see, and then click the name of the format you want to use. In the area labeled **Attributes**, specify the overall width (the longest number of characters that will be allowed for this variable), and, for numeric variables, the number of decimal places. The area labeled **Example** shows a sample of how this format will look. See section 1.10 for a list of commonly used formats.

In this Formats window, the category Date has been selected, along with the format WEEKDATE*w.d*, an overall width of 17, and no decimal places. This format can be written as WEEKDATE17.0.

When you are satisfied with the format, click **OK**. Then click **OK** in the Properties window, and click **Run** in the task window.

Results Here is the beginning of the report using the new format for StartDate. Any formats you apply in a task are not saved in the original data set and will not be used in other tasks.

Report Listing

Row number	Volcano	StartDate	VEI
1	Barren Island	Sun, Dec 20, 1795	2
2	Barren Island	Tue, Dec 20, 1994	2
3	Erebus	Thu, Dec 12, 1912	2
4	Erebus	Mon, Jan 3, 1972	1
5	Etna	Sat, Feb 6, 1610	2
6	Etna	Mon, Jun 4, 1787	4
7	Etna	Mon, Jan 30, 1865	2
8	Etna	Fri, Jun 17, 1994	3
9	Fuji	Fri, Dec 16, 1707	5
10	Grimsvotn	Fri, Oct 31, 1603	2

3.3 Defining Your Own Character Formats

Even with all the standard formats provided by SAS Enterprise Guide, there are times when you need something different. In those cases, you can create a user-defined format. Basically, user-defined formats allow you to specify a set of labels that will be substituted for specific values or ranges of values in your data. To do this, open the Create Format window by selecting **Data ▶ Create Format** from the menu bar.

Create Format window To create a format for a character variable, select a **Format type** of **Character**. Then type a name for the new format in the **Format name** box. This name must be 31 characters or fewer in length, cannot start or end with a numeral, and can contain only letters, numerals, or underscores. This example shows a character format named RegionName being created.

Any formats stored in the WORK library (the default) will be deleted when you exit SAS Enterprise Guide. To save your format, specify a location to store the format by choosing a server and library. If you choose to leave your format in the WORK library, you can always regenerate it later by rerunning the Create Format task. If you have more than one SAS server, be sure to save your format on the same server where you run

tasks. When you are satisfied, click **Define formats** in the selection pane on the left.

Defining formats

You define formats in a stepwise fashion following the instructions in the Create Format window. First, click **New Label** and type a label in the **Label** box. Then click **New Range,** and under **Values** type the data value that corresponds to that label. Data values are case-sensitive, so "Yes" is not the same as "yes." Repeat these steps for the second label, and so on, until you have created all labels you wish. If you want to specify a range of data values (such as A–F), click the down arrow next to **Discrete** and select **Range** from the pull-down list. In this example, you can see that the label Africa is being applied to the data value Af.

You can specify a label to be used for missing values or for all other values by clicking the arrow in the box labeled **Values**. In this window, you can see that the label Error will be applied to all other data values. When you are satisfied with the format labels and ranges, click **Run** to create the format. All character format names begin with a dollar sign, and end with a period, so this format will be named $RegionName. A more detailed example of creating a character format appears in Tutorial C.

Using custom formats   You can apply a user-defined format to a variable in the same ways you apply standard formats: in a Data Grid, a task, or a query. Section 3.5 shows the $RegionName. format being used in a List Data task.

3.4 ▶ Defining Your Own Numeric Formats

The previous section showed how to create a user-defined format for a character variable. Creating a user-defined format for a numeric variable is similar, but you have a few more options. Start by selecting **Data ▶ Create Format** from the menu bar to open the Create Format window.

Create Format window

Select a **Format type** of **Numeric**. Then type a name for the new format in the **Format name** box. This name must be 32 characters or fewer in length, cannot start or end with a numeral, and can contain only letters, numerals, or underscores. This example shows a numeric format named HeightGroup being created.

Any formats stored in the WORK library (the default) will be deleted when you exit SAS Enterprise Guide. To save your format, specify a location to store the format by choosing a server and library. If you choose to leave your format in the WORK library, you can always regenerate it later by rerunning the Create Format task. If you have more than one SAS server, be sure to save your format on the same server where you run tasks. When you are satisfied, click **Define formats** in the selection pane on the left.

Defining formats

You define formats in a stepwise fashion. First, click **New Label** and type a label in the **Label** box. Then click **New Range** and enter the data values corresponding to that label. Repeat these steps for the second label, and so on, until you have created all the labels you wish.

When you specify a range, you have some choices. Under **Type,** click the down arrow to open the pull-down list and select either **Discrete** (if you have a single value) or **Range**. In this example, you can see the label Pip-squeak will be substituted for a range of data values up to 500.

You can make ranges inclusive or exclusive. In this example, the label Middling has been mapped to data values from 500 up to (but excluding) 4000. If you see a red X over ranges at the top of the window, it means that your ranges are overlapping and you will probably want to make one of them exclusive.

You can specify a label to be used for special values by clicking the arrow in the box labeled **Values.** For discrete values, you can select **All Other Values** or **Missing Values**; for ranges, you can select **Low** (the lowest possible value) and **High** (the highest). In this window, the label Stupendous has been mapped to data values from 4000 to High.

When you are satisfied with the format labels and ranges, click **Run** to create the format. Unlike character formats, numeric formats do not begin with a dollar sign. However, they do end with a period, so the name of this format will be HeightGroup.

Using custom formats You can apply a user-defined format to a variable in the same ways you apply standard formats: in a Data Grid, a task, or a query. The next section shows the HeightGroup. format being applied in a List Data task.

3.5 ▷ Applying User-Defined Formats

You apply user-defined formats in exactly the same ways you apply standard formats: in a Data Grid, a task, or a query. In this example, two user-defined formats, $RegionName. and HeightGroup. (from sections 3.3 and 3.4), are applied in a List Data task.

Here is a simple report from a List Data task using the Volcanoes data set. The variables Volcano, Region, and Height have been assigned to serve in the List variables role. Notice that the data values are unformatted.

You can apply a format when you first run a task, or to change an existing report, right-click the task icon in the Project Explorer or Project Designer and select **Open** to open the task window.

Report Listing

Row number	Volcano	Region	Height
1	Altar	SA	5321
2	Arthur's Seat	Eu	251
3	Barren Island	As	354
4	Elbrus	Eu	5633
5	Erebus	An	3794
6	Etna	Eu	3350
7	Fuji	As	3776

Opening the Properties window   To apply a format in a task, right-click the name of the variable you want to change in the Task Roles page (in either the **Variables to assign** area or the **Task roles** area), and select **Properties** from the pop-up window. In this example, **Properties** is being selected for the variable Region.

Using custom formats In the Properties window, click **Change** to open the Formats window for that variable. Then, in the Formats window, select the **User Defined** category. All the formats you have created will be listed.

Here is the Formats window for the variable Region. Because Region is character, only character formats are listed. In this case, $REGIONNAME. is being selected. Once you have selected the correct format, click **OK** in the Formats window and click **OK** in the Properties window.

From the task window, you can assign formats to other variables.

Here is the Formats window for the variable Height. Because Height is numeric, only numeric formats are listed. In this example, HEIGHTGROUP. is being selected. Once you have selected the correct format, click **OK** in the Formats window and click **OK** in the Properties window. Once you have applied all the formats you want, click **Run** in the task window.

Results Here is the new report with user-defined formats. You can see how the values of Region and Height are now displayed with the user-defined formats.

Report Listing

Row number	Volcano	Region	Height
1	Altar	South America	Stupendous
2	Arthur's Seat	Europe	Pip-squeak
3	Barren Island	Asia	Pip-squeak
4	Elbrus	Europe	Stupendous
5	Erebus	Antarctica	Middling
6	Etna	Europe	Middling
7	Fuji	Asia	Middling

CHAPTER 4

Modifying Data Using the Query Builder

4.1 Selecting Columns in a Query

To run a query, you must tell SAS Enterprise Guide which columns to include in the result. When you first open the Query Builder, no columns are selected. You select columns in the Select Data tab of the Query Builder window where you can also set properties for columns.

Here is a sample of the Volcanoes data table which contains six columns of data about volcanoes around the world. To create a query, click the data icon in the Project Explorer or Project Designer to make it active, and select **Data ▶ Filter and Query** from the menu bar. The Query Builder opens with the **Select Data** tab on top. You can also open the Query Builder by right-clicking the data icon and selecting **Filter and Query** from the pop-up menu.

Selecting the data When you open the Query Builder window, the Select Data tab is on top, and no columns are selected. To select a column for the query, click the column name in the box on the left and drag it to the box on the right under the **Select Data** tab. You can also right-click the column and choose **Add to Selection** from the pop-up menu. To add more than one column at a time, hold down the control key (or shift if you want to select a whole group) when you click the column names. You can also add all the columns in a table to the query, by clicking the table name and dragging it to the Select Data tab. If you want to remove a column listed in

the Select Data tab, click the column name in the Select Data tab and click the delete button [X] on the right side of the window. You can also change the order of the columns using the up and down arrow buttons [⇧] [⇩].

Setting properties for columns

You can change the properties of a column in a query by clicking the column name in the Select Data tab and clicking the Properties button located on the right side of the window. This opens the Properties window for the column where you can change the alias, label, and format for the column. Here the **Height** column is given the label **Height in Meters**. Click **OK** to return to the Query Builder window. After selecting columns and setting properties, click **Run** in the Query Builder window to run the query.

Results The result is a new data table which is given a name starting with the letters QUERY and is stored in a default location. You can change the location or name of the data table by clicking the **Change** button next to the output name in the Query Builder window. In this result, notice the label given to the column Height does not appear in the Data Grid. By default, the Data Grid displays the column names instead of the labels.

	Volcano	Country	Region	Height
1	Altar	Ecuador	SA	5321
2	Arthur's Seat	UK	Eu	251
3	Barren Island	India	As	354
4	Elbrus	Russia	Eu	5633
5	Erebus		An	3794
6	Etna	Italy	Eu	3350
7	Fuji	Japan	As	3776
8	Garibaldi	Canada	NA	2678
9	Grimsvotn	Iceland	Eu	1725
10	Illimani	Bolivia	SA	6458

QUERY_FOR_VOLCANOES_0005 (read-only)

4.2 Sorting Data in a Query

If all you want to do is create a sorted version of a data table, then you might want to use the Sort task (discussed in section 2.9). But, if you also want to select columns, filter the data, or create new columns, then you can do all of these in the Query Builder.

Here is a sample of the data table created in the previous section. This table contains the Volcano, Country, Region, and Height columns from the Volcanoes data table, and is currently sorted by the name of the volcano. To sort these data using the Query Builder, re-open the query by right-clicking the **Query for Volcanoes** icon in the Project Explorer or Project Designer and selecting **Open**. The Query Builder opens with the Select Data tab on top. Click the **Sort Data** tab.

	Volcano	Country	Region	Height
1	Altar	Ecuador	SA	5321
2	Arthur's Seat	UK	Eu	251
3	Barren Island	India	As	354
4	Elbrus	Russia	Eu	5633
5	Erebus		An	3794
6	Etna	Italy	Eu	3350
7	Fuji	Japan	As	3776
8	Garibaldi	Canada	NA	2678
9	Grimsvotn	Iceland	Eu	1725
10	Illimani	Bolivia	SA	6458

Sorting the data   At first there are no columns listed in the Sort Data tab on the right, but all the columns in the data table are listed in the box on the left. Notice that even columns (Activity and Type) not selected for the query are listed. You can use columns for sorting even if they don't appear in the result. To sort the data, click the desired column in the list on the left and drag it to the Sort Data tab. You can sort by more that one column by dragging multiple columns to the Sort Data tab.

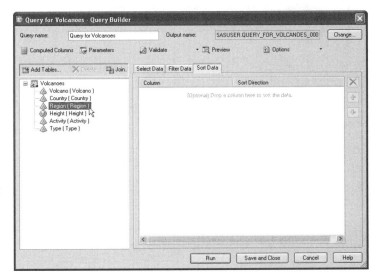

If you choose more than one column for sorting, the order of the columns in the Sort Data tab will determine how the data are sorted. The data will be sorted by the first column in the list. Then, within unique values of the first column, the data will be sorted by the second column. You can change the sort order by clicking the column name in the Sort Data tab and clicking the up or down arrow buttons ⬆ ⬇ to move the columns. To change the sort direction, click the column name in the Sort Data tab, then click the down arrow ⌄ next to the sort direction for that column and select either Ascending or Descending from the drop-down list. In this query, the data will be sorted first by Region in Ascending order, then by Height in Descending order. Click **Run** in the Query Builder window to create a sorted SAS data table.

Results Notice that the data are sorted first by Region. Then, within Region, by descending Height. Missing values are always lowest in the sort order, so if Region were missing for any volcanoes, those volcanoes would appear first in this list.

	Volcano	Country	Region	Height
1	Mauna Loa	USA	AP	4170
2	Ruapehu	NZ	AP	2797
3	Kilauea	USA	AP	1222
4	Warning	Australia	AP	1125
5	Kilimanjaro	Tanzania	Af	5895
6	Kenya	Kenya	Af	5199
7	Nyiragongo	DRCongo	Af	3470
8	Nyamuragira	DRCongo	Af	3058
9	Erebus		An	3794
10	Kliuchevskoi	Russia	As	4835

4.3 Creating Columns Using Mathematical Operators in the Expression Editor

Sometimes you need to create a new column based on data values in other columns. To do this, add a computed column in the Query Builder. Use the Advanced Expression Editor to specify the expression to use for the values in the new column.

This example uses the Eruptions data table which contains start and end dates for volcano eruptions around the world. To open the Query Builder, click the data icon in the Project Explorer or Project Designer to make it active, and then select **Data ▶ Filter and Query** from the menu bar. The Query Builder opens with the Select Data tab on top. Select the columns for the query. In this case, they are Volcano, StartDate, and EndDate.

	Volcano	StartDate	EndDate	VEI
1	Barren Island	12/20/1795	12/21/1795	2
2	Barren Island	12/20/1994	06/05/1995	2
3	Erebus	12/12/1912	.	2
4	Erebus	01/03/1972	.	1
5	Etna	02/06/1610	08/15/1610	2
6	Etna	06/04/1787	08/11/1787	4
7	Etna	01/30/1865	06/28/1865	2
8	Etna	06/17/1994	07/17/2001	3
9	Fuji	12/16/1707	02/24/1708	5
10	Grimsvotn	10/31/1603	11/01/1603	2

Creating a new column To create a new column, click the **Computed Columns** button located near the top of the window. This opens the Computed Columns window. Click **New** and select **Build Expression**. This opens the Advanced Expression Editor window where you specify the expression to use for the new column.

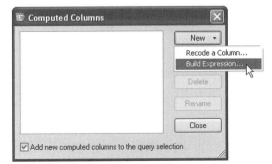

Building the expression

The Advanced Expression Editor has a large box at the top of the window. You can simply type the expression in this box, or you can let SAS Enterprise Guide help you build the expression. The bottom part of the window has a tab for **Data** and a tab for **Functions**. The **Available variables** box of the Data tab shows all the data tables and columns in the query. When you click an item in the Available variables list, all the possible values of the item are listed in the **Variable values** box on the right. If you click a data table, as in this example, all the columns in the data table appear in the Variable values box. If you click a column name in the Available variables list, all unique values for that column in the data table appear in the Variable values box. To add items to the expression you are building, click the item in the Variable values box, and then click **Add to Expression**. You can use the various operator buttons that appear below the Expression text box to build your expression. In this example, you want the length of the eruption in days. Because the StartDate and EndDate are both SAS date values (the number of days since January 1, 1960), you can simply subtract the start date from the end date and add one. Click **OK** to return to the Computed Columns window. The column is given the name Calculation1. To rename the column, click **Rename** and enter a new name, LengthOfEruption in this example. Click **Close** and then click **Run** in the Query Builder window to run the query.

Results The Query Builder creates a new SAS data table that contains the new column. The new data table is given a name starting with the letters QUERY and is stored in a default location. You can change the location or name of the data table using the **Change** button in the Query Builder window. Here are the results of the query which now include the new column LengthOfEruption.

	Volcano	StartDate	EndDate	LengthOfEruption
1	Barren Island	12/20/1795	12/21/1795	2
2	Barren Island	12/20/1994	06/05/1995	168
3	Erebus	12/12/1912		
4	Erebus	01/03/1972		
5	Etna	02/06/1610	08/15/1610	191
6	Etna	06/04/1787	08/11/1787	69
7	Etna	01/30/1865	06/28/1865	150
8	Etna	06/17/1994	07/17/2001	2588
9	Fuji	12/16/1707	02/24/1708	71
10	Grimsvotn	10/31/1603	11/01/1603	2

4.4 ▸ Creating Columns Using Functions in the Expression Editor

SAS Enterprise Guide has many built-in functions you can use to build expressions when creating new columns. A function takes a value and turns it into another related value. For example, the MONTH function will take a date and return just the month. The LOG function will return the natural log of a number. There are many functions to choose from in over 20 different categories including: arithmetic, character, date and time, descriptive statistics, financial, trigonometric, and truncation. Some of the commonly used functions are listed in the next section. Use the Query Builder to create new columns using functions.

Here is a portion of the Bookings Excel file which has been converted to a SAS data table. The Deposit_Date column is a datetime value. To create a column that just has date values, you can use the DATEPART function. To open the Query Builder, click the data icon in the Project Explorer or Project

Designer to make it active, and then select **Data ▸ Filter and Query** from the menu bar. The Query Builder opens with the Select Data tab on top. Select the columns for the query, in this case all of them.

Creating a new column As discussed in the previous section, to create a new column, click the **Computed Columns** button in the Query Builder window. This opens the Computed Columns window. Click **New** and select **Build Expression**. This opens the Advanced Expression Editor window where you specify the expression to use for the new column.

Choosing a function

Click the **Functions** tab to list all available functions. These functions are grouped by category. Click a category, and all the functions in that category will be listed in the box on the right under Functions. To insert a function into an expression, click the function name, and then click **Add to Expression**. In this example, the help text at the bottom of the Functions tab tells you that the DATEPART function extracts the date (the number of days since January 1, 1960) from a datetime value (the number of seconds since midnight on January 1,1960).

Defining arguments for functions Most functions take some sort of argument. When the function is inserted into the expression, a placeholder for the argument appears in the expression. You must replace the placeholder in the function with a valid argument. If the function calls for a character value, that value can be a column of type character, or a character string enclosed in quotes. If the function calls for a numeric value, that value can be a column of type numeric, or a number.

Click the **Data** tab to insert column names or values into the expression. Click the name of the column to insert into the function from the **Variable values** list, and then highlight the placeholder in the function—<numValue> for this example. Click **Add to Expression** and the placeholder will be replaced by the column you selected, in this case the Deposit_Date column from the Bookings table.

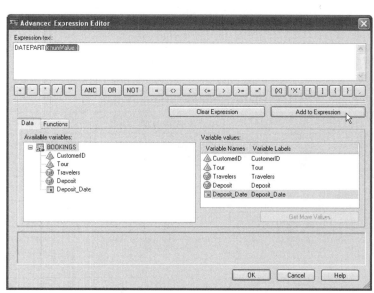

Here is what the expression looks like after replacing the placeholder. When you are satisfied with your expression, click **OK** to return to the Computed Columns window where you can rename the column if you like. For this example, rename the column DateOfDeposit.

Click **Close** in the Computed Columns window, and then click **Run** in the Query Builder.

Results Notice here how the values for the new column, DateOfDeposit, are simple numbers. These numbers are dates represented as the number of days since January 1, 1960. To display the numbers as readable dates, give the column a date display format in the Properties window for the column.

	CustomerID	Tour	Travelers	Deposit	Deposit_Date	DateOfDeposit
1	SL28	SH-43	10	425	05JUL2006:12:00:00 AM	16987
2	DE27	PS27	6	75	11JUL2006:12:00:00 AM	16993
3	SL34	FJ12	4	200	19JUL2006:12:00:00 AM	17001
4	DI33	SH-43	4	150	23JUL2006:12:00:00 AM	17005
5	BU12	SH-43	2	75	23JUL2006:12:00:00 AM	17005
6	DE31	FJ12	3	175	25JUL2006:12:00:00 AM	17007
7	WI48	FJ12	2	100	26JUL2006:12:00:00 AM	17008
8	NG17	PS27	5	65	26JUL2006:12:00:00 AM	17008

4.5 Selected Functions

The following table lists the definition and form of commonly used functions.

Function name	Form of function	Definition
Mathematical		
LOG	LOG(numValue)	Natural logarithm
LOG10	LOG10(numValue)	Logarithm to the base 10
Descriptive Statistics		
MAX	MAX(numValue,numValue,...)	Largest non-missing value
MEAN	MEAN(numValue,numValue,...)	Arithmetic mean of non-missing values
MIN	MIN(numValue,numValue,...)	Smallest non-missing value
SUM	SUM(numValue,numValue,...)	Sum of non-missing values
Character		
LENGTH	LENGTH(charValue)	Returns the length of a character value not counting trailing blanks (missing values have a length of 1)
SUBSTR{Extract}	SUBSTR(charValue,position,n)	Extracts a substring from a character value starting at 'position' for 'n' characters or until end if no 'n'
TRANSLATE	TRANSLATE(charValue,to-1, from-1,...to-n,from-n)	Replaces 'from' characters in character value with 'to' characters (one-to-one replacement only—you cannot replace one character with two, for example)
UPCASE	UPCASE(charValue)	Converts all letters in character value to uppercase
Date and Datetime[1]		
DATEPART	DATEPART(SAS-datetime-value)	Converts a datetime to a SAS date value
DAY	DAY(SAS-date-value)	Returns the day of the month from a SAS date value
MDY	MDY(month,day,year)	Returns a SAS date value from month, day, and year values
MONTH	MONTH(SAS-date-value)	Returns the month (1–12) from a SAS date
QTR	QTR(SAS-date-value)	Returns the yearly quarter (1–4) from a SAS date value
TODAY	TODAY()	Returns the current date as a SAS date value

---

[1] A SAS date value is the number of days since January 1, 1960. A SAS datetime is the number of seconds since midnight January 1, 1960.

Here are examples using the selected functions.

Function name	Example	Result	Example	Result
Mathematical				
LOG	LOG(1)	0.0	LOG(10)	2.30259
LOG10	LOG10(1)	0.0	LOG10(10)	1.0
Descriptive Statistics				
MAX	MAX(9.3,8,7.5)	9.3	MAX(−3,.,5)	5
MEAN	MEAN(1,4,7,2)	3.5	MEAN(2,.,3)	2.5
MIN	MIN(9.3,8,7.5)	7.5	MIN(−3,.,5)	−3
SUM	SUM(3,5,1)	9.0	SUM(4,7,.)	11
Character				
LENGTH	LENGTH('hot lava')	8	LENGTH('eruption')	8
SUBSTR{Extract}	SUBSTR('(916)734-6281',2,3)	'916'	SUBSTR('Tour12',5)	'12'
TRANSLATE	TRANSLATE ('6/16/2004','-','/')	'6-16-2004'	TRANSLATE ('hot lava', 'j','l')	'hot java'
UPCASE	UPCASE('St. Helens')	'ST. HELENS'	UPCASE('Fuji')	'FUJI'
Date and Datetime				
DATEPART	DATEPART(86400)	1	DATEPART(31536000)	365
DAY	DAY(0)	1	DAY(290)	17
MDY	MDY(1,1,1960)	0	MDY(10,17,1960)	290
MONTH	MONTH(0)	1	MONTH(290)	10
QTR	QTR(0)	1	QTR(290)	4
TODAY	TODAY()	*today's date*	TODAY()−1	*yesterday's date*

4.6 Adding a Grand Total to a Data Table

Using the Query Builder, you can create columns that contain summary statistics for existing columns. For example, you may want to calculate a grand total over all the rows of data and put the result in a new column. Then you could compute the percent of the total for each row because the one grand total value is repeated for each row in the data.

Here is a sample of the AdResults data which contains the amounts spent on advertising for the Fire and Ice Tours company for both its Seattle and Portland offices. To create a new column that has the total amount spent for both offices for the time period, click the data icon in the Project Explorer or Project Designer to make it active, and then open the Query Builder by selecting **Data ▶ Filter and Query** from the menu bar.

	City	Month	AdDollars	Bookings
8	Seattle	8	250	17
9	Seattle	9	250	22
10	Seattle	10	325	20
11	Seattle	11	400	25
12	Seattle	12	500	31
13	Portland	1	325	25
14	Portland	2	290	19
15	Portland	3	250	17
16	Portland	4	300	18

Summarizing the data First select the columns for the query, in this case all the columns in the AdResults table. To summarize data in a column, click the column name in the Select Data tab. When you do this, the summary function for the column will appear in the Summary cell. Initially all columns have a summary function of NONE. Click the down arrow in the summary cell for the column to choose the summary function you want to use from the drop-down list. For this example, choose **SUM**.

Adding back the original column After you choose a summary statistic, the original column will be replaced by the newly summarized column. The name for the new column combines the summary statistic and the old column name. If you don't like the name that SAS Enterprise Guide gives the column, you can change the name in the Properties window. Click

the column name, then click the Properties button ⬚⬚ on the right side of the Query Builder window to open the Properties window. Because the newly computed column replaces the original column, the original column will not be in the result of the query unless you add it back. If you want to keep the original column, as well as the newly computed column, click the original column name in the box on the left and drag it over to the Select Data tab. Use the up or down arrow buttons on the right side of the window to position the original column where you want. In this example, the original column, AdDollars, has been added back in the query and positioned above the Bookings column. When you are satisfied, click **Run**.

Results When you run the query, it creates a SAS data table containing the newly computed column. The new data table is given a name starting with the letters QUERY and is stored in a default location. You can change the location or name of the data table by clicking the **Change** button on the Query Builder window. Notice that the new column, SUM_OF_

	City	Month	SUM_OF_AdDollars	AdDollars	Bookings
8	Seattle	8	7845	250	17
9	Seattle	9	7845	250	22
10	Seattle	10	7845	325	20
11	Seattle	11	7845	400	25
12	Seattle	12	7845	500	31
13	Portland	1	7845	325	25
14	Portland	2	7845	290	19
15	Portland	3	7845	250	17
16	Portland	4	7845	300	18

AdDollars, has the same value for all the rows—the grand total of AdDollars.

4.7 Adding Subtotals to a Data Table

The previous section showed how you can create new columns that summarize all the rows in a data table. This section shows how to summarize all the rows that belong to a group. The steps are the same as adding a grand total, with the additional step of selecting a group column.

Here is a sample of the results from the previous section where the SUM_OF_AdDollars column contains the total of the AdDollars column. To calculate the total amount spent by each office instead of the grand total, all you need to do is add a group column to the query. Re-open the query by right-clicking the query icon in the Project Explorer or Project Designer and selecting **Open**. This opens the Query Builder window.

	City	Month	SUM_OF_AdDollars	AdDollars	Bookings
8	Seattle	8	7845	250	17
9	Seattle	9	7845	250	22
10	Seattle	10	7845	325	20
11	Seattle	11	7845	400	25
12	Seattle	12	7845	500	31
13	Portland	1	7845	325	25
14	Portland	2	7845	290	19
15	Portland	3	7845	250	17
16	Portland	4	7845	300	18

Project Designer   QUERY_FOR_ADRESULTS_0000 (read-only)

Summarizing the data   Here is the query from the previous section which contains all the columns from the AdResults table and the SUM_OF_AdDollars column which is the grand total for the AdDollars column. To change the SUM_OF_AdDollars column to a sub-total by City, click the **Edit Groups** button. This opens the Edit Groups window.

Selecting groups In the Edit Groups window, select the column or columns to use for the groups. Click the column name, City for this example, in the **Available columns** list and drag it to the **Group by** list. Click **OK** to return to the Query Builder window.

Notice that the name for the summarized column, in this case SUM_OF_AdDollars, does not change. But now the grouping column, City from the AdResults table, appears in the area labeled **Summary Groups** near the bottom of the window. Click **Run** to run the query.

Results Notice that now the SUM_OF_AdDollars column has the same value for all the rows with the same value of the grouping column, City. Also the resulting data table is sorted by the grouping column.

	City	Month	SUM_OF_AdDollars	AdDollars	Bookings
8	Portland	3	3665	250	17
9	Portland	1	3665	325	25
10	Portland	10	3665	350	24
11	Portland	12	3665	400	33
12	Portland	4	3665	300	18
13	Seattle	7	4180	150	17
14	Seattle	3	4180	525	32
15	Seattle	6	4180	325	18
16	Seattle	12	4180	500	31

4.8 Creating Summary Data Tables in a Query

The previous section showed how you can create new columns that summarize all the rows belonging to a group. The summarized values were repeated for each row that belonged to the group. But if you want only one row for each group showing just the summarized values, you can do this in a query by eliminating all columns that are not either grouped or summarized.

Here is a sample of the AdResults data which contains the amounts spent on advertising for the Fire and Ice Tours company for its Seattle and Portland offices. To create a new table that has the total number of bookings for each office and the total amount spent by each office, click the **AdResults** data icon in the Project Explorer or Project Designer to make it active, and then open the Query Builder by selecting **Data ▶ Filter and Query** from the menu bar.

	City	Month	AdDollars	Bookings
8	Seattle	8	250	17
9	Seattle	9	250	22
10	Seattle	10	325	20
11	Seattle	11	400	25
12	Seattle	12	500	31
13	Portland	1	325	25
14	Portland	2	290	19
15	Portland	3	250	17
16	Portland	4	300	18

Select the summary and group columns When selecting columns for a query that will produce a summary data table, select only columns that will be either summarized or grouped. Choose the type of summarization from the drop-down list that appears when you double-click the Summary cell for the column on the Select Data tab. In this example the AdDollars and the Bookings columns are summed. Then click **Edit Groups** to set the grouping column.

In the Edit Groups window, select the column to be used for the groups. In this example, the City column is the grouping column. Click **OK** to return to the Query Builder window.

After assigning all the columns that you want to keep to either grouping or summary roles, you are ready to run your query. In this example, the Query Builder window shows that the AdDollars and Bookings columns are summed, and since the City column is listed in the area labeled Summary groups, it is the grouping column. Click **Run**.

Results When you run the Query Builder, it creates a SAS data table containing the summarized data. The new data table is given a name starting with the letters QUERY and is stored in a default location. You can change the location or name of the data table by clicking the **Change** button in the Query Builder window. Notice that the new table contains only one row for each value of the grouping column, City.

4.9 Filtering Data

Sometimes you don't want to use all the rows in your data table for your reports or analyses. If you need to exclude certain rows based on the value of a column, then filter your data before you run your report or analysis.

Here are the first 10 rows of the Volcanoes data table. The goal is to create a subset of the data containing only volcanoes in North America and South America. To filter the data, click the data icon in the Project Explorer or Project Designer to make it active, and then select **Data ▶ Filter and Query** from the menu bar. This opens the Query Builder window, with the Select Data tab on top.

Select all the columns that you want in the query result (in this example every column except Type), then click the **Filter Data** tab.

Select the column that you want to use for filtering purposes and drag it over to the box under the Filter Data tab. Notice that you can filter by columns that are not even part of the query result. In this example, drag **Region** to the filter area. When you drop the column, the Edit Filter window opens automatically.

Defining the filter In the Edit Filter window, you can see the name of the column you dragged to the filter area. Initially, the operator is **Equal to**. You would use this operator if you wanted to filter all the rows that equal a particular value. But you are not limited to the Equal to operator. There are several operators to choose from when filtering your data. When you click the down arrow to the right of the **Operator** box, you can choose a different operator. In this example, the **In a list of values** operator is the most useful because it allows you to specify a list of unique values for Region.

After choosing an operator, you will need to choose a value or values for your filter condition. You can type the values for your condition in the **Values** box if you like, but SAS Enterprise Guide can help you select values for your condition. Click **Add** next to the **Values** box. This opens a window where you can get all the values for the column. Click **Get Values**. You will see a list of all possible values for the column you selected, and the label on the Get Values button will change to More Values. Highlight one or more values by holding down the control key as you select values. In this example, select **NA** and **SA**, and then click **OK**. The values will be inserted into the Values box of the Edit Filter window. If you want to compare the value of the column being filtered to the value in a different column, then you can click the **Columns** tab to get a list of available columns and insert the column into the filter. This is not an option for the **In a list of values** operator.

Once you have set the filter condition, click **OK** and the filter will appear in the Filter Data tab of the Query Builder window. Notice that the box for the filter states what the filter does. In this case, it selects all rows from the Volcanoes table where Region has the value of NA or SA. Click **Run** to run the query.

Results Here is the result of the query with just the volcanoes from North and South America. The new data table is given a name starting with the letters QUERY and is stored in a default location. You can change the location or name of the data table by clicking the **Change** button in the Query Builder window. This new data table is now ready for any analysis or report you want to create.

4.10 Creating Compound Filters

When you create a filter condition, sometimes it's not enough to base the filter on only one condition. If you want to create a filter based on two or more conditions, you can do this in the Query Builder. You can add conditions to a filter using either AND logic or OR logic. If you use AND logic, rows must meet both conditions of the filter to be included in the result. If you use OR logic, rows need to meet only one condition or the other.

In the previous section, the Volcanoes data were filtered so that only the volcanoes in North America and South America appeared in the result. Suppose you also want the volcanoes that are in Japan. For this result, you need to select rows where the region is North America or South America, or where the country is Japan. To modify the existing query, right-click the query icon

in the Project Explorer or Project Designer and select **Open**. Click the **Filter Data** tab.

Adding conditions to a filter

To add a condition to an existing filter, click and drag the column for the new condition from the column list on the left to the Filter Data tab on the right. For this example, drag the Country column to the **Filter Data** tab. When you drop the column, the Edit Filter window will open.

Editing the Filter The procedure for specifying the additional condition is the same as if you were creating a single condition filter. First, choose an appropriate operator for your condition, and then either type the desired value in the **Value** box, or click the down arrow next to the Value box to get a list of values to choose from. In this example, the filter will choose rows where the Country column from the Volcanoes table is equal to the value **Japan**. When you are satisfied with your condition, click **OK**.

Setting the logic After you create the additional condition, it will be added to the existing filter condition in the Filter Data tab. The filter now has two conditions. When you add new conditions to your filter, SAS Enterprise Guide automatically chooses AND logic. To change to OR logic, click **Combine Filters** to open the Filter Combination window. This window shows a diagram of the current filter conditions. To change the logic for the filter, click the word **AND** with the arrow next to it, and select **Change to OR** from the drop-down list. Click **OK** to return to the Query Builder window, and click **Run** to run the query.

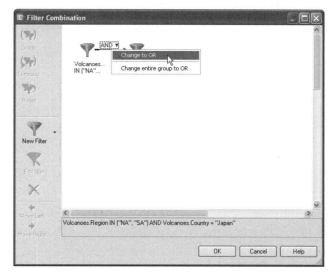

Results Here is the Volcanoes data set after filtering. Now, all the volcanoes from North America and South America are included, as well as all the volcanoes in Japan. The new data table is given a name starting with the letters QUERY and is stored in a default location. You can change the location or name of the data table by clicking the **Change** button in the Query Builder window. Now you can use this new data table for any analysis or report you want to create.

	Volcano	Country	Region	Height	Activity
1	Altar	Ecuador	SA	5321	Extinct
2	Fuji	Japan	As	3776	Active
3	Garibaldi	Canada	NA	2678	
4	Illimani	Bolivia	SA	6458	Extinct
5	Lassen	USA	NA	3187	Active
6	Poas	Costa Rica	NA	2708	Active
7	Popocatepetl	Mexico	NA	5426	Active
8	Reventador	Ecuador	SA	3562	Active
9	Sabancaya	Peru	SA	5976	Active
10	Shishaldin	USA	NA	2857	Active
11	St. Helens	USA	NA	2549	Active
12	Villarrica	Chile	SA	2847	Active

4.11   Filtering Based on Grouped Data

In the Query Builder, you can summarize data by group. Once the data are summarized, you can subset the data based on the summarized values. To do this, use the **Filter the summarized data** area of the Filter Data tab.

Summarizing the data To filter your data based on summarized values in a group, you first need to create the summarized values. Click the desired data icon in the Project Explorer or Project Designer to make it active, and then select **Data ▶ Filter and Query** from the menu bar. This opens the Query Builder window with the Select Data tab on top. Select the columns for the query. In this example, all columns from the Volcanoes table except Activity and Type are selected. Click the column you want to summarize in the Select Data tab, then select the type of summarization from the drop-down list in the Summary column. Next click the **Edit Groups** button to open a window where you can select the grouping column. In this example, the Height column is averaged producing a computed column named AVG_OF_Height and the grouping column is Region. The original Height column is also part of the query.

Creating the group filter In the Query Builder, click the **Filter Data** tab to bring it forward. There are two parts to the Filter Data tab: **Filter the raw data** and **Filter the summarized data**. To filter based on a summarized column, you must use the **Filter the summarized data** area of the window. Click the summarized column. In this example, use AVG_OF_Height, and drag it to the **Filter the summarized data** portion of the window. This opens the Edit Filter window. Choose an operator from the drop-down list of operators, and then type a value in the **Value** box. Or,

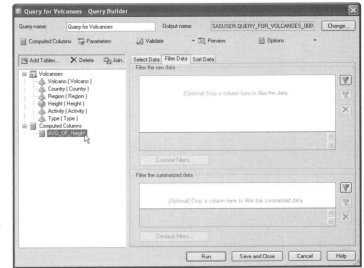

instead of typing in a value, you can choose from a list by clicking the down arrow next to the **Value** box. This opens another window where you can select from a list of values, columns, or parameters. In this example, the **Greater than** operator is selected and the value is **4000**.

Click **OK** and the filter will appear in the **Filter the summarized data** portion of the Filter Data tab. Click **Run** to run the query.

Results When you run the query, the result is a data table that has a name starting with the letters QUERY and is stored in a default location. If you want to give the data table another name, or choose a different location, you can do this by clicking the **Change** button in the Query Builder window. Here is the result of the query that contains only the rows from the Volcanoes data table where the average volcano height for the region is greater than 4000 meters. Note that the heights of some individual volcanoes are less than 4000 meters, but the average for the whole region is greater than 4000 meters.

	Volcano	Country	Region	AVG_OF_Height	Height
1	Kilimanjaro	Tanzania	Af	4405.5	5895
2	Nyamuragira	DRCongo	Af	4405.5	3058
3	Nyiragongo	DRCongo	Af	4405.5	3470
4	Kenya	Kenya	Af	4405.5	5199
5	Villarrica	Chile	SA	4832.8	2847
6	Sabancaya	Peru	SA	4832.8	5976
7	Reventador	Ecuador	SA	4832.8	3562
8	Altar	Ecuador	SA	4832.8	5321
9	Illimani	Bolivia	SA	4832.8	6458

4.12   Recoding Values in a Query

If you want to group data together based on a set of values in a column, you can do this by recoding a column in the Query Builder. For example, if you have sales offices from several different cities, you may want to group them by region. If region is not already defined in the data, then you can define it using the Query Builder. Recoding a column is similar to creating and applying user-defined formats to a column. But, when you recode a column, you create a newly computed column where the data values are actually changed. When you use formats, only the way the data values are displayed is changed.

Here are a few rows from the Latlong data table, which gives the latitude and longitude of volcanoes from around the world. Using the recode feature of the Query Builder you can group the volcanoes by zone, according to the value of the column Latitude. Click the data icon in the Project Explorer or Project Designer, and then select **Data ▶ Filter and Query** from the menu bar. This opens the Query Builder window, with the Select Data tab on top. Select the columns for the query. In this case, all the columns in the table are selected.

	Name	Latitude	Longitude
1	Altar	-1.67	-78.42
2	Barren Island	12.28	93.52
3	Elbrus	43.33	42.45
4	Erebus	-77.53	167.17
5	Etna	37.73	15
6	Fuji	35.35	138.73
7	Garibaldi	49.85	-123
8	Grimsvotn	64.42	-17.33
9	Illimani	-16.39	-67.47
10	Kenya	-0.09	37.18

Creating the recoded column   In the Query Builder window, right-click the column to recode (Latitude for this example) in the list of columns on the left and select **Recode**.   This opens the Recode Column window. (You can also get to the Recode Column window through the Computed Columns button.) The new column is automatically given a name starting with Recode. You can give the column a different name here if you like.   Click **Add** to add replacement definitions.

Specify a Replacement

Replace Values | Replace a Range

☑ Set a lower limit:

-90

☑ Set an upper limit:

-66.5

With this value:

Antarctic

Tip: Missing values are represented by a period.

OK   Cancel   Help

Defining the replacements Choose either to make a one-to-one replacement using the **Replace Values** tab or replace a range of values using the **Replace a Range** tab. It probably makes the most sense to use the range feature for numeric data, but it can be used for character data if you want to replace a set of values that fall into a consecutive range alphabetically. For this example, click the **Replace a Range** tab. Enter the lower and upper limits of the range of values to replace in the appropriate boxes. If you want to see what the current values are, then you can click the down arrow to the right of the box and a window will open showing all the values. In the box labeled **With this value**, type the new value that you want to replace the old range of values. When the specification for the replacement is complete, click **OK**.

Recode Column - Latlong.Latitude

New column name: Recode_Latitude

Replacements: Add...   Remove

Replace	With
-23.49...23.49	Tropical
23.5...66.49	N. Temperate
-66.49...-23.5	S. Temperate
66.5...90	Arctic
-90...-66.5	Antarctic

Other values

Replace all other values with:

○ The current value

◉ A missing value

○ This value:

New column type

◉ Character   ○ Numeric

OK   Cancel   Help

The replacement logic you defined will appear in the list of replacements in the Recode Column window. Click **Add** again to add another replacement and repeat this procedure for all the replacements you want to make. If you made a mistake with any of the replacements, you can highlight the replacement in the list, click **Remove,** and start over. At the bottom of the window, choose the type for the new column: Character or Numeric. For this example, choose **Character**. You can also choose what to do with values that do not fall into the ranges you specified. For this example, replacing with **A missing value** is fine. When you are finished, click **OK** in the Recode Column window, then click **Run** in the Query Builder window to run the query.

Project Designer | **Query_for_Latlong [read-only]**

	Name	Latitude	Longitude	Recode_Latitude
1	Altar	-1.67	-78.42	Tropical
2	Barren Island	12.28	93.52	Tropical
3	Elbrus	43.33	42.45	N. Temperate
4	Erebus	-77.53	167.17	Antarctic
5	Etna	37.73	15	N. Temperate
6	Fuji	35.35	138.73	N. Temperate
7	Garibaldi	49.85	-123	N. Temperate
8	Grimsvotn	64.42	-17.33	N. Temperate
9	Illimani	-16.39	-67.47	Tropical
10	Kenya	-0.09	37.18	Tropical

Results Here is a sample of the query result. Notice that both the Latitude column and the new column, Recode_Latitude, are part of the query result. The values for Recode_Latitude reflect the replacements defined in the Recode Column window.

4.13 Changing the Result Type of Queries

When you run a query using the Query Builder, you have a choice about the type of result the query produces. A query can produce a SAS data table, an HTML report, or a SAS data view. A SAS data view is similar to a SAS data table, except it does not contain any data. Instead, SAS data views contain information about where to find the data.

Setting the default result type When you first install SAS Enterprise Guide, the default result type for queries is a data table. But you can change the default result type in the Options window. Open the Options window by selecting **Tools ▶ Options** from the menu bar. Click the **Query** group of options in the selection pane on the left to open the Query page. Near the bottom of this page is a drop-down list under **Save query result set as**. Select the desired result type. All subsequent queries you build will use this as the default result type.

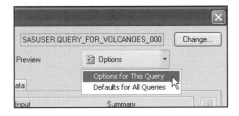

Setting the result type for each query If you want to change the result type of an individual query, you can do this in the Result Options window for the query. Click the **Options** button in the Query Builder window and select **Options for This Query**. Note that you can also change the default options from this window by selecting **Defaults for All Queries** which opens the same Options page you see above.

In the Result Options window, check **Override preferences set in Tools -> Options**, and then select the type of result you want for the query. You can choose a data table, data view, or report. The default action is to use the setting defined in the Options window. Changes made in the Result Options window affect only the results of the current query. All other queries will use the default result type.

Query report All the query examples so far in this book have shown the result as a data table. Here is what a result would look like if you chose a report instead.

CHAPTER 5

Combining Data Tables

Chapter 5

5.1 Appending Tables

In SAS Enterprise Guide, there are two basic ways to combine data tables: appending and joining. You append tables when they contain the same (or almost the same) columns. For example, if you had sales data for January, February, and March in three separate tables, you could append the tables to create one table for the entire quarter.

In this example, a customer living in southern Washington is interested in traveling with the Fire and Ice Tours company. Because this customer lives between Seattle and Portland, she wants to see prices for flights from each city. Here are two data tables, one showing flights from Portland and the other from Seattle.

	Origin	Destination	FlightNo	FlightPrice
1	Portland	Catania	L469	$679.00
2	Portland	Hilo	HA25	$603.00
3	Portland	Nairobi	KLM6034	$1,733.00
4	Portland	Rome	D1576	$544.00
5	Portland	San Jose	CA1210	$394.00
6	Portland	Tokyo	UA383	$605.00

	Origin	Destination	FlightNo	FlightPrice
1	Seattle	Catania	BA48	$702.00
2	Seattle	Hilo	HA21	$577.00
3	Seattle	Jakarta	AA119	$1,715.00
4	Seattle	Nairobi	KLM6034	$1,661.00
5	Seattle	Quito	CA1086	$733.00
6	Seattle	Rome	USA6	$496.00
7	Seattle	San Jose	CA1100	$380.00
8	Seattle	Tokyo	UA875	$621.00

Looking at these two data tables, you can see they contain the same columns, making them good candidates for appending. To append tables, in the Project Explorer or Project Designer, click one data table to make it active. Then select **Data ▶ Append Table** from the menu bar.

Appending tables The Append Table window opens, showing the active table. To open a second table, click **Add Table**, navigate to the table you want to add, and click **OK**. Continue adding tables until all the tables you want to combine are listed in the Append Table window.

Table Name	File Location
PORTLAND	C:\EG Data\Portland.sas7bdat

Add a table to the list.

At this point, you can click **Run** and SAS Enterprise Guide will create the new table, store it in a default location, and give it the name **Append_Table**. (If you have more than one appended table in that location, SAS Enterprise Guide will add numbers to the name.) To choose a different name or location, click the **Results** option in the selection pane on the left. Then click **Browse** to open the Save As window.

In the Save As window, type a name for the new data table in the **File name** box and choose a library. To see the available libraries, click the down arrow in the **Save in** box at the top of the window. In this example, the new data table will be named Port_Sea and saved in the SASUSER library. Once you have specified the library and filename, click **Save**.

In the Append Table window, click **Run**. SAS Enterprise Guide will display the results in a Data Grid.

Results Here is the new data table. Notice that SAS Enterprise Guide concatenated the Portland and Seattle tables by matching the columns.

	Origin	Destination	FlightNo	FlightPrice
1	Portland	Catania	L469	$679.00
2	Portland	Hilo	HA25	$603.00
3	Portland	Nairobi	KLM6034	$1,733.00
4	Portland	Rome	D1576	$544.00
5	Portland	San Jose	CA1210	$394.00
6	Portland	Tokyo	UA383	$605.00
7	Seattle	Catania	BA48	$702.00
8	Seattle	Hilo	HA21	$577.00
9	Seattle	Jakarta	AA119	$1,715.00
10	Seattle	Nairobi	KLM6034	$1,661.00
11	Seattle	Quito	CA1086	$733.00
12	Seattle	Rome	USA6	$496.00
13	Seattle	San Jose	CA1100	$380.00
14	Seattle	Tokyo	UA875	$621.00

Chapter 5

5.2 Joining Tables

When you append tables, you match columns. But often, instead of matching columns, you need to match rows. For example, a teacher might record grades from homework in one table and grades from tests in another. To compute final grades you would need to match the homework and test scores for each student. This is called joining tables, and you do it with a query.

In the preceding section, two tables were appended to create one table containing all the data about flights. Now the data for each tour can be joined with the matching data for flights. In the Project Explorer or Project Designer, click the **Tours** data table to make it active. Then select **Data ▸ Filter and Query** from the menu bar. The Query Builder window will open.

	Origin	Destination	FlightNo	FlightPrice
1	Portland	Catania	L469	$679.00
2	Portland	Hilo	HA25	$603.00
3	Portland	Nairobi	KLM6034	$1,733.00
4	Portland	Rome	D1576	$544.00
5	Portland	San Jose	CA1210	$394.00
6	Portland	Tokyo	UA383	$605.00
7	Seattle	Catania	BA48	$702.00
8	Seattle	Hilo	HA21	$577.00
9	Seattle	Jakarta	AA119	$1,715.00
10	Seattle	Nairobi	KLM6034	$1,661.00
11	Seattle	Quito	CA1086	$733.00
12	Seattle	Rome	USA6	$496.00
13	Seattle	San Jose	CA1100	$380.00
14	Seattle	Tokyo	UA875	$621.00

	Volcano	Departs	Days	Price	Difficulty
1	Etna	Catania	7	$1,025	m
2	Fuji	Tokyo	2	$195	c
3	Kenya	Nairobi	6	$780	m
4	Kilauea	Hilo	1	$45	e
5	Kilimanjaro	Nairobi	9	$1,260	c
6	Krakatau	Jakarta	7	$850	e
7	Poas	San Jose	1	$50	e
8	Reventador	Quito	4	$525	m
9	St. Helens	Portland	2	$157	e
10	Vesuvius	Rome	6	$950	e

Adding tables When you open the Query Builder, it will show the active table. To open a second table, click the **Join** button. The Tables and Joins window will open. In the Tables and Joins window, click the **Add Tables** button and navigate to the table you want to add.

When you add a second table, SAS Enterprise Guide will automatically look for columns with the same name and type. If SAS Enterprise Guide does not find any columns with the same name and type, then a warning message will appear telling you to join the columns manually.

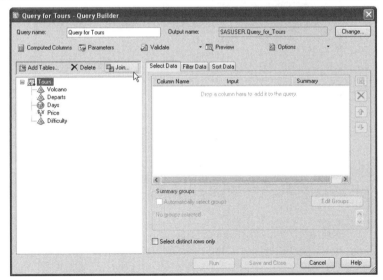

To join two tables manually, click the first table, then right-click the name of one column and select the name of the matching column from the pop-up menu. SAS Enterprise Guide will draw a line from one column to the other. To correctly match the Tours data table and the Port_Sea table, the destination of a flight must match the city from which a tour departs. To join these tables, click the Tours table, and then right-click the column Departs and select Port_Sea and Destination in the pop-up menu. When you are satisfied, click **Close**. You can join up to 32 tables at once.

Running the query Before you run a query, you must select the columns to be included in the output table. To include all columns, click each data table name and drag it to the area under the Select Data tab. You can also click and drag individual column names. Once you have selected the columns you want, click **Run**. SAS Enterprise Guide will display the results in a Data Grid.

Results This Data Grid shows the result from joining the two data tables. SAS Enterprise Guide gives the new table a name starting with QUERY and saves it in a default location. To give the table a different name or location, use the **Change** button in the Query Builder window.

	Volcano	Departs	Days	Price	Difficulty	Origin	Destination	FlightNo	FlightPrice
1	Etna	Catania	7	$1,025	m	Portland	Catania	L469	$679.00
2	Etna	Catania	7	$1,025	m	Seattle	Catania	BA48	$702.00
3	Fuji	Tokyo	2	$195	c	Portland	Tokyo	UA383	$605.00
4	Fuji	Tokyo	2	$195	c	Seattle	Tokyo	UA875	$621.00
5	Kenya	Nairobi	6	$780	m	Portland	Nairobi	KLM6034	$1,733.00
6	Kenya	Nairobi	6	$780	m	Seattle	Nairobi	KLM6034	$1,661.00
7	Kilauea	Hilo	1	$45	e	Portland	Hilo	HA25	$603.00
8	Kilauea	Hilo	1	$45	e	Seattle	Hilo	HA21	$577.00
9	Kilimanjaro	Nairobi	9	$1,260	c	Portland	Nairobi	KLM6034	$1,733.00
10	Kilimanjaro	Nairobi	9	$1,260	c	Seattle	Nairobi	KLM6034	$1,661.00
11	Krakatau	Jakarta	7	$850	e	Seattle	Jakarta	AA119	$1,715.00
12	Poas	San Jose	1	$50	e	Portland	San Jose	CA1210	$394.00
13	Poas	San Jose	1	$50	e	Seattle	San Jose	CA1100	$380.00
14	Reventador	Quito	4	$525	e	Seattle	Quito	CA1086	$733.00
15	Vesuvius	Rome	6	$950	e	Portland	Rome	D1576	$544.00
16	Vesuvius	Rome	6	$950	m	Seattle	Rome	USA6	$496.00

Because there are two tours departing from Nairobi, and two flights with a destination of Nairobi, this is a many-to-many match merge. SAS Enterprise Guide kept only the rows that matched. This is the default type of join in SAS Enterprise Guide. To keep rows that don't match, use a modified join as described in the next section.

5.3 Modifying a Join

By default, when you join tables, SAS Enterprise Guide keeps only rows for which a match is found. Sometimes that may be just what you want, but at other times, you may want to keep all the rows regardless of whether they match, or all the rows from one table, but not the other. To do this, use a modified join.

Reopening the Query window To change a query that you have already run, right-click the query icon in the Project Explorer or Project Designer and select **Open** from the pop-up menu. The Query Builder window will open. Click the **Join** button to open the Tables and Joins window.

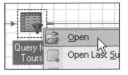

To modify a join, right-click the join indicator between the two tables and select **Modify Join** from the pop-up menu. The Modify Join window will open.

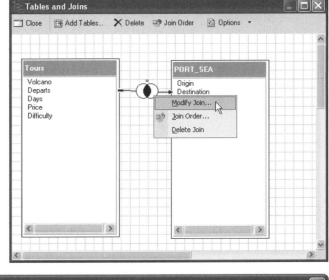

Modify Join window In the Modify Join window, you can choose from four types of joins: matching rows only, all rows from the left data table, all rows from the right data table, or all rows from both data tables. In this Modify Join window, **All rows from the left table** has been selected. Tours is the table on the left, so all rows from Tours will be included regardless of whether there is a matching row in the

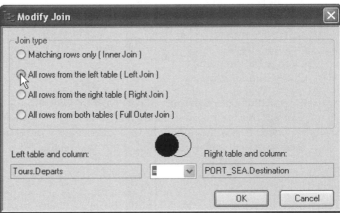

Port_Sea table. When you are satisfied with the join, click **OK**.

When you return to the Tables and Joins window, you will see that the join indicator between the two tables has changed. In this example, the circle on the left is filled in, indicating that all rows from the Tours data table will be included. When you are satisfied, click **Close**.

Running the query If you have not already selected the columns to be included in the results, then drag those columns to the Select Data area in the Query Builder window. When you are satisfied, click **Run**. SAS Enterprise Guide will display the results in a Data Grid.

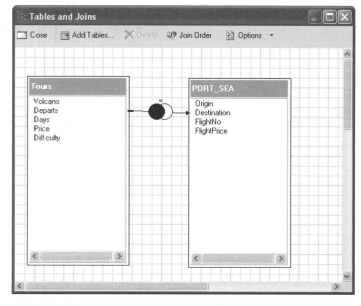

Results This Data Grid shows the result of the modified join. This table contains all the tours, including the one for St. Helens. Because the customer lives near St. Helens, she doesn't need a flight to go on that tour. SAS Enterprise Guide gives the new table a name starting with the word Query and saves it in a default location. To give the table a different name or location, use the **Change** button in the Query Builder window.

	Volcano	Departs	Days	Price	Difficulty	Origin	Destination	FlightNo	FlightPrice
1	Etna	Catania	7	$1,025	m	Portland	Catania	L469	$679.00
2	Etna	Catania	7	$1,025	m	Seattle	Catania	BA48	$702.00
3	Kilauea	Hilo	1	$45	e	Portland	Hilo	HA25	$603.00
4	Kilauea	Hilo	1	$45	e	Seattle	Hilo	HA21	$577.00
5	Krakatau	Jakarta	7	$850	e	Seattle	Jakarta	AA119	$1,715.00
6	Kenya	Nairobi	6	$780	m	Seattle	Nairobi	KLM6034	$1,661.00
7	Kilimanjaro	Nairobi	9	$1,260	c	Seattle	Nairobi	KLM6034	$1,661.00
8	Kenya	Nairobi	6	$780	m	Portland	Nairobi	KLM6034	$1,733.00
9	Kilimanjaro	Nairobi	9	$1,260	c	Portland	Nairobi	KLM6034	$1,733.00
10	St. Helens	Portland	2	$157	e				
11	Reventador	Quito	4	$525	m	Seattle	Quito	CA1086	$733.00
12	Vesuvius	Rome	6	$950	e	Seattle	Rome	USA6	$496.00
13	Vesuvius	Rome	6	$950	e	Portland	Rome	D1576	$544.00
14	Poas	San Jose	1	$50	e	Seattle	San Jose	CA1100	$380.00
15	Poas	San Jose	1	$50	e	Portland	San Jose	CA1210	$394.00
16	Fuji	Tokyo	2	$195	c	Seattle	Tokyo	UA875	$621.00
17	Fuji	Tokyo	2	$195	c	Portland	Tokyo	UA383	$605.00

ooo Project Designer | Query1_for_Tours (read-only)

CHAPTER 6

Producing Simple Lists and Reports

Chapter 6

6.1 ▶ Creating Simple Lists of Data

A simple list report has one line for each observation in the data set. It's the kind of report you need when you just want to see your data. You can select some variables and not others, group the data by a particular variable, and insert totals, but as long as you have one line for each observation, it is still a list report, and to create it you use the List Data task.

This example creates a report listing the Bookings data. In the Project Explorer or Project Designer, click the data icon to make it active. Then select **Describe ▶ List Data** from the menu bar. The List Data window will open, displaying the Task Roles page.

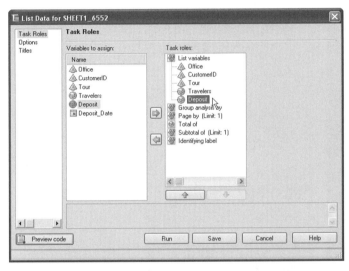

Assigning task roles

You assign variables to roles by clicking the name of a variable and dragging it to the role you want to give it. For the List Data task, you must assign at least one variable to serve as a list variable. In this window, the variables Office, CustomerID, Tour, Travelers, and Deposit have been assigned to serve as list variables.

Choosing options

If you click **Options** in the selection pane on the left, you will see options for the List Data task. By default, the List Data task will print the row number for each line in the report. If you don't want row numbers, then uncheck **Print the row number**. For this report, the default values are fine. When you are satisfied with the options, click **Run**.

Results Here is the simple list report of the Bookings data with the five selected variables. Notice that the report includes row numbers, and a default title and footnote. The next section shows how to customize titles and footnotes.

§sas. | Enterprise Guide.

The Power to Know.

Report Listing

Row number	Office	CustomerID	Tour	Travelers	Deposit
1	Portland	SL28	SH43	10	425
2	Portland	DE27	PS27	6	75
3	Portland	SL34	FJ12	4	200
4	Portland	DI33	SH43	4	150
5	Portland	BU12	SH43	2	75
6	Portland	DE31	FJ12	3	175
7	Portland	WI48	FJ12	2	100
8	Portland	NG17	PS27	5	65
9	Portland	RA28	PS27	2	30
10	Portland	ME11	PS27	2	30
11	Portland	GI08	SH43	8	300
12	Portland	HI15	SH43	4	150
13	Portland	MA09	SH43	2	75

Generated by the SAS System (Local, XP_PRO) on 23MAY2006 at 1:35 PM

6.2 Customizing Titles and Footnotes

By default, reports in SAS Enterprise Guide have titles that describe the type of report, such as "Summary Statistics" or "Analysis of Variance," and footnotes that show the date and time the task was run. That's a good start, but in most cases, you will want titles and footnotes that reflect your unique report. You can easily customize titles and footnotes in any task that produces a report.

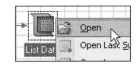

This example takes the report that was produced in the previous section and gives it a custom title and footnote. You can change a title when you first run a task or, to change the titles and footnotes for an existing report, right-click the task icon in the Project Explorer or Project Designer and select **Open**. The task window will open. In the task window, click **Titles** in the selection pane on the left to display the Titles page.

Titles page The area labeled **Section** lists all the titles and footnotes for the task. For the List Data task, you can choose **Report Titles** or **Footnote**. Some tasks have other types of titles you can change. The Summary Statistics task, for example, offers Analysis, Histogram, and Box and Whisker Plot titles, plus Footnote. You can change any of these using the Titles page.

To change a title, click its name in the area labeled **Section**. Then uncheck the **Use default text** option and type up to 10 new titles in the box below. In this example, the title "Report Listing" has been replaced with two titles: "Bookings for Portland" and "July."

To change a footnote, click **Footnote** in the area labeled **Section**. Then uncheck the **Use default text** option and type up to 10 new footnotes in the box below. In this example, the footnote has simply been deleted.

When you are satisfied with the new titles and footnotes, click **Run** in the task window.

Titles

Section:
✓ Report Titles
✓ Footnote

Text for section: Footnote
☐ Use default text

Checked sections will be generated based on current task settings.

Results Here is the report with the new titles and no footnote.

If you find yourself changing titles and footnotes a lot, you may want to change the default values. You do this using the Options window (see section 1.15). To open the Options window, select **Tools ▶ Options** from the menu bar. Then select **Tasks General** from the selection pane on the left to display the Tasks > Tasks General page. In this page you can specify a new title that will be inserted before the existing default titles in your results. You can also set the footnote to blank, or specify a new footnote to replace the default footnote.

§sas. | Enterprise Guide.

The Power to Know.

**Bookings for Portland
July**

Row number	Office	CustomerID	Tour	Travelers	Deposit
1	Portland	SL28	SH43	10	425
2	Portland	DE27	PS27	6	75
3	Portland	SL34	FJ12	4	200
4	Portland	DI33	SH43	4	150
5	Portland	BU12	SH43	2	75
6	Portland	DE31	FJ12	3	175
7	Portland	WI48	FJ12	2	100
8	Portland	NG17	PS27	5	65
9	Portland	RA28	PS27	2	30
10	Portland	ME11	PS27	2	30
11	Portland	GI08	SH43	8	300
12	Portland	HI15	SH43	4	150
13	Portland	MA09	SH43	2	75

6.3 Adding Groups to Lists of Data

Most tasks that produce reports allow you to assign one or more variables to serve as grouping variables. When you do this, SAS Enterprise Guide divides your data into groups based on the values of the grouping variables, and handles the groups separately. That way, you can get a report for each salesperson, or statistics for each state, or a chart for each quarter.

This example creates a grouped listing report using the Bookings data. In the Project Explorer or Project Designer, click the data icon to make it active. Then select **Describe ▶ List Data** from the menu bar. The List Data window will open, displaying the Task Roles page.

Assigning a variable to the grouping task role
To produce a report with observations divided into groups, assign one or more variables to the **Group analysis by** task role. Each time you drag a variable name to the **Group analysis by** role, two items will appear on the right: a pull-down list for the sort order, and a box labeled **Sort by variables**. You use these options to tell SAS Enterprise Guide whether you want the report to be sorted by that grouping variable and, if so, whether in ascending or descending order. In the List Data window above, the variable Tour is a grouping variable, and the variables Office, CustomerID, Travelers, and Deposit are list variables. When you are satisfied with the variables and their task roles, click **Run**.

Results
Here is the beginning of the report with Tour as a grouping variable. Notice that there is a separate section of the report for each value of Tour.

List Data for SHEET1_6552

Task Roles / Options / Titles

Task Roles

Variables to assign:

Name
- Office
- CustomerID
- Tour
- Travelers
- Deposit
- Deposit_Date

Task roles:
- List variables
  - Office
  - CustomerID
  - Travelers
  - Deposit
- Group analysis by
  - Tour
- Page by (Limit: 1)
- Total of
- Subtotal of (Limit: 1)
- Identifying label

Tour sort order:
Ascending

☑ Sort by variables

When you assign one or more variables to this role, the table is sorted by the selected variable or variables, and a listing is generated for each distinct value, or BY group, in the variable or combination of variables.

Preview code | Run | Save | Cancel | Help

§sas. | Enterprise Guide.

The Power to Know.

Bookings for Portland
July

Tour=FJ12

Row number	Office	CustomerID	Travelers	Deposit
1	Portland	SL34	4	200
2	Portland	DE31	3	175
3	Portland	WI48	2	100

Tour=PS27

Row number	Office	CustomerID	Travelers	Deposit
4	Portland	DE27	6	75
5	Portland	NG17	5	65
6	Portland	RA28	2	30
7	Portland	ME11	2	30

Tour=SH43

Row number	Office	CustomerID	Travelers	Deposit
8	Portland	SL28	10	425

Assigning a variable to the identifying label role Many tasks allow you to assign a variable to the **Group analysis by** role. The List Data task also allows you to assign a variable to the **Identifying label** role. You can use these two task roles together to create an attractive report. In this List Data window, the variable Tour has been assigned to both the Group analysis by role and the Identifying label role. When you are satisfied with the variables and their task roles, click **Run**.

Results Here is the report with Tour serving as a grouping variable and as an identifying variable. Notice that this report is more compact than the previous one, and that the row numbers have been replaced by the identifying variable.

Bookings for Portland
July

Tour	Office	CustomerID	Travelers	Deposit
FJ12	Portland	SL34	4	200
	Portland	DE31	3	175
	Portland	WI48	2	100
PS27	Portland	DE27	6	75
	Portland	NG17	5	65
	Portland	RA28	2	30
	Portland	ME11	2	30
SH43	Portland	SL28	10	425
	Portland	DI33	4	150
	Portland	BU12	2	75
	Portland	GI08	8	300
	Portland	HI15	4	150
	Portland	MA09	2	75

6.4 ▶ Adding Totals to Lists of Data

List reports have one line for each observation in a data set, but it is possible to add some summary data to these reports. Using the Total of task role, you can add subtotals for groups and a grand total at the bottom of the report.

This example creates a list report with totals using the Bookings data set. In the Project Explorer or Project Designer, click the data icon to make it active. Then select **Describe** ▶ **List Data** from the menu bar. The List Data window will open, displaying the Task Roles page.

Assigning a variable to the total task role   To produce a list report with totals, assign one or more variables to the Total of task role. To do this, click a variable name and drag it to the **Total of** role. Because this variable will be summed, it must be numeric.

The List Data window above shows the List Data task for the Bookings data. The variables Travelers and Deposit have been assigned to the Total of role. In addition, the variables Office and CustomerID have been selected as list variables, and Tour has been selected as both a grouping and identifying variable. When you are satisfied with the variables and their roles, click **Run**.

Results Here is a list report of the Bookings data with the variables Travelers and Deposit totaled. Notice that there are totals for each value of the grouping variable, Tour, and a grand total at the bottom of the report. If this report did not have a grouping variable, then only the grand total would appear.

§sas. | Enterprise Guide⌀

The Power to Know.

Bookings for Portland
July

Tour	Office	CustomerID	Travelers	Deposit
FJ12	Portland	SL34	4	200
	Portland	DE31	3	175
	Portland	WI48	2	100
FJ12			9	475
PS27	Portland	DE27	6	75
	Portland	NG17	5	65
	Portland	RA28	2	30
	Portland	ME11	2	30
PS27			15	200
SH43	Portland	SL28	10	425
	Portland	DI33	4	150
	Portland	BU12	2	75
	Portland	GI08	8	300
	Portland	HI15	4	150
	Portland	MA09	2	75
SH43			30	1175
			54	1850

6.5 Creating Frequency Reports

If you have ever wondered exactly how many different values a particular variable has, then a one-way frequency table is what you need. Frequencies are also called counts because you can produce a basic frequency table by simply counting the number of times each data value occurs. To produce frequencies for an individual variable in SAS Enterprise Guide, use the One-Way Frequencies task.

This example uses the Volcanoes data set to produce frequencies for the variables Activity and Region. In the Project Explorer or Project Designer, click the data icon to make it active. Then select **Describe ▶ One-Way Frequencies** from the menu bar. The One-Way Frequencies window will open, displaying the Task Roles page.

Assigning task roles You assign variables to roles by clicking the name of a variable and dragging it to the role you want to give it. For the One-Way Frequencies task, you must assign at least one variable to serve as an analysis variable. In this example, the variables Activity and Region are designated as analysis variables.

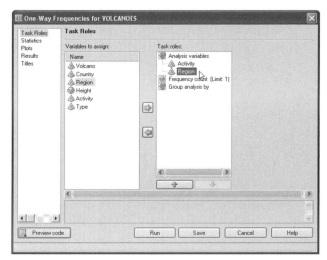

Choosing statistics If you click **Statistics** in the selection pane on the left, you will see options for this task. By default, the results will include frequencies and percentages, along with cumulative frequencies and percentages. You can choose different combinations of statistics. The default results exclude any missing values. If you want to include missing values in the resulting table, then check the option **Show frequencies** in the **Missing values** section. For this report, the default values are fine. When you are satisfied with the options, click **Run**.

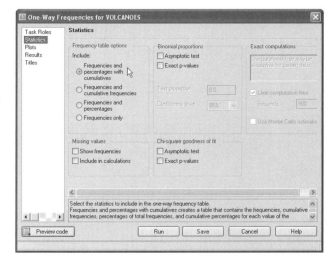

Results Here are the one-way frequencies for Activity and Region. Notice that there are two separate tables, one for each variable. The variable Activity has two missing values. These missing values are not included in the table, but are mentioned in a note below the table. The variable Region doesn't have any missing values, so there is no note below the second table.

One-Way Frequencies Results

The FREQ Procedure

Activity				
Activity	Frequency	Percent	Cumulative Frequency	Cumulative Percent
Active	23	76.67	23	76.67
Extinct	7	23.33	30	100.00

Frequency Missing = 2

Region				
Region	Frequency	Percent	Cumulative Frequency	Cumulative Percent
AP	4	12.50	4	12.50
Af	4	12.50	8	25.00
An	1	3.13	9	28.13
As	5	15.63	14	43.75
Eu	7	21.88	21	65.63
NA	6	18.75	27	84.38
SA	5	15.63	32	100.00

6.6 Creating Crosstabulations

When you have counts for one variable, they are called one-way frequencies. When you create counts by crossing two or more variables, they are called two-way, three-way, and so on, up to *n*-way frequencies; or simply crosstabulations. To produce crosstabulations, use the Table Analysis task.

This example is similar to the one in the previous section, but, instead of having one table for Activity and one for Region, it produces a single table showing Activity by Region. In the Project Explorer or Project Designer, click the data to make it active. Then select **Describe ▶ Table Analysis** from the menu bar. The Table Analysis window will open, displaying the Task Roles page.

Assigning task roles You assign variables to roles by clicking the name of a variable and dragging it to the role you want to give it. For the Table Analysis task, you must assign at least two variables to serve as table variables. In this window, the variables Activity and Region have been designated as table variables.

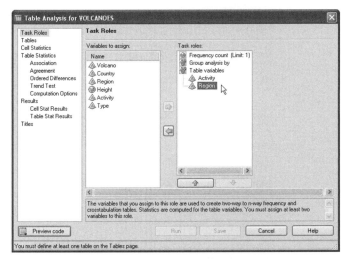

Arranging your table Click **Tables** in the selection pane on the left to display the Tables page. In this page, you will see an area labeled **Variables permitted in table**, and an area labeled **Preview**. To arrange your table, click the name of a variable and drag it to the Preview area. When you drag a variable to the Preview area, its name will disappear from the list of variables permitted in the table.

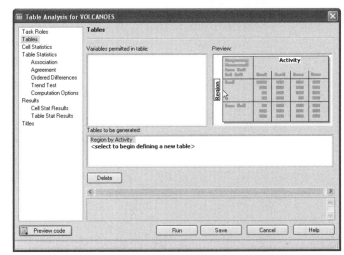

The values of the first variable dragged over will be used for rows, the second for columns, and the third for pages, but you can switch them around by dragging them within the Preview area. In the preceding window, the variable Region has been assigned to the rows, and Activity to the columns.

Choosing cell statistics If you click **Cell Statistics** in the selection pane on the left, you will see options for basic statistics. By default, the results will include column percentages and cell frequencies. You can choose different combinations of statistics. The Table Analysis task also offers many other statistics, including the chi-square test. See section 8.3 for a discussion of more advanced statistical options. For this report, the default values are fine. When you are satisfied with the options, click **Run**.

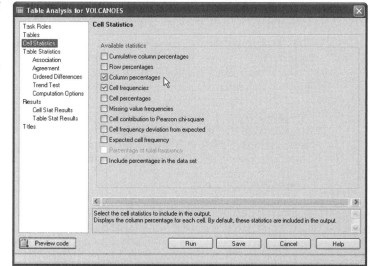

Results Here is the two-way frequency table for Region by Activity. Because the variable Activity has two missing values, there is a note at the bottom saying that two observations are missing.

Table Analysis Results

The FREQ Procedure

Frequency Col Pct	Table of Region by Activity		
		Activity(Activity)	
Region(Region)	Active	Extinct	Total
AP	3 13.04	1 14.29	4
Af	2 8.70	1 14.29	3
An	1 4.35	0 0.00	1
As	5 21.74	0 0.00	5
Eu	4 17.39	3 42.86	7
NA	5 21.74	0 0.00	5
SA	3 13.04	2 28.57	5
Total	23	7	30
Frequency Missing = 2			

6.7 ▶ Creating Simple Summary Reports

Once you have run a list or frequency report, there's a good chance you'll want to see some summary statistics. Statistics like the mean, standard deviation, and minimum and maximum values not only give you a feel for your data, but can alert you to unexpected values or errors in your data. SAS Enterprise Guide offers many ways to summarize data, and the Summary Statistics task is a good place to start.

This example summarizes the Volcanoes data set by finding summary statistics for Height within each Type of volcano. In the Project Explorer or Project Designer, click the data icon to make it active. Then select **Describe ▶ Summary Statistics** from the menu bar. The Summary Statistics window will open, displaying the Task Roles page.

Assigning task roles You assign variables to roles by clicking the name of a variable and dragging it to the role you want to give it. For the Summary Statistics task, you must assign at least one variable to the Analysis variables role, and all analysis variables must be numeric. SAS Enterprise Guide will summarize the analysis variables.

Classification variables are optional and may be numeric or character. If you assign a variable to the Classification variables role, then SAS Enterprise Guide will produce separate summary statistics for each combination of the classification variables. When you drag a variable to the classification role, options will appear on the right. You can choose the sort order (ascending or descending) and whether to include missing values. The default is to exclude any observations with missing values for the classification variables. The Group analysis by role is similar to the classification role, but it produces a separate table for each combination of the grouping variables.

Here the variable Height has been designated as an analysis variable, and Type as a classification variable. This example uses the default options for sort order (Unformatted values, Ascending) and missing values (Exclude).

Choosing statistics Click **Basic** under the **Statistics** group of options in the selection pane on the left to display the Statistics > Basic page. Here you can choose statistics and set the number of decimal places to be displayed in the report. The Summary Statistics task offers many other statistics, including the coefficient of variation and percentiles. See section 8.2 for a discussion of more advanced options. In this case, the default statistics are fine. When you are satisfied with the settings, click **Run**.

Results Here is the report showing the default summary statistics for Height within each Type of volcano. Notice that there are only 30 volcanoes because the two volcanoes with missing values for Type were excluded.

Summary Statistics
Results

The MEANS Procedure

		Analysis Variable : Height				
Type	N Obs	Mean	Std Dev	Minimum	Maximum	N
Caldera	2	1269.00	644.8813844	813.0000000	1725.00	2
Cinder Cone	1	1464.00	.	1464.00	1464.00	1
Complex	1	1281.00	.	1281.00	1281.00	1
Shield	5	1988.40	1570.44	367.0000000	4170.00	5
Stratovolcano	21	3759.95	1586.47	354.0000000	6458.00	21

6.8 Creating Summary Data Sets in a Task

Sometimes you may want to save summary data so you can use it for further analysis or join it with other data sets. Many tasks can save summary data, including the Query Builder, Table Analysis, Summary Tables, and Summary Statistics.

The previous section used the Volcanoes data set to find summary statistics for the variable Height within each Type of volcano. These summary statistics can be saved in a data set. To open an existing task so you can make changes, right-click the task icon in the Project Explorer or Project Designer and select **Open**. The task window will open. Click **Results** in the selection pane on the left to display the Results page.

Results page In the Results page, you will see options that affect both your printed report and output data set. To save an output data set, check the **Save statistics to data set** option. SAS Enterprise Guide gives the data set a name such as MEANSummaryStats-VOLCANOES and stores it in a default location. To specify a different name or location, click **Browse**. This opens the Save As window.

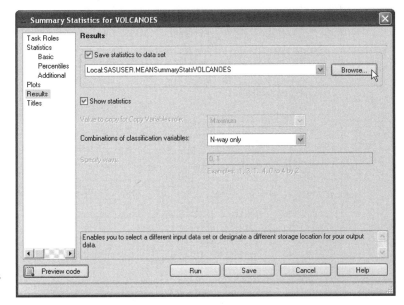

Save As window In the Save As window, choose a library, and then type a name for your file in the **File name** box. In this window, the data set has been named VolcanoStats and will be saved in the SASUSER library. When you are satisfied, click **Save** to return to the Results page.

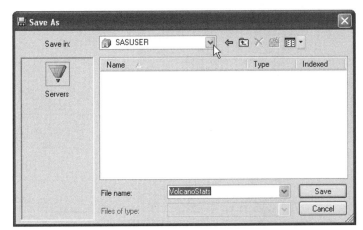

Choosing options In the Results page, you will see the new data set name. Before you run the report, you may want to make some other changes. Because you are creating an output data set, you may not care about the standard Summary Statistics report. To turn off the report, uncheck the **Show statistics** box.

You can choose the combinations of classification variables that will be included. **N-way only** (the default) tells SAS Enterprise Guide to include only results for the highest interaction of the classification variables. In this case, with only one classification variable, the highest interaction will produce summary statistics by Type of volcano. You can choose all combinations, or specific combinations.

If you have many classification variables, then you will have many possible combinations. When you are satisfied with the settings, click **Run**.

Results Here is the output data set displayed in a Data Grid. The data set contains summary statistics for Height within each level of Type of volcano. Notice that SAS Enterprise Guide has created new variables for the summary statistics: Height_Mean, Height_StdDev, Height_Min, Height_Max, and Height_N. In addition, the variable _FREQ_ tells you how many observations contributed to each group, while _WAY_ and _TYPE_ reflect the type of combination. See the SAS Enterprise Guide Help for more information about these automatic variables.

	Type	_WAY_	_TYPE_	_FREQ_	Height_Mean	Height_StdDev	Height_Min	Height_Max	Height_N
1	Caldera	1	1	2	1269	645	813	1725	2
2	Cinder Cone	1	1	1	1464	.	1464	1464	1
3	Complex	1	1	1	1281	.	1281	1281	1
4	Shield	1	1	5	1988	1570	367	4170	5
5	Stratovolcano	1	1	21	3760	1586	354	6458	21

CHAPTER 7

Producing Complex Reports in Summary Tables

7.1 Creating Summary Tables with Frequencies

The Summary Tables task is the most powerful and flexible of the reporting tasks in SAS Enterprise Guide. It gives you not only control over what data appear in your table, but also over how data are arranged, summarized, labeled, and even colored.

This example uses the Volcanoes data set to create a table showing the number of active and extinct volcanoes for each region. In the Project Explorer or Project Designer, click the data icon to make it active. Then select **Describe ▶ Summary Tables** from the menu bar. The Summary Tables window will open, displaying the Task Roles page.

Assigning task roles To produce a summary table showing frequencies, assign one or more variables to the classification role. These variables may be character or numeric. SAS Enterprise Guide will divide the data into categories based on the values of the classification variables. The following window shows the Volcanoes data set with the variables Region and Activity serving as classification variables.

When you drag a variable to the classification role, a box will appear on the right. In this box, you can select options for that variable, including how to handle missing data. By default, missing values are included as valid rows and columns, which may or may not be what you want. In this case, two volcanoes have a missing value for Activity. To avoid having an entire row devoted to missing values, click **Missing values** and select **Exclude** for the variable Activity.

Once you exclude missing values for a variable, observations with missing values for that variable will be excluded from the report even if you decide not to use that particular variable. Because of this, it's a good idea to assign variables to the classification role only if you intend to use them in the current report.

Arranging your table Before you can run a report, you must tell Summary Tables how to arrange it. Start by clicking the **Summary Tables** option in the selection pane on the left. In the Summary Tables page, you will see areas labeled **Available variables** and **Preview**. To assign a variable to serve as a row or column in your report, drag the variable name from the list of available variables to the Preview area. It may take a little practice to get variables where you want them. The trick is to watch the cursor. If the cursor looks like the universal not-allowed symbol, $\oslash$, then you cannot drop the variable. If the cursor is a line or a box, then you can drop the variable.

The undo ⟲ and redo ⟳ buttons in the upper-right corner of the Preview area can be quite useful. If you want to switch the row variables with the column variables, use the pivot button. You can drag the ALL variable to the Preview area to tell SAS Enterprise Guide where to insert totals. In the preceding window, the values of the variable Activity form the rows, and the values of Region form the columns. When you are satisfied with the arrangement of your table, click **Run**.

Results Here is the report of Activity by Region. Notice that the values in the cells are frequencies. The number of volcanoes that are in each category and totals appear in the column and row labeled All.

Summary Tables

	Region							All
	AP	Af	An	As	Eu	NA	SA	
	N	N	N	N	N	N	N	N
Activity								
Active	3	2	1	5	4	5	3	23
Extinct	1	1	.	.	3	.	2	7
All	4	3	1	5	7	5	5	30

7.2 Adding Statistics to Summary Tables

The previous section showed how to produce a table containing simple counts. Sometimes that's all you need, but often you want more. You might want to know total sales by region, or the mean test score for each class. In summary tables, you can compute sums and means, plus a long list of other statistics, including maximum and minimum values, percentages, medians, quartiles, standard deviations, and variances.

This example uses the Tours data set to create a report showing the minimum number of days, maximum number of days, and mean price for each level of difficulty. In the Project Explorer or Project Designer, click the data icon to make it active. Then select **Describe ▶ Summary Tables** from the menu bar. This opens the Summary Tables window displaying the Task Roles page.

Assigning task roles There are a few statistics you can compute for classification variables. These include N (the default), and ColPctN and RowPctN, the percentage of frequency for each column or row. However, most statistics can only be computed for analysis variables. Analysis variables must be numeric. (It's simply not possible to compute a mean using character values like Active and Extinct.) To produce a summary report containing sums and means, assign one or more variables to the analysis role. The following window shows the Tours data set with the variable Difficulty serving as a classification variable, and the variables Days and Price serving as analysis variables.

Arranging your table You arrange analysis variables in your table the same way you arrange classification variables. First, click the **Summary Tables** option in the selection pane on the left. In the Summary Tables page, you will see areas labeled **Available variables** and **Preview**. To assign a variable to serve as a row or column in your report, drag the variable name from the list of available variables to the Preview area. In the following window, the values of Difficulty form the rows, and the values of Days and Price form the columns.

Choosing statistics The default statistic for classification variables is N (the number of non-missing values). The default statistic for analysis variables is Sum. You can choose many other statistics from the box labeled **Available statistics**. To add a statistic to your report, click the name of the statistic and drag it to the **Preview** area. Be sure to watch your cursor carefully. If the cursor looks like the universal not-allowed symbol, ⊘, then you cannot drop the statistic. If the cursor is a line or a box, then you can drop the statistic.

In the preceding window, the statistics Min and Max have been placed under the variable Days, and the statistic Mean has been placed under the variable Price. When you are satisfied with the arrangement of your table, click **Run**.

Results Here is the report of Difficulty by Days and Price. Notice that the values in the cells are the minimum and maximum number of Days, and the mean of Price.

Summary Tables			
	Days		Price
	Min	Max	Mean
Difficulty			
c	2.00	9.00	727.50
e	1.00	7.00	410.40
m	4.00	7.00	776.67

7.3 Changing Heading Properties in Summary Tables

Once you've constructed a summary table, put each variable in its proper place, and selected statistics, you may want to change the way the table looks. From the Preview area, you can change many properties of headers and data values.

To modify an existing report, right-click the **Summary Tables** task icon in the Project Explorer or Project Designer and select **Open**. The Summary Tables window will open. To display the Preview area, click the **Summary Tables** option in the selection pane on the left.

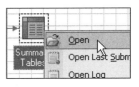

Heading Properties To change headings that are the names of variables or statistics, use the Heading Properties window. For example, to change the heading Min to Minimum, you would right-click **Min** in the **Preview** area and select **Heading Properties** from the pop-up menu. The Heading Properties window will open.

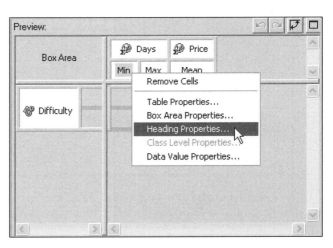

Using the **General** tab of the Heading Properties window, you can type a new label for the variable or statistic you have selected. In this window, the word Minimum has been typed in the **Label** box. Using the **Font** tab, you can change the font, font style, size, foreground color, background color, and other attributes of headings. When you are satisfied with the changes, click **OK**.

You can now change other properties. For this example, change the statistic name Max to Maximum using the Heading Properties window for Max.

Box Area Properties Summary Tables reports always contain a box in the upper-left corner. By default, this box is empty, but you can put a label in that box and this often gives reports a nicely polished look. To do this, right-click anywhere in the **Preview** area and select **Box Area Properties** from the pop-up menu.

Using the **General** tab of the Box Area Properties window, you can type the text you want printed in the box area. In this Box Area Properties window, the words Volcano Tours have been typed in the text box. Using the **Font** tab, you can change the font, font style, size, foreground color, background color, and other attributes of the text to be printed in the box area.

When you are satisfied with the changes, click **OK**. You can then change other properties, or click **Run** to see the new results.

Results Here is the report. Notice that the labels Min and Max have been replaced with Minimum and Maximum, and the words Volcano Tours have been inserted in the box area.

Summary Tables

Volcano Tours	Days		Price
	Minimum	Maximum	Mean
Difficulty			
c	2.00	9.00	727.50
e	1.00	7.00	410.40
m	4.00	7.00	776.67

7.4 Changing Class Level Headings and Properties in Summary Tables

The previous section showed how to change headings that are the names of variables or statistics, but classification variables also use data values as headings. These data values are called class level headings. When you change class level headings, you are changing the way those data values are displayed. To change the way data values are displayed, you use a format.

To modify an existing report, right-click the **Summary Tables** task icon in the Project Explorer or Project Designer and select **Open**. The Summary Tables window will open.

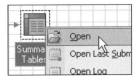

Applying a format to a classification variable To change headings that are data values, you specify a format in the Task Roles page. Click the name of the classification variable you want to change. A box will open on the right listing options for that variable. Click the words **Heading for** and a small box containing three dots will appear ⬚. Click the box to open a Format window for that variable. In this example, the heading for the variable Difficulty is being selected.

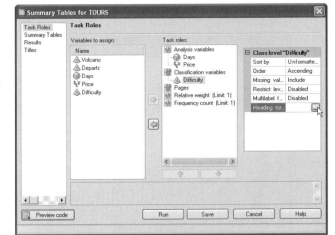

In the Select Column Format window, choose the category of formats you want to see, and then choose the name of the format you want to use. In most cases, to change a class level heading you will need a user-defined format. In this example, the user-defined format $DIFF. has been selected. The $DIFF. format was created in Tutorial C. Sections 3.3 and 3.4 also discuss creating a user-defined format. Once you are satisfied, click **OK**.

Class Level Properties To change other properties of class level headings, click the **Summary Tables** option in the selection pane on the left. Then right-click the name of the classification variable in the **Preview** area and select **Class Level Properties** from the pop-up menu. This example shows Class Level Properties being selected for the variable Difficulty. The Class Level Properties window will open.

Using the **Font** tab, you can change the font, font style, size, foreground color, background color, and other attributes of headings. For this report, the background color has been changed to Gray–25%. When you are satisfied with the changes, click **OK**. Click **Run** to see the new results.

Results Here is the report. Notice that the labels c, e, and m have been replaced with Challenging, Easy, and Moderate (the values of the $DIFF. format), and have a medium gray background.

Summary Tables

Volcano Tours	Days		Price
	Minimum	Maximum	Mean
Difficulty			
Challenging	2.00	9.00	727.50
Easy	1.00	7.00	410.40
Moderate	4.00	7.00	776.67

7.5 Changing Table Properties in Summary Tables

In addition to changing headers and labels, you can make changes to the data cells in a table. To make a change that will apply to all the cells, use the Table Properties window.

To modify an existing report, right-click the **Summary Tables** task icon in the Project Explorer or Project Designer and select **Open**. The Summary Tables window will open. Click the **Summary Tables** option in the selection pane on the left to display the Preview area.

To make changes to all the data cells of a table, right-click anywhere in the **Preview** area and select **Table Properties** from the pop-up menu.

General tab Using the **General** tab of the Table Properties window, you can specify options for the treatment of missing values and class variable levels. By default, missing values are displayed as a period (.). You can specify a more meaningful label. In this example, the label none has been assigned to missing values.

Format tab Using the Format tab of the Table Properties window, you can choose a format for the data in the cells of the table. Here the basic numeric format, *w.d*, has been specified with an overall width of 4 characters, and no decimal places.

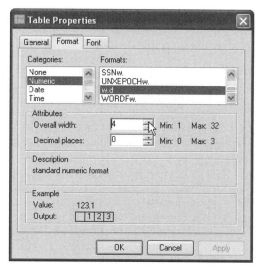

Font tab Using the **Font** tab of the Table Properties window, you can change the font, font style, size, foreground color, background color, and other attributes of the data cells in your table. In this case, the font has been set to Courier New, the style to Bold, the foreground color to white, and the background color to Gray–50%.

When you are satisfied with the changes, click **OK**. You can then change other properties, or click **Run** to see the new results.

Results Here is the new report. Notice that the data cells have a dark gray background and white foreground. Also, the data are displayed in bold Courier New, and with no decimal places.

Summary Tables

Volcano Tours	Days		Price
	Minimum	Maximum	Mean
Difficulty			
Challenging	2	9	728
Easy	1	7	410
Moderate	4	7	777

Chapter 7

7.6   Changing Data Value Properties in Summary Tables

Using the Table Properties window, you can make changes to all the data cells in a report, but sometimes you may want to choose different formats or fonts for different variables or statistics. To do that, use the Data Value Properties window.

To modify an existing report, right-click the **Summary Tables** task icon in the Project Explorer or Project Designer and select **Open**. The Summary Tables window will open. Click the **Summary Tables** option in the selection pane on the left to display the Preview area.

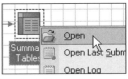

To make changes to a particular row or column, right-click the header for that row or column in the **Preview** area and select **Data Value Properties** from the pop-up menu. In this Preview area, Data Value Properties is being selected for the column Price.

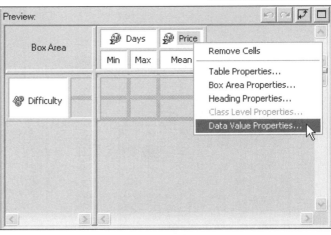

Format tab Using the **Format** tab of the Data Value Properties window, you can choose a format for the data values in the row or column. In this example, the category Currency has been selected, and SAS Enterprise Guide has listed all the available formats for currency data. The format DOLLAR*w.d* is selected, with an overall width of **7** characters, and 2 decimal places.

Font tab Using the **Font** tab of the Data Value Properties window, you can change the font, font style, size, foreground color, background color, and other attributes of the data cells in the row or column. In this example, the font for Price has been set to Courier New, the style to Bold, the foreground color to white, and the background color to black.

When you are satisfied with the changes, click **OK**. You can now change other properties, or click **Run** to see the new results.

Results Here is the report. Notice that the column for Mean Price looks different from the columns for Minimum and Maximum Days. The background color is black instead of gray, and the numbers have dollar signs in front of them and two decimal places.

Volcano Tours	Days		Price
	Minimum	Maximum	Mean
Difficulty			
Challenging	2	9	$727.50
Easy	1	7	$410.40
Moderate	4	7	$776.67

Summary Tables

CHAPTER 8

Basic Statistical Analysis

Chapter 8

8.1 Distribution Analysis

When you are doing statistical analysis, generally your goal is to examine the relationship between two or more variables. You may want to know how length of day affects the growth of plants, or how an advertising campaign influences sales. But before you start testing hypotheses, it's a good idea to pause and do a little exploration. The Distribution Analysis task is a good place to start. Distribution Analysis produces statistics describing the distribution of a single variable.

This example explores the distribution of the variable Height in the Volcanoes data set. In the Project Explorer or Project Designer, click the data icon to make it active. Then select **Describe** ▶ **Distribution Analysis**. The Distribution Analysis window will open, displaying the Task Roles page.

Assigning task roles For Distribution Analysis, you must assign at least one variable to serve as an analysis variable, and that variable must be numeric. In this example, the variable Height has been assigned to the Analysis variables role.

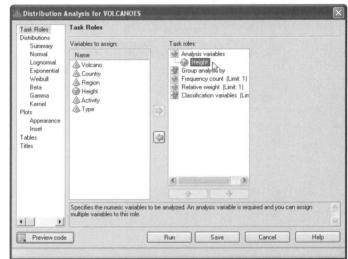

Choosing statistics There are many options in Distribution Analysis for choosing different summary statistics and examining different types of distributions. In the Tables page, you can choose sets of statistics. For this example, select Basic confidence intervals, Basic measures, Tests for location, Moments, and Quantiles. When you are satisfied with your selections, click **Run**.

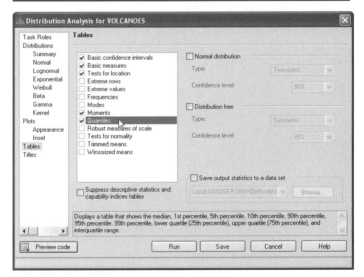

Results The resulting report starts with basic information about the distribution of the variable: the number of observations (N), mean, and standard deviation. Skewness indicates how symmetrical the distribution is (whether it is more spread out on one side than the other), while kurtosis indicates how flat or peaked the distribution is. Other sections of the report contain the mean, the median, and the mode (in this case, there is no mode because no two volcanoes had the same value of Height); confidence limits assuming normality; tests of the hypothesis that the mean is zero; and quantiles.

Distribution analysis of: Height

The UNIVARIATE Procedure
Variable: Height

Moments			
N	32	Sum Weights	32
Mean	3113.5625	Sum Observations	99634
Std Deviation	1806.35239	Variance	3262908.96
Skewness	0.16096928	Kurtosis	-0.9518867
Uncorrected SS	411366864	Corrected SS	101150178
Coeff Variation	58.0156137	Std Error Mean	319.321006

Basic Statistical Measures			
Location		Variability	
Mean	3113.563	Std Deviation	1806
Median	2957.500	Variance	3262909
Mode	.	Range	6207
		Interquartile Range	3028

Basic Confidence Limits Assuming Normality			
Parameter	Estimate	95% Confidence Limits	
Mean	3114	2462	3765
Std Deviation	1806	1448	2402
Variance	3262909	2097164	5767244

Tests for Location: Mu0=0				
Test		Statistic	p Value	
Student's t	t	9.750572	Pr > |t|	<.0001
Sign	M	16	Pr >= |M|	<.0001
Signed Rank	S	264	Pr >= |S|	<.0001

Quantiles (Definition 5)	
Quantile	Estimate
100% Max	6458.0
99%	6458.0
95%	5976.0
90%	5633.0
75% Q3	4502.5
50% Median	2957.5
25% Q1	1475.0
10%	813.0
5%	354.0
1%	251.0
0% Min	251.0

8.2 Summary Statistics

There are many ways to summarize data in SAS Enterprise Guide. The Summary Statistics task gives you basic descriptive statistics like the mean, minimum, and maximum. You can also request more advanced statistics such as the coefficient of variation and quartiles. The Distribution Analysis task produces many of the same statistics, but the Summary Statistics task gives you more control over which specific statistics are produced, and formats the results differently.

The Fire and Ice Tours company has weather data by month for both its Seattle and Portland offices, along with the number of tour bookings for each month. Here is a sample of the data set, NWweather. To produce summary statistics, click the data icon in the Project Explorer or Project Designer to make it active. Then select **Describe ▶ Summary Statistics** from the menu bar. The Summary Statistics window will open, displaying the Task Roles page.

	City	Month	AvgTemp	FromNormal	InchesRain	Bookings
1	Seattle	1	45.8	4.9	8.39	32
2	Seattle	2	41.7	-1.6	1.76	19
3	Seattle	3	46.8	0.6	6.34	23
4	Seattle	4	48.9	-1.3	2.74	18
5	Seattle	5	54.8	-1	1.16	21
6	Seattle	6	62.8	2.1	0.51	18
7	Seattle	7	67.9	2.6	0.06	17
8	Seattle	8	66.4	0.8	0.32	17
9	Seattle	9	62.6	1.5	0.89	22
10	Seattle	10	54.3	1.6	8.96	20
11	Seattle	11	42.8	-2.4	6.77	25
12	Seattle	12	41.8	1.1	3.88	31
13	Portland	1	44.8	4.9	7.64	22
14	Portland	2	44.3	1.2	2.37	19
15	Portland	3	49	1.8	5.75	17
16	Portland	4	50.8	-0.4	4.37	18

Assigning task roles You should assign to the Analysis Variables role all the numeric variables you want summarized. If you choose a classification variable, then you will get separate analyses for each value of the classification variable. The Group analysis by role produces the same result as the Classification variables role, but the output is formatted differently. In this example, the variables InchesRain and Bookings have been assigned to the Analysis variables role, and the variable City has been assigned to the Classification variables role.

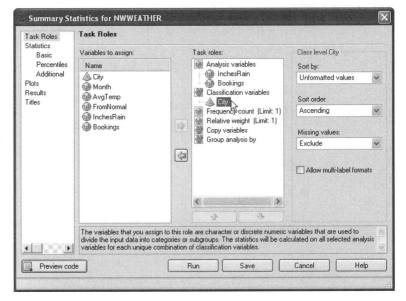

Choosing statistics The statistics for this task are grouped into Basic, Percentiles, and Additional. Several statistics in the Statistics > Basic page are chosen by default: mean, standard deviation, minimum, maximum, and number of observations. In the Statistics > Percentiles page, you can choose from various percentile statistics, including the median. The Statistics > Additional page has five more statistics, including confidence limits of the mean. If you choose confidence limits, then you can also choose the confidence level. In the Plots page, you can request histograms and box plots of your data. In this example, **Median** has been chosen in the Percentiles page, and **Confidence limits of the mean** in the Additional page.

Results The Summary Statistics task will produce a table with all the statistics you choose. Each analysis variable will have its own entry in the table, and if you include a classification or grouping variable, then each analysis variable will have a separate entry for each level of the classification or grouping variable. In this example, City is a classification variable so there are separate statistics for Portland and Seattle.

Summary Statistics
Results

The MEANS Procedure

City	N Obs	Variable	Mean	Std Dev	Minimum	Maximum	N	Median	Lower 95% CL for Mean	Upper 95% CL for Mean
Portland	12	InchesRain	3.1266667	2.7501879	0	7.6400000	12	2.6900000	1.3792807	4.8740527
		Bookings	20.9156667	5.4515775	13.0000000	33.0000000	12	20.0000000	17.4528996	24.3804337
Seattle	12	InchesRain	3.4816667	3.2946453	0.0600000	8.9600000	12	2.2500000	1.3883489	5.5749844
		Bookings	21.9156667	5.1071845	17.0000000	32.0000000	12	20.5000000	18.6717165	25.1616169

8.3 Table Analysis

The Table Analysis task produces crosstabulations and statistics for categorical data. You can choose measures of association, including chi-square, and you can request additional tests such as trend tests and measures of agreement.

Here is the OnTimeStatus data set, which shows the number of flights between Seattle and Chicago in the winter months. The data are broken down by the time of day, and whether flights had a delayed departure of 15 minutes or more. The objective is to determine if there is an association between the flights' time of day and punctuality. In the Project Explorer or Project Designer, click the data icon to make it active. Then select **Describe ▶ Table Analysis**. The Table Analysis window will open, displaying the Task Roles page.

	Month	Departure	TimeOfDay	NumOfFlights
1	Dec	OnTime	AfterNoon	25
2	Dec	Late	AfterNoon	33
3	Dec	OnTime	BeforeNoon	80
4	Dec	Late	BeforeNoon	13
5	Jan	OnTime	AfterNoon	15
6	Jan	Late	AfterNoon	12
7	Jan	OnTime	BeforeNoon	30
8	Jan	Late	BeforeNoon	13
9	Feb	OnTime	AfterNoon	20
10	Feb	Late	AfterNoon	8
11	Feb	OnTime	BeforeNoon	43
12	Feb	Late	BeforeNoon	1

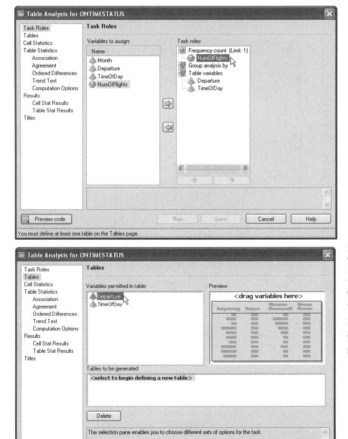

Assigning task roles For a two-way table, you must have two table variables. In this example, the variables TimeOfDay and Departure have been assigned to the Table variables role. Because each row in this table represents multiple flights, the variable NumOfFlights has been assigned to the Frequency count role. If each row in your data represents one count, then do not use the Frequency count role.

Creating the table To arrange your table, click the **Tables** option in the selection pane on the left. The first variable you drag to the **Preview** area will form the columns of the table. The second variable you drag will form the rows. In this example, Departure is on the top, and TimeOfDay on the side.

Choosing statistics You can choose many different statistics in the Table Analysis task. The different categories of statistics are listed under **Table Statistics** in the selection pane on the left. Click **Association** and choose the tests you want. In this example, Chi-square tests has been chosen.

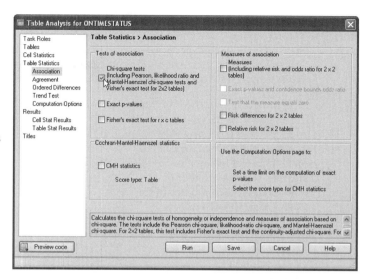

Results The output starts with a frequency table and is followed by the tests of association, including a table for Fisher's Exact Test since this is a 2x2 table. In this example, it appears that late departures tend to be more frequent in the afternoon hours. The probability of obtaining a chi-square value this large or larger by chance alone is less than 0.0001.

Table Analysis Results

The FREQ Procedure

Frequency Col Pct	Table of TimeOfDay by Departure		
	Departure		
TimeOfDay	Late	OnTime	Total
AfterNoon	53 66.25	60 28.17	113
BeforeNoon	27 33.75	153 71.83	180
Total	80	213	293

Statistics for Table of TimeOfDay by Departure

Statistic	DF	Value	Prob
Chi-Square	1	35.5961	<.0001
Likelihood Ratio Chi-Square	1	35.1538	<.0001
Continuity Adj. Chi-Square	1	34.0070	<.0001
Mantel-Haenszel Chi-Square	1	35.4746	<.0001
Phi Coefficient		0.3486	
Contingency Coefficient		0.3291	
Cramer's V		0.3486	

Fisher's Exact Test	
Cell (1,1) Frequency (F)	53
Left-sided Pr <= F	1.0000
Right-sided Pr >= F	3.428E-09
Table Probability (P)	2.772E-09
Two-sided Pr <= P	3.966E-09

Sample Size = 293

8.4 Correlations

The Correlations task produces correlation coefficients that measure relationships between numeric variables. A correlation coefficient of one means two variables are perfectly correlated, while a correlation coefficient of zero means there is no relationship between the two variables.

Here is a portion of the NWweather data set showing the average temperature, the deviation from the normal average temperature, the inches of rain, and the number of bookings for the Fire and Ice Tours company for each month for both Seattle and Portland. Using the Correlations task, you can measure the relationship between local weather and the number of tours booked each month. In the Project Explorer or Project Designer, click the data icon to make it active. Then select **Analyze ▶ Multivariate ▶ Correlations**. The Correlations window will open, displaying the Task Roles page.

	City	Month	AvgTemp	FromNormal	InchesRain	Bookings
8	Seattle	8	66.4	0.8	0.32	17
9	Seattle	9	62.6	1.5	0.89	22
10	Seattle	10	54.3	1.6	8.96	20
11	Seattle	11	42.8	-2.4	6.77	25
12	Seattle	12	41.8	1.1	3.88	31
13	Portland	1	44.8	4.9	7.64	22
14	Portland	2	44.3	1.2	2.37	19
15	Portland	3	49	1.8	5.75	17
16	Portland	4	50.8	-0.4	4.37	18
17	Portland	5	57.3	0.2	1.49	21

Assigning task roles For correlations, variables assigned to the Analysis variables role will appear across the top of the table, while variables assigned to the Correlate with role will appear down the side of the table. If there are no Correlate with variables, then the Analysis variables will appear both across the top and down the side of the table. In this example, the three weather variables AvgTemp, FromNormal, and InchesRain have been assigned to the Analysis variables role, and Bookings has been assigned to the Correlate with role.

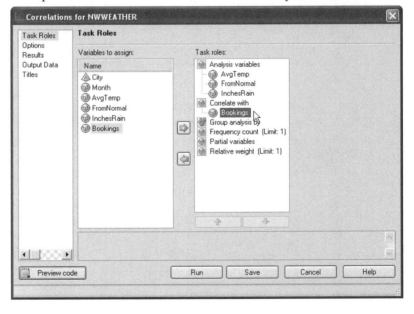

Choosing statistics and plots To run a correlation, all you need to do is assign variables to the task roles. However, you may want to choose some additional statistics. The Options page allows you to choose the type of correlation: Pearson (the default), Hoeffding, Kendall, or Spearman. There are additional options for Pearson correlations. For this example, leave the type of correlation set to Pearson.

Correlations for NWWEATHER

Task Roles
Options
Results
Output Data
Titles

Options

Correlation types
- ☑ Pearson
- ☐ Hoeffding
- ☐ Kendall
- ☐ Spearman

Pearson correlation options
- ☐ Cronbach's coefficient alpha
- ☐ Covariances
- ☐ Sums of squares and cross products
- ☐ Corrected sums of squares and cross products
- ☐ Suppress Pearson correlations from results

Divisor for variance:
Degrees of freedom

☐ Omit rows with missing values for variables being correlated

Preview code   Run   Save   Cancel   Help

If you click **Results** in the selection pane on the left, you can request plots and choose the statistics to be included in the results.

When you are satisfied with all the settings, click **Run**.

Results The output starts with a list of the analysis variables, followed by basic statistics. Next are the correlation coefficients. The default type of correlation is Pearson, but if you checked other types in the Options page, those correlations will appear also. In this example, two variables—AvgTemp and InchesRain—are correlated with the number of bookings. AvgTemp is negatively correlated, while InchesRain is positively correlated. The FromNormal variable is not significantly correlated with Bookings.

Correlation Analysis

The CORR Procedure

1 With Variables:	Bookings
3 Variables:	AvgTemp FromNormal InchesRain

Simple Statistics

Variable	N	Mean	Std Dev	Sum	Minimum	Maximum
Bookings	24	21.41667	5.19127	514.00000	13.00000	33.00000
AvgTemp	24	54.30417	10.21284	1303	41.70000	71.60000
FromNormal	24	1.41250	1.99659	33.90000	-2.40000	4.90000
InchesRain	24	3.30417	2.97348	79.30000	0	8.96000

Pearson Correlation Coefficients, N = 24
Prob > |r| under H0: Rho=0

	AvgTemp	FromNormal	InchesRain
Bookings	-0.60049	0.09931	0.57642
	0.0019	0.6443	0.0032

8.5 Linear Regression

In SAS Enterprise Guide, you can perform many different types of regression analysis, and the models that you build can be quite complex. You can choose linear, nonlinear, logistic, and generalized linear models. In addition, within each type of regression, there are many options for customizing your analysis. This section shows how to do a simple linear regression with one dependent and one explanatory variable. You must have SAS/STAT software installed on your SAS server to perform regression analysis.

The Fire and Ice Tours company started a local advertising campaign in both Seattle and Portland. It wants to see if the money spent on advertising is increasing the number of tour bookings. Here is a sample of the AdResults data set with data for the dollars spent on advertising and the number of bookings for each month and city. A linear regression analysis will show if there is a relationship between dollars spent and bookings. In the Project Explorer or Project Designer, click the data icon to make it active. Then select **Analyze ►**

	City	Month	AdDollars	Bookings
7	Seattle	7	150	17
8	Seattle	8	250	17
9	Seattle	9	250	22
10	Seattle	10	325	20
11	Seattle	11	400	25
12	Seattle	12	500	31
13	Portland	1	325	25
14	Portland	2	290	19
15	Portland	3	250	17
16	Portland	4	300	18

Regression ► Linear from the menu bar. The Linear window will open, displaying the Task Roles page.

Assigning task roles

For a simple linear regression, you must assign one variable to the Dependent variable role, and one to the Explanatory variables role. Both the dependent and the explanatory variables must be numeric. This example tests whether the number of bookings can be explained by the dollars spent on advertising. So, the variable Bookings has been assigned to the Dependent variable role, and the variable AdDollars has been assigned to the Explanatory variables role.

Choosing statistics Because you can perform many different types of regression analysis using this task, there are a lot of options listed in the selection pane on the left. In the Model page, you can choose the model selection method, including forward, backward, stepwise, and several methods based on R-squared. The Statistics page gives choices for additional statistics, including details on estimates, correlations, and diagnostics. For this simple example, there is no need to change the model type, or to request additional statistics.

Selecting plots Options for plots are divided into three groups: Predicted, Residual, and Influence. To produce a simple scatter plot of the dependent and explanatory variables with the regression line and confidence limits, select the **Predicted** group of options in the selection pane on the left. Then, in the **Scatter plots** area, select **Observed vs independents** and **Confidence limits**.

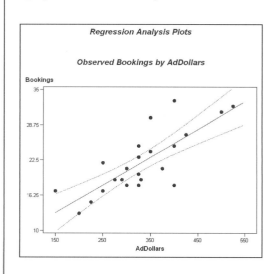

Results The results of the regression analysis start with the number of observations used for the

analysis, followed by the Analysis of Variance table, statistics, and Parameter Estimates. In this example, the model is significant with a *p*-value of less than 0.0001. The scatter plot gives a graphic view of the analysis.

Linear Regression Results

The REG Procedure
Model: Linear_Regression_Model
Dependent Variable: Bookings

Number of Observations Read	24
Number of Observations Used	24

Analysis of Variance

Source	DF	Sum of Squares	Mean Square	F Value	Pr > F
Model	1	436.59983	436.59983	36.56	<.0001
Error	22	262.73350	11.94243		
Corrected Total	23	699.33333			

Root MSE	3.45578	R-Square	0.6243
Dependent Mean	21.83333	Adj R-Sq	0.6072
Coeff Var	15.82801		

Parameter Estimates

Variable	DF	Parameter Estimate	Standard Error	t Value	Pr > |t|
Intercept	1	5.70295	2.75946	2.07	0.0507
AdDollars	1	0.04935	0.00816	6.05	<.0001

8.6 Analysis of Variance

SAS Enterprise Guide can perform several types of analysis of variance, including one-way ANOVA and nonparametric one-way ANOVA, as well as mixed and linear models. This section shows the One-Way ANOVA task, which performs analysis of variance tests, and comparisons of means. You must have SAS/STAT software installed on your SAS server to use any of the ANOVA tasks.

The Fire and Ice Tours company wants to know if the tours it offers, with the three difficulty ratings, attract customers from different age groups. Ten customers were surveyed in each of the three difficulty categories to find their ages. Here is a sample of the resulting data set, Ages. In the Project Explorer or Project Designer, click the data icon to make it active. Then select **Analyze ▶ ANOVA ▶ One-Way ANOVA** from the menu bar. The One-Way ANOVA window will open, displaying the Task Roles page.

Ages (read-only)		
	Difficulty	Age
1	e	45
2	e	38
3	e	65
4	e	43
5	e	29
6	e	72
7	e	66
8	e	57
9	e	39
10	e	33
11	m	26
12	m	37

Assigning task roles For one-way ANOVA, you must assign one variable to the Dependent variables role, and one to the Independent variable role. The dependent variable is a numeric variable whose means you want to test. The independent variable determines the different categories. In this example, the variable Age has been assigned to the Dependent variables role. The variable Difficulty has been assigned to the Independent variable role. If you want to test more than one variable at a time, you can assign several variables to the Dependent variables role, but each variable will be analyzed separately.

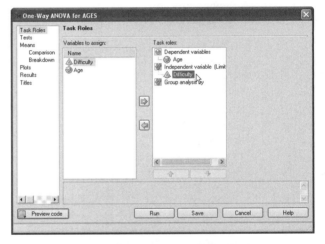

Choosing statistics The One-Way ANOVA task offers several groups of options in the selection pane on the left. In the Tests page, you can select tests for equal variance. In the Plots page, you can request box-and-whisker or means plots. You can choose descriptive statistics for the dependent variables in the Means > Breakdown page. If you want to do any comparison of means tests, choose them in the Means > Comparison page. In this example, Scheffe's multiple comparison procedure has been selected from the list of possible methods.

Results The output starts with information about the number of classes (categories) and the number of observations in the data. Next is the result of the analysis of variance, followed by the results of Scheffe's test. Scheffe's test includes the comparison of the means between the three levels of difficulty. Letters are used to group the means, where means labeled with different letters are significantly different from each other. In this case, people in the challenging tours are significantly older than people in the moderate tours. However, while people in the challenging tours are also older than people in the easy tours, they are not significantly older. In this example, the *p*-value of 0.0053 shows that the overall model is also significant.

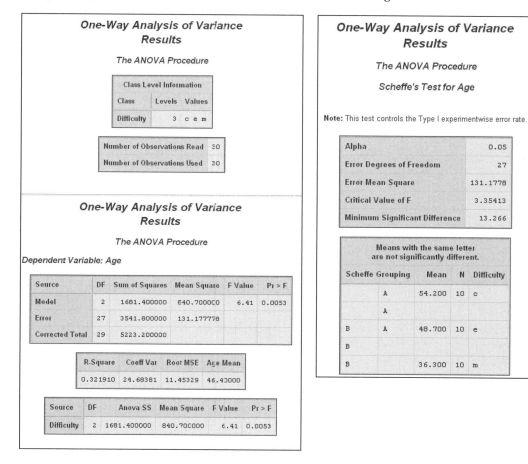

One-Way Analysis of Variance Results

The ANOVA Procedure

Class Level Information		
Class	Levels	Values
Difficulty	3	c e m

Number of Observations Read	30
Number of Observations Used	30

One-Way Analysis of Variance Results

The ANOVA Procedure

Dependent Variable: Age

Source	DF	Sum of Squares	Mean Square	F Value	Pr > F
Model	2	1681.400000	840.700000	6.41	0.0053
Error	27	3541.800000	131.177778		
Corrected Total	29	5223.200000			

R-Square	Coeff Var	Root MSE	Age Mean
0.321910	24.68381	11.45329	46.40000

Source	DF	Anova SS	Mean Square	F Value	Pr > F
Difficulty	2	1681.400000	840.700000	6.41	0.0053

One-Way Analysis of Variance Results

The ANOVA Procedure

Scheffe's Test for Age

Note: This test controls the Type I experimentwise error rate.

Alpha	0.05
Error Degrees of Freedom	27
Error Mean Square	131.1778
Critical Value of F	3.35413
Minimum Significant Difference	13.266

Means with the same letter are not significantly different.			
Scheffe Grouping	Mean	N	Difficulty
A	54.200	10	c
A			
B A	48.700	10	e
B			
B	36.300	10	m

CHAPTER 9

Producing Graphs

9.1 ▶ Bar Charts

Bar charts can be an effective way to present data when you want to show the frequency, percentage, sum, or mean of values in your data, broken into groups. You must have SAS/GRAPH software installed on your SAS server to create bar charts.

The Eruptions data set contains the volcano name and the Volcanic Explosivity Index (VEI) for selected eruptions. Here is a sample of the data. Notice that the column VEI ranges in value from 0 to 6. From these data, you can create a bar chart showing the number of eruptions for each value of VEI. In the Project Explorer or Project Designer, click the data icon to make it active, and then select **Graph ▶ Bar Chart**. The Bar Chart window will open, displaying the Bar Chart page.

	Volcano	StartDate	EndDate	VEI
12	Grimsvotn	12/18/1998	12/28/1998	3
13	Kilauea	05/30/1840	06/25/1840	0
14	Kilauea	05/24/1969	07/22/1974	0
15	Kliuchevskoi	09/25/1737	11/04/1737	2
16	Kliuchevskoi	03/25/1931	03/27/1931	4
17	Kliuchevskoi	01/20/2005	04/07/2005	2
18	Krakatau	05/20/1883	10/21/1883	6
19	Krakatau	07/04/1938	07/02/1940	3
20	Krakatau	05/29/2000	10/30/2000	1

Choosing the type of bar chart There are many different types of bar charts you can create. Scroll down to see all the available types. For this example, select **Simple Vertical Bar,** and then click **Task Roles** in the selection pane on the left to assign roles to columns.

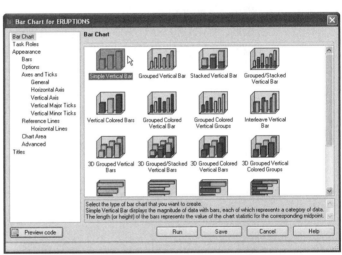

Assigning task roles For all kinds of bar charts, you must assign a column to the **Column to chart** role. For stacked or grouped bar charts, you also need to assign columns to stacking and grouping roles. In this example, the VEI column is the Column to chart. This will produce bars whose lengths are determined by the frequency of eruptions for each value of VEI. If you choose a **Sum of** column, then instead of getting frequencies, you will get the sum of whichever column you choose.

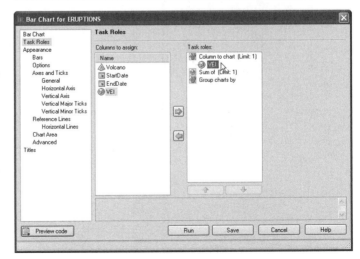

Customizing a bar chart As you can see from the list of options in the selection pane on the left, there are many options for bar charts. You can make changes to the axes and tick marks, add or remove reference lines, specify the size of your chart, change the background color, choose the shape and size of the bars in your chart, and change the order of the bars. If you want to display the mean instead of the sum (or the percentage instead of the frequency), you can change the statistic in the Appearance > Advanced page.

The Appearance > Bars page allows you to change the color or texture of the bars, and to specify the number of bars. If the column you are charting is character, then you will get a bar for each value of the column. If your column is numeric, then SAS Enterprise Guide will determine an appropriate number of bars for your chart, and label the bars with the midpoint in the range. You can override this behavior by specifying the number of bars. In this example, the column charted—VEI—is numeric, but it has only seven discrete values. So, it makes sense to have one bar for each value. To do this, check **Specify number of bars**, and select **One bar for each unique data value**. When you are satisfied with the options, click **Run**.

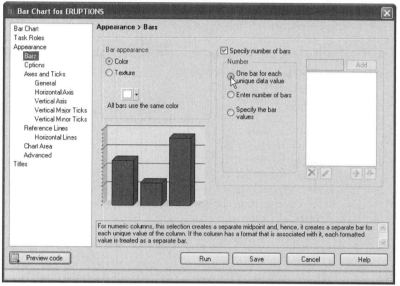

Results Here is the resulting bar chart of VEI. There is a bar for each unique value of VEI, and the lengths of the bars show a simple count of eruptions for each value of VEI.

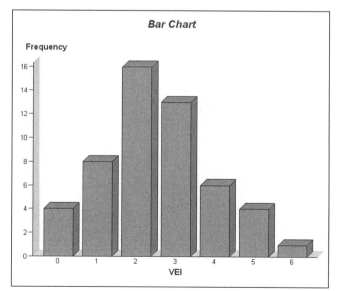

9.2 Pie Charts

Pie charts are similar to bar charts. With both types of charts, you can show the frequency, percentage, sum, or mean of values in your data, broken into groups. The type of chart you use depends on your personal preference. You must have SAS/GRAPH software installed on your SAS server to create pie charts.

To create a pie chart of the Volcanoes data, click the data icon in the Project Explorer or Project Designer to make it active. Then select **Graph ▶ Pie Chart**. This opens the Pie Chart window, displaying the Pie Chart page.

Choosing the type of pie chart Before assigning columns to task roles, you must select the type of pie chart you want to create. If you want one pie chart that shows the frequency or percentage of rows that fall into different categories, then select a Simple Pie chart. If you have a grouping column and you want a separate pie for each level of the group, then you may want to select the Group Pie. The Stacked Pie is similar to a Group Pie, except the pies are stacked one on top of the other instead of side by side. Use a Group/Stacked Pie if you have more than one grouping column. In this example, select **Simple Pie** and then click **Task Roles** in the selection pane on the left to assign roles to columns.

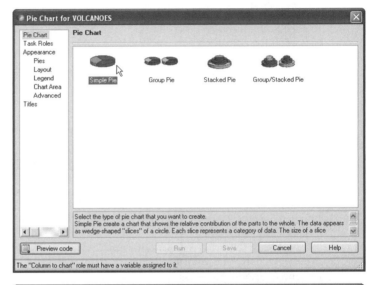

Assigning task roles For simple pie charts, all you need is a column to chart. Drag the column you want to summarize to the **Column to chart** role. Use the **Sum of** role if you want the size of the pie slice to represent a sum or mean value, instead of simple counts or percentages. The **Group charts by** role is similar to using a Group Pie chart, except that selecting a Group Pie will produce pies side by side on the same page, whereas the Group charts by role will produce one pie per page. In this example, Region has been assigned to the Column to chart role.

Other chart options

In the Appearance > Pies page, you can specify the color scheme to use for the chart, as well as the number of slices for the pie. In the Layout page, you can make the pies two- or three-dimensional, control placement of labels on the pies, specify how pies are placed on the page for grouped pies, and control the "other" slice of pie. Use the Legend page to control the legend, the Chart Area page to control the size and background color of the chart, and the Advanced page to specify if the pie slices should be frequencies or percentages. In this example, on the Appearance > Layout page, the position of the label for the **Statistic value** has been changed from Outside (the default) to Inside. When you are satisfied with the options, click **Run**.

Results Here is the result of the Pie Chart task. Because Region is the Column to chart, each slice of the pie shows the number of volcanoes from the data set that are in that region. The label for the statistic value was specified to be inside, so the actual number of volcanoes appears inside each pie slice.

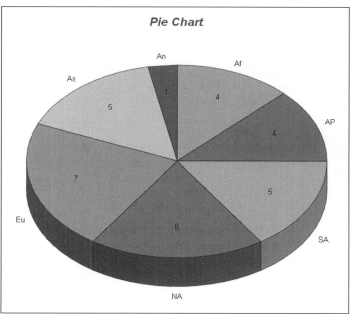

9.3 Simple Line Plots

There are many different types of line plots you can produce using SAS Enterprise Guide. You can plot one or several plots on the same graph, and you can specify different types of interpolation for your plot. If you use a type of interpolation for your plot where the points are connected, make sure that it makes sense to connect the points. You must have SAS/GRAPH software installed on your SAS server to create line plots.

Here is a portion of the NWweather data set, which has been filtered so that only the Seattle data are in the data set. Three variables have been kept: City, Month, and FromNormal (the degrees from normal for the month).

	City	Month	FromNormal
1	Seattle	1	4.9
2	Seattle	2	-1.6
3	Seattle	3	0.6
4	Seattle	4	-1.3
5	Seattle	5	-1
6	Seattle	6	2.1
7	Seattle	7	2.6
8	Seattle	8	0.8
9	Seattle	9	1.5
10	Seattle	10	1.6
11	Seattle	11	-2.4
12	Seattle	12	1.1

Query_for_NWweather (read-only)

To create a line plot, click the data icon in the Project Explorer or Project Designer to make it active. Then select **Graph ▶ Line Plots**. This opens the Line Plot window displaying the Line Plot page.

Choosing the type of line plot Before assigning columns to task roles, you must select the type of line plot you want to create. There are many different types of plots. Choosing the plot type will automatically change other settings in the Line Plot window to fit that type of plot. For this example, select **Line Plot,** and then click **Task Roles** in the selection pane on the left to assign roles to columns.

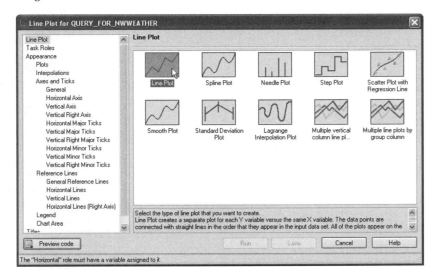

Assigning task roles

For a basic line plot, you must assign one column to the **Horizontal** role and one to the **Vertical** role. In this example, Month has been assigned to the Horizontal role and FromNormal to the Vertical role.

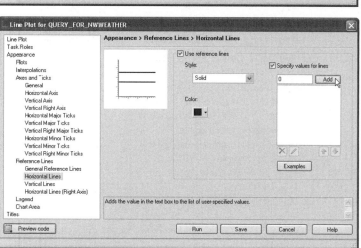

Other plot options

The selection pane on the left lists many categories of options. You can specify the line style, the interpolation method, axes and tick marks, reference lines, the legend, and the size and background color of your plot. For this example, click **Horizontal Lines** in the selection pane on the left. Then click the boxes labeled **Use reference lines** and **Specify values for lines**. Type the number 0 into the box next to the Add button, and click the **Add** button. When you are satisfied with the options, click **Run**.

Results

Here is the result of the Line Plot task. Month is on the horizontal axis and FromNormal on the vertical. The horizontal reference line is set at zero.

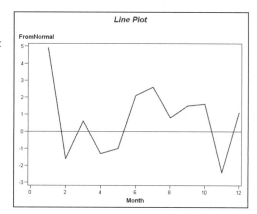

9.4 Multiple Line Plots

Sometimes you may want to put more than one line on a plot. You can plot two different columns on the vertical axes by choosing a column for the left vertical axis and a column for the right. You can also plot only one column, but with separate lines for unique values of a third column. This type of plot is called a multiple line plot by group column. You must have SAS/GRAPH software installed on your SAS server to create line plots.

Here is a portion of the NWweather data set. To create a line plot of the data with separate lines for Seattle and Portland, click the data icon in the Project Explorer or Project Designer to make it active, and select **Graph ▸ Line Plots**. This opens the Line Plot window displaying the Line Plot page.

	City	Month	AvgTemp	FromNormal	InchesRain	Bookings
9	Seattle	9	62.6	1.5	0.89	22
10	Seattle	10	54.3	1.6	8.96	20
11	Seattle	11	42.8	-2.4	6.77	25
12	Seattle	12	41.8	1.1	3.88	31
13	Portland	1	44.8	4.9	7.64	22
14	Portland	2	44.3	1.2	2.37	19
15	Portland	3	49	1.8	5.75	17
16	Portland	4	50.8	-0.4	4.37	18
17	Portland	5	57.3	0.2	1.49	21
18	Portland	6	66.1	3.4	0.31	19
19	Portland	7	71.6	3.5	0	13

Choosing the type of line plot Before assigning columns to task roles, you must select the type of line plot you want to create. You may need to scroll down to see all the types of plots. In this example, select **Multiple line plots by group column,** and then click **Task Roles** in the selection pane on the left to assign roles to columns.

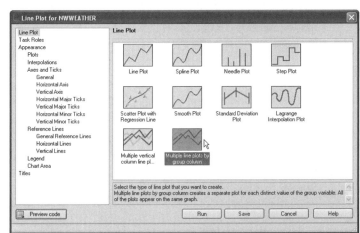

Assigning task roles For this type of plot, you need to assign one column to the **Horizontal** role and one to the **Vertical** role. Then assign the grouping column to the **Group** role. There will be one line for each unique value of the grouping column. In this example, Month has been assigned to the Horizontal role, AvgTemp to the Vertical role, and City to the Group role.

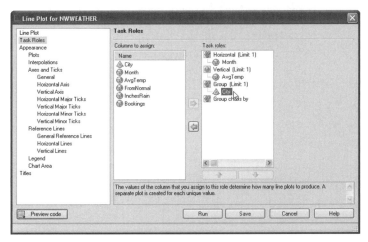

Other plot options

As with simple line plots, there are many options you can specify, such as the type of interpolation, axes and tick marks, reference lines, legends, and the size and background color of your plot. For this example, click **Plots** in the selection pane on the left. By default, all lines are solid, with no data point markers, but different colors. In the Appearance > Plots page, you can assign different symbols and line styles to the values of the grouping column making it easier to identify the lines. There are two values for the grouping variable City: Portland and Seattle. Click the city name to choose styles for that city, and select the desired attributes for the line and data point markers. In this example, Seattle will have a dashed line with the star symbol, and Portland a solid line with the diamond symbol. When you are satisfied with the options, click **Run**.

Results Here is the result of the Line Plot task. Month is on the horizontal axis and AvgTemp on the vertical. There is a separate line for each city.

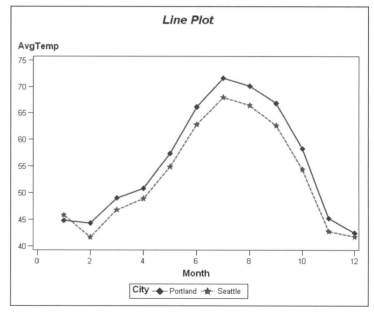

9.5 Scatter Plots

Scatter plots are similar to line plots, but in a scatter plot you do not connect the points. You may simply display the points without any interpolation, or you may add a regression line showing the relationship between two columns. You can produce a scatter plot with a regression line using regression analysis, but the Scatter Plot task gives you more control over the appearance of your plot. You must have SAS/GRAPH software installed on your SAS server to create scatter plots.

This example produces a simple scatter plot using the AdResults data set. This data set contains the amount spent on advertising and the number of tour bookings for each month. To create a scatter plot of the data, click the data icon in the Project Explorer or Project Designer to make it active. Then select **Graph ▶ Scatter Plot**. This opens the Scatter Plot window, displaying the Scatter Plot page.

	City	Month	AdDollars	Bookings
1	Seattle	1	350	30
2	Seattle	2	330	19
3	Seattle	3	525	32
4	Seattle	4	400	18
5	Seattle	5	375	21
6	Seattle	6	325	18
7	Seattle	7	150	17
8	Seattle	8	250	17

Choosing the type of scatter plot Before assigning columns to task roles, you must select the type of scatter plot you want to create. You can choose a two-dimensional scatter plot, a three-dimensional scatter plot, or a three-dimensional needle plot. For this example, select **2D Scatter Plot**, and then click **Task Roles** in the selection pane on the left to assign roles to columns.

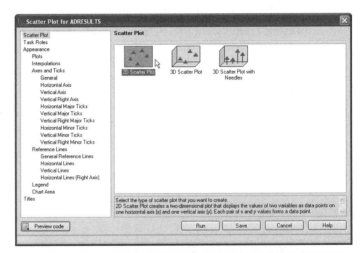

Assigning task roles For a two-dimensional scatter plot, you must assign one column to the **Horizontal** role and one to the **Vertical** role. In this example, AdDollars is assigned to the horizontal axis, and Bookings to the vertical axis.

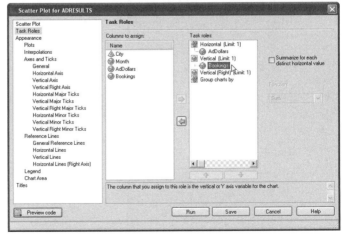

Other plot options

As with line plots, there are many options you can specify, such as the type of interpolation (including regression), axes and tick marks, reference lines, and legends. The Chart Area page controls the size and background color of your plot. In the Plots page, you can select line styles and point markers. By default, the axes are labeled with the column names. For this

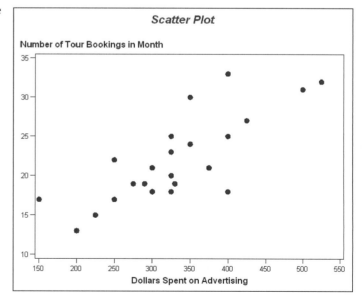

example, change the axis labels. In the Appearance > Axes and Ticks > Horizontal Axis page (as shown here), type **Dollars Spent on Advertising** in the **Label** box. Then in the Appearance > Axes and Ticks > Vertical Axis page, type **Number of Tour Bookings in Month** in the **Label** box. When you are satisfied with the options, click **Run**.

Results Here is the result of the Scatter Plot task. AdDollars is on the horizontal axis and Bookings is on the vertical. Instead of column names, labels appear on both axes.

9.6 Selecting the Graph Output Format

The graphics tasks in SAS Enterprise Guide can produce graphs in several different formats.

Setting the default graph format The default output format for graphs is ActiveX. If you want to change the default output format, then select **Tools ▶ Options** from the menu bar to open the Options window. Select the **Graph** page under **Results**. Here you can select the **Graph Format** and set other options specific to each format. Any changes you make here will affect all subsequent graphs produced using SAS Enterprise Guide.

Setting the graph format in a task To change the graph format of a particular task, right-click the task icon in the Project Explorer or Project Designer and select **Properties**. Open the **Results** page of the Properties window and check **Override the preferences set in Tools -> Options**. Then you can select an alternate graph format for the task. Rerun the task to see the result using the new graph format.

ActiveX and Java formats Both the ActiveX and Java formats give the viewer of the graph interactive controls. ActiveX graphs can be viewed on computers running the Windows operating environment using Microsoft Internet Explorer, while Java graphs can be viewed in any Web browser that supports Java. The charts on this page were rendered in ActiveX format.

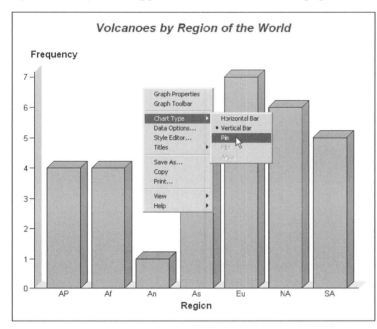

For both Java and ActiveX, when the viewer right-clicks the graph, a pop-up menu displays several options that the viewer can change, including graph properties, chart type, and style elements. The viewer of the graph can make any of these changes without needing SAS Enterprise Guide or SAS on his or her computer. In this graph, the **Chart Type** is being changed from **Vertical Bar** to **Pie**.

Here is the vertical bar chart shown above, converted to a pie chart. When the cursor is moved over a graph element, details about that graph element appear in a flyover box. Because the cursor is over the NA region of this chart, the box displays the frequency and percent for the NA region.

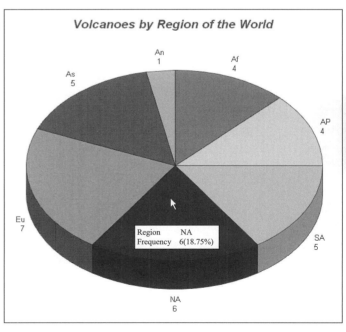

CHAPTER **10**

Changing Output Styles and Types

Chapter 10

10.1 Changing the Output Format

When you run a task that produces output, by default SAS Enterprise Guide creates that output in HTML format. But, you don't have to confine yourself to HTML. SAS Enterprise Guide can produce output in RTF, which can be opened in Microsoft Word; PDF, which can be opened using Adobe Acrobat or Adobe Reader; SAS Report format, which can be used to create customized reports; and plain text, which can be opened in any text editor.

Setting the default output format To set the default output type, select **Tools ▶ Options** from the menu bar. This opens the Options window. There are many options you can set in this window, covering a wide variety of categories. Click **Results General** under **Results** to open the Results General page of options. The available output types are listed under the heading **Result Formats** on this page. Select one or more output types by clicking the box next to the type. Once you make this

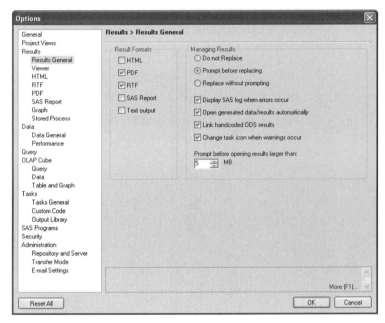

change, it will affect all subsequent results. In this example, because both **PDF** and **RTF** are checked, any task that you run will produce results in both PDF and RTF format.

Volcano Tours

Volcano	Departs	Days	Price	Difficulty
Etna	Catania	7	$1,025	m
Fuji	Tokyo	2	$195	c
Kenya	Nairobi	6	$780	m
Kilauea	Hilo	1	$45	e
Kilimanjaro	Nairobi	9	$1,260	c
Krakatau	Jakarta	7	$850	e
Poas	San Jose	1	$50	e
Reventador	Quito	4	$525	m
St. Helens	Portland	2	$157	e
Vesuvius	Rome	6	$950	e

Results When you run a task with alternate output formats designated, the results will appear in the workspace of SAS Enterprise Guide, just like when the output is in HTML format. You get an icon in the Project Explorer and Project Designer for each output type you specify. If you specify more than one output type, all results may not open automatically. To open a result in SAS Enterprise Guide, double-click the icon for the result. This is what the results of the List Data task look like in PDF format. Note that the style for PDF is quite different from the style for HTML.

Changing the result type of a
task If you change the result type in the Options window, then the results of all tasks are affected. If you want to change output formats for individual tasks, then right-click the task icon in the Project Explorer or Project Designer, and select **Properties**. This opens the Properties window for the task. Click **Results** in the selection pane on the left to open the Results page, and then check **Override the preferences set in Tools -> Options**. Now you can choose result formats and styles for the task's results. In this example, this task will produce results in RTF format only.

Saving or sending results
If you want, you can save results to a file either on your local computer or on a SAS server. Right-click the icon for the results in the Project Explorer or Project Designer, and select **Export**. If you choose **Export** *result-name*, then the file will be saved just once. If you choose **Export** *result-name* **As A Step In Project**, then a step will be added to the project so that every time you run the project the result will be exported. You can also choose to attach the results to an e-mail message by right-clicking the results icon and selecting **Send To ▶ E-Mail Recipient** or **E-Mail Recipient as a Step in Project**.

10.2   Changing the Output Style

The output style determines the overall look for your output. The colors, fonts, and layout of your output are all defined in the style. SAS Enterprise Guide comes with many different styles, so if you don't like the style of your output, you can change it. The only output type that does not have a style associated with it is the text output type. But for the other output types— HTML, RTF, PDF, and SAS Report—you can choose from a number of styles.

Setting the default output style   When you first install SAS Enterprise Guide, the default style for HTML and SAS Report output is EGDefault. This style includes the SAS logo at the top, and the words "SAS Enterprise Guide." The RTF and PDF output types also come with default styles. If you want to change the default style for any of the HTML, RTF, PDF, or SAS Report output types, you can do this in the Options window. Open the Options window by selecting **Tools ► Options** from the menu bar. Click the type of output (HTML, RTF, PDF, or SAS Report) in the selection pane on the left to open the page for that type of output. Then select the style you want for that output type from the **Style** drop-down list. Once you make this change, every task you run will use the style you select for that output type.

Changing the output style for a task

If you want to change the output style for the results of a particular task, you can do this in the Properties window for the task. Right-click the task icon in the Project Explorer or Project Designer and select **Properties**. Then click **Results** in the selection pane on the left to open the Results page of the Properties window. Check the box next to **Override the preferences set in Tools -> Options**, and then you can select the result format and a style from the drop-down list for each format.

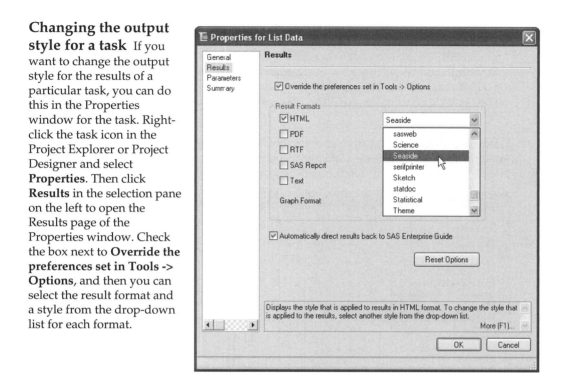

Results

Here is what HTML output looks like using the Seaside style.

<table>
<tr><td colspan="5" align="center">Volcano Tours</td></tr>
<tr><th>Volcano</th><th>Departs</th><th>Days</th><th>Price</th><th>Difficulty</th></tr>
<tr><td>Etna</td><td>Catania</td><td>7</td><td>$1,025</td><td>m</td></tr>
<tr><td>Fuji</td><td>Tokyo</td><td>2</td><td>$195</td><td>c</td></tr>
<tr><td>Kenya</td><td>Nairobi</td><td>6</td><td>$780</td><td>m</td></tr>
<tr><td>Kilauea</td><td>Hilo</td><td>1</td><td>$45</td><td>e</td></tr>
<tr><td>Kilimanjaro</td><td>Nairobi</td><td>9</td><td>$1,260</td><td>c</td></tr>
<tr><td>Krakatau</td><td>Jakarta</td><td>7</td><td>$850</td><td>e</td></tr>
<tr><td>Poas</td><td>San Jose</td><td>1</td><td>$50</td><td>e</td></tr>
<tr><td>Reventador</td><td>Quito</td><td>4</td><td>$525</td><td>m</td></tr>
<tr><td>St. Helens</td><td>Portland</td><td>2</td><td>$157</td><td>e</td></tr>
<tr><td>Vesuvius</td><td>Rome</td><td>6</td><td>$950</td><td>e</td></tr>
</table>

10.3 Customizing Output Styles Using the Style Manager

Although SAS Enterprise Guide supplies you with many output styles, you still might not be able to find a style that fits your needs. You can use the Style Manager to modify existing styles for HTML and SAS Report output, and you can add styles to your project that you may have created outside SAS Enterprise Guide. You cannot modify styles for use with RTF or PDF output types.

Opening the Style Manager Open the Style Manager by selecting **Tools ▶ Style Manager** from the menu bar. The Style Manager provides you with a list of available styles in the box on the left. When you click a style, you will see a preview of the style in the box on the right.

Editing an existing style To edit an existing style, first create a copy of the style. Click the style in the Style Manager window, and then click **Create a Copy**. This opens the Save Style As window where you give the new style a name and choose a storage location. Now you can edit the copy of the style you just saved. Click the new style name in the Style Manager window, and click **Edit**.

This opens the Style Editor window. There are several elements of the output where you can control the style. The preview area on the left shows the current style of these elements. Choose the element you want to edit by clicking it in the preview area on the left, or selecting it from the **Active element** drop-down list. Then select the attributes to use for that element in the area on the right. In this example, the **SAS System Title** is given a **Bold** text style, **14pt** font text size, and a background color. In addition to changing the style of the text, you can control borders using the Borders tab, and add images to your style using the Images tab. Click **OK** when you are finished making changes to the style. Then click **OK** in the Style Manager window to save your changes.

Using the new style The new style you created will appear in the **My Styles** section of the list of styles. You can select it for any HTML or SAS Report output, or set it to be the default style. See section 10.2 for details about changing the output style.

10.4 Combining Results into a Single HTML Document

The Document Builder allows you to create an HTML document that contains selected items from your project. You can include any HTML results, project notes, links to other documents, and lines separating the items. If you like, you can also include a table of contents for your HTML document, and select an overall style.

Here is the process flow from a project that contains three results. The goal is to produce an HTML document with the results from the List Data task and the Scatter Plot task. To open the Document Builder, select **Tools ▶ Create HTML Document** from the menu bar. This opens the Document Builder window.

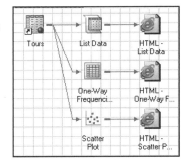

Building a document From the Document Builder window, you can add items to your document, give the document a name, choose a style for the document, and specify the type of table of contents. To add results, click **Add**.

This opens the Add Results window. All the HTML results in your project will appear in this window. Select the results you want to add to your document and click **OK**. If you want to look at results before you add them to the document, highlight the results, and click **Preview**.

You can add other types of items to your document by choosing the item type from the drop-down list next to the **Add** button. In this example, there are no notes in the project, so that item type is not available.

In this Document Builder window, the results of the List Data task are followed by a Separator, which is followed by the results of the Scatter Plot task. The document will have a table of contents to the side of the document, and it uses the Meadow style. If you want to preview the document before you create it, click **Preview**. When you are satisfied with your document, click **OK**.

Viewing a document After creating the document, you won't automatically see it in the workspace of your project. What you will see is an icon added to the Project Explorer and Project Designer. You can preview the document in SAS Enterprise Guide by right-clicking the document icon and selecting **Preview**. If you want to save the document as an HTML file outside your project, right-click the document icon and select **Export**.

Results Here is how the document looks when you preview it. Notice that there is a table of contents on the left, and the two results on the right are separated by a line. The table of contents is hyperlinked to the rest of the document, so when you click an item in the table of contents, it will take you directly to that item in the document.

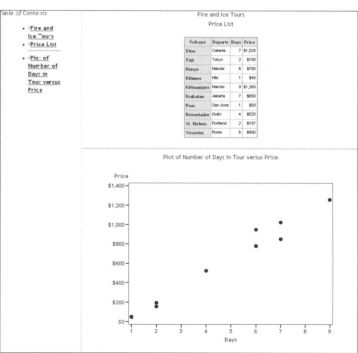

10.5 Creating a Customized Report

The report editor in SAS Enterprise Guide allows you to combine results created in the SAS Report format along with text, images, and headers and footers. These reports can be printed, copied, and pasted into other applications such as Word and Excel (although some formatting may be lost). The reports can also be shared with other SAS applications such as SAS Web Report Studio.

Selecting and arranging items for the report To create a report, first generate the desired results in the SAS Report format, and then select **File ▶ New ▶ Report** from the menu bar. This opens the New Report window. All results in SAS Report format appear in the **Select SAS items** box. Drag the desired items to the **Report layout** box. You can also insert text or images by clicking the **Insert Text** or **Insert Image** buttons. In this example, text has been added above the List Data and Bar Chart results. To change the relative size of an item, click and drag the handle on the edge of the item's box. When you have all the items you want in the report, click **OK**.

Fitting items on a page After you close the New Report window, a Report tab will appear in the workspace. The Report tab has four options: Edit Report, Header & Footer, Page Setup, and Page View. If you click **Page View**, you will see what your report will look like when printed. If you want all the report elements on one page, you may need to resize some items. You can resize graphs and charts, but you cannot resize tables. You can't make any changes to the report in page view mode, so click **Page View** again to return

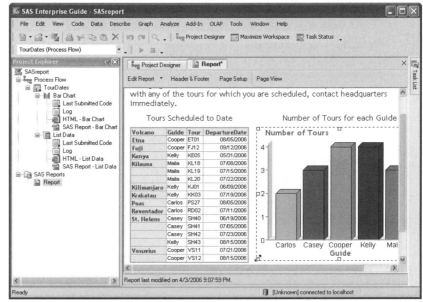

to edit mode. Click a report item on the Report tab to select it, and then resize it if needed. You can also add new elements to your report by clicking **Edit Report**.

Adding headers and footers

To add headers or footers to your report, click **Header & Footer** in the Report tab. This opens the Header & Footer window. You can enter and format text in the text box, add and position images, and add lines above or below the header or footer. Any headers or footers you add to the report will appear on each page of the report. In the Titles & Footnotes tab it is also possible to remove (but not edit) the titles and footnotes generated by SAS Enterprise Guide tasks. In this example, a header is added to the report, along with an image to the right of the header text and a line below. When you are finished making changes to the header and footer, click **OK**.

Results After arranging the items for your report and adding any headers or footers, you can preview your report by choosing **File ▶ Print Preview for Report** from the menu bar, or simply clicking **Page View** in the Report tab. Here is what the report will look like when printed. To print the report, choose **File ▶ Print Report** from the menu bar. All report contents generated by SAS Enterprise Guide tasks will be automatically refreshed when you rerun the tasks in the project. If you do not want the results refreshed, then create a report snapshot by right-clicking the report icon in the Project Explorer and selecting **Create Report Snapshot**. To share your report with other SAS Enterprise Guide users, you can export the

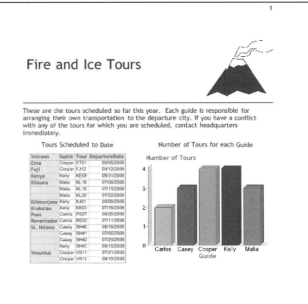

report by right-clicking the report icon in the Project Explorer or Project Designer and choosing **Export**. Exported report files can be opened in SAS Enterprise Guide by choosing **File ▶ Open ▶ Other** from the menu bar.

CHAPTER 11

Adding Flexibility with Parameters

11.1   Creating Parameters for Data Values

Parameters allow you to develop projects that are flexible. For example, when you run a query with a filter condition that uses a parameter, a box will appear, prompting you to specify a value for that parameter. The query will be filtered according to the value you enter. This allows you to create one query that can generate many different results.

There are three places you can use parameters in SAS Enterprise Guide: in a query, in a task, and in SAS code. The example in this section creates a parameter that will then be used in a query in section 11.2. Sections 11.3 and 11.4 discuss creating and using a parameter in a task. Section 11.5 shows how to use parameters in SAS code.

To create a parameter, select **Tools ▶ Parameters (Macro Variable) Manager** from the menu bar. You can also open the Parameters Manager window from the Query Builder by clicking the Parameters button. In the Parameters Manager, click **Add** to open the Add New Parameter window.

Setting the parameter type and properties In the General tab of the Add New Parameter window, you specify a **Display name**, **SAS code name**, **Description**, and **Data type** for the new parameter. The display name will be used to prompt you for a value when you run the query. The SAS code name is the actual name of the parameter. The SAS code name must be 32 characters or fewer in length; start with a letter or underscore; and contain only letters, numerals, and underscores. If you do not enter a SAS code name, then SAS Enterprise Guide will simply use the display name, substituting underscores for any spaces or special characters. The description is displayed only when the parameter is being created or edited, and is optional. There are several types of parameters you can choose, including character strings, integers, and dates. The type of parameter you choose depends on how it will be used. For this example, integer is appropriate since the parameter will be used to filter data based on the value of a numeric column, Height, from the Volcanoes data table. After giving the parameter a name and data type, click the **Data Type and Values** tab.

Setting valid values for the parameter

In the Data Type and Values tab, select the **Data value type**. For this example, select **A range of values**. When you select a range of values as the data value type, new options will appear in the lower part of the window. These options allow you to enter minimum and maximum values for the range as well as a step value. When users are prompted for a value, the values will be incremented by the step value each time they click the up or down arrows in the selection box. For this example, the **Minimum value** is zero, the **Maximum value** is 6400, and the **Step** is 100. Since the tallest volcano is 6458 meters, setting the maximum value at 6400 ensures that at least one row of the Volcanoes table will always be selected after filtering. If users select a value outside the specified range, then they will get a message saying their value is outside the allowed range.

When you have set all the properties for the parameter, click **Add and Close**. The parameter you created will appear in the Parameters Manager window. Click **Close** and your parameter will be ready to use.

11.2 Using Parameters in Filter Conditions

The previous section showed how to create a parameter for a data value. This section shows how to use that parameter in a filter and how to run the new query.

Setting the Filter Condition To open the Query Builder, click the data icon in the Project Explorer or Project Designer to make it active, and select **Data ▶ Filter and Query** from the menu bar. Then select the columns you desire in the Select Data tab. For this example, use the Volcanoes data table for the query, and select all the columns. Then click the **Filter Data** tab and create the filter just like you would any other filter. Drag the desired column into the **Filter Data** tab of the Query Builder. For this example, drag the column Height from the Volcanoes data table to the **Filter Data** tab. This opens the Edit Filter window.

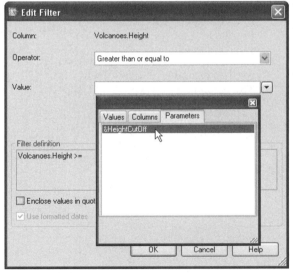

In the Edit Filter window, choose the appropriate operator for the condition, in this case **Greater than or equal to**. Click the down arrow next to the Value box, then click the **Parameters** tab to select the desired parameter. Notice that the parameter name is preceded by an ampersand (&). The ampersand indicates that this is the name of a parameter, not a column. In this example, the filter will select all rows where the Height column is greater than or equal to the **&HeightCutOff** parameter.

After you click **OK** in the Edit Filter window, the filter, including the parameter, will appear in the **Filter Data** tab of the Query Builder window. Click **Run**.

Running the query

When you run the query, a window will open, prompting you to select a value for the parameter. In this example, you can either type in a value for height in the selection box, or use the up or down arrows to select the desired height. Because the &HeightCutOff parameter has a data type of **A range of values**, and the step value is 100, when you click the up or down arrows in the selection box, the value will be incremented by 100 and will not move below the minimum (zero) or above the maximum (6400). If you type a value outside the allowable range into the box and click Run, then you will get an error message.

Results

Here is the data table with results from selecting 5000 for the cut-off value for height. This table includes all the rows from the Volcanoes table where Height is greater than or equal to 5000. Any tasks that use this data table will reflect the selection made in the query. The next time you run the query, you will be prompted again for the cut-off value for Height.

	Volcano	Country	Region	Height	Activity	Type
1	Alter	Ecuador	SA	5321	Extinct	Stratovolcano
2	Elbrus	Russia	Eu	5633	Extinct	Stratovolcano
3	Illimani	Bolivia	SA	6458	Extinct	Stratovolcano
4	Kenya	Kenya	Af	5199	Extinct	
5	Kilimanjaro	Tanzania	Af	5895		Stratovolcano
6	Popocatepetl	Mexico	NA	5426	Active	Stratovolcano
7	Sabancaya	Peru	SA	5976	Active	Stratovolcano

11.3 Creating Parameters for Variables Names

The previous two sections showed how to create a parameter for a data value and then use it in a filter condition in a query. This section shows how you can create a parameter for a variable name, and the next section shows how you can use this parameter in a task. This example creates a parameter that will allow a user to choose a grouping variable when a task is run.

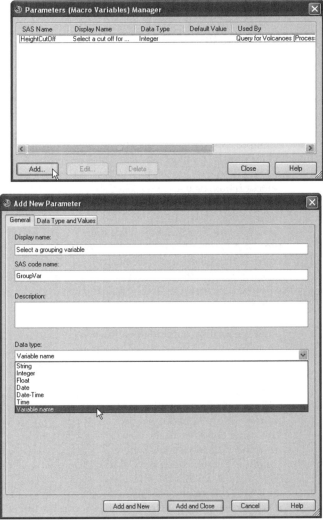

To create a parameter, select **Tools ▶ Parameters (Macro Variable) Manager** from the menu bar. The Parameters Manager will open. In this case, the Parameters Manager window lists the &HeightCutOff parameter that was created in section 11.1. Click the **Add** button to open the Add New Parameter window.

Setting the parameter type and properties In the General tab of the Add New Parameter window, you specify a **Display name**, **SAS code name**, **Description**, and **Data type** for the new parameter. The display name will be used to prompt you for a value when you run the task. The SAS code name is the actual name of the parameter. The SAS code name must be 32 characters or fewer in length; start with a letter or underscore; and contain only letters, numerals, and underscores. If you do not enter a SAS code name, then SAS Enterprise Guide will simply use the display name, substituting underscores for any spaces or special characters. The description is displayed only when the parameter is being created or edited, and is optional. There are several data types you can choose, but for tasks you must choose a data type of **Variable name**. In this window, the display name is **Select a grouping variable**, the SAS code name is **GroupVar**, the description is blank, and the data type is **Variable name**. After you specify the display name, SAS code name, and data type, click the **Data Type and Values** tab.

Setting valid values for the parameter For a variable name parameter, users can either type a value or choose values from a list. For this example, select a **Data value type** of **A list of values**. When you select a list of values as the data value type, new options will appear in the lower part of the window. In the section labeled **Options** on the right, you can choose the variable type. The default variable type is character. If you click the **Load Values** button near the bottom of the window and navigate to a data set, you will get a list of all the variables of that type for that data set. In this example, all the character variables in the Volcanoes data set have been listed in the section labeled **Value list**. Delete from the list any variables that would not be appropriate for your parameter. In this example, only the variables Region, Activity, and Type make sense as grouping variables. To delete unwanted variables, highlight their names, and click the delete

button. It is possible to choose a different variable type (such as numeric or date), and click Load Values again so that the list will include variables of more than one type. For this example, only three character variables (Region, Activity, and Type) are needed.

When you have set all the properties for the parameter, click **Add and Close**. The parameter you created will appear in the Parameters Manager window. Click **Close** and your parameter will be ready to use.

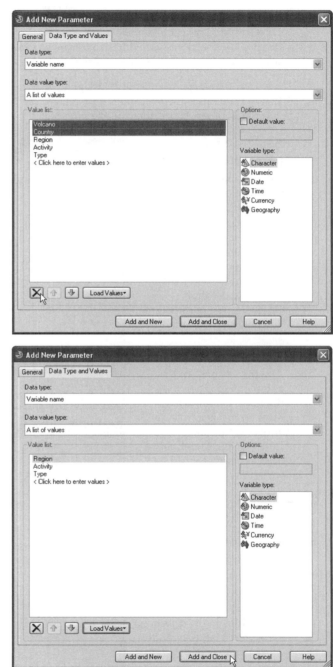

11.4 Using Parameters in Tasks

The previous section showed how to create a parameter for a variable name. This section shows how to assign that parameter to a task role, and how to run the new task.

In the Project Explorer or Project Designer, click the data icon to make it active. Then open a task. This example uses the Volcanoes data set and the List Data task. To open the List Data task, select **Describe ▶ List Data** from the menu bar.

Assigning a parameter to a task role

In the task roles page, notice that the list of variables includes not only the regular variables, but also any variable name parameters you have created for this project. The ampersand (&) in the data icon indicates that GroupVar is a parameter, not a regular variable.

Assign variables and parameters to roles by dragging them to task roles. In this example, the variables Volcano, Country, and Height have been assigned to the List variables role. The parameter GroupVar has been assigned to the Group analysis by and Identifying label roles.

Using parameters in titles

You can use parameters to create custom titles or footnotes. Click **Titles** in the selection pane on the left to open the Titles page.

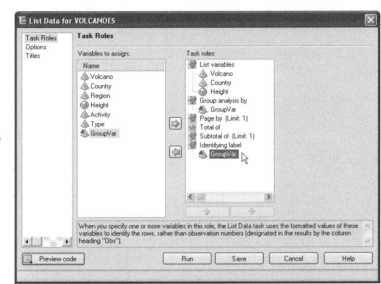

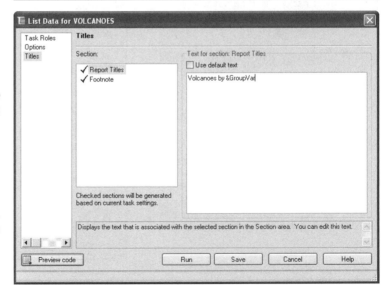

The Titles page opens, displaying the default title for that particular task. To change the title, uncheck the **Use default text** box and type the new title in the text box. In this example, the title has been changed to "Volcanoes by &GroupVar." When you are satisfied with the settings, click **Run**.

Running the task Every time you run the task, a window will open, prompting you to select a value for the parameter. In this window, the variable Type is being selected from a pull-down list of three possible grouping variables. Select the parameter value, and click **Run** to run the task.

Results Here are the results from selecting Type as the grouping variable. This is a List Data report organized by type of volcano. Notice that the value of the parameter (in this case Type) also appears in the title. The next time you run the task, you will be prompted again to choose a grouping variable.

Volcanoes by Type

Type	Volcano	Country	Height
	Arthur's Seat	UK	251
	Kenya	Kenya	5199
Caldera	Grimsvotn	Iceland	1725
	Krakatau	Indonesia	813
Cinder Cone	Puy de Dome	France	1464
Complex	Vesuvius	Italy	1281
Shield	Kilauea	USA	1222
	Mauna Loa	USA	4170
	Nuamuragira	DRCongo	3058

11.5 Using Parameters in SAS Code

The previous sections showed how to create parameters and use them in queries or tasks. This section shows how you can create flexible SAS code by using the same parameters. When you run the SAS code, SAS Enterprise Guide will prompt you for the values of the parameters.

Adding parameters to SAS code Here is a simple SAS program written in a Code window in SAS Enterprise Guide.

```
PROC FREQ DATA = 'C:\EG Data\Volcanoes';
    WHERE  Height >= &HeightCutOff;
    TABLES &GroupVar;
    TITLE1 "Number of Volcanoes &HeightCutOff Meters or Higher";
    TITLE2 "For Each Value of &GroupVar";
RUN;
```

This program uses both the data value parameter created in section 11.1 (&HeightCutOff) and the variable name parameter created in section 11.4 (&GroupVar). &HeightCutOff is used in a WHERE statement to select only rows where the values of the Height column are greater than or equal to the parameter value. &GroupVar is used in a TABLES statement so the data will be summarized based on the values of the grouping variable. Then both parameters are used again in the TITLE statements, so that the values of the parameters will appears in the titles for the report.

Setting the properties of the code Because the parameters have been defined outside the code, you need to associate the parameters with the code. To do this, right-click the Code icon in the Project Explorer or Project Designer and select **Properties**. Then, in the Properties for Code window, click **Parameters** in the selection pane on the left to display the Parameters page. Click the **Add** button. This opens the Select Parameters window.

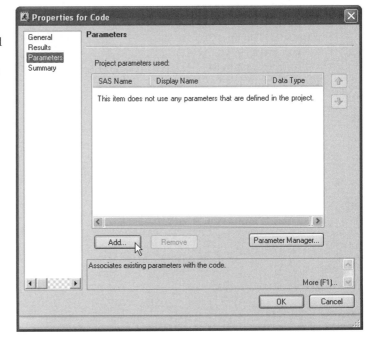

The Select Parameters window lists all the parameters currently defined in the project. Use control-click to highlight the names of the parameters used in the code. Then click **OK** to return to the Properties for Code window.

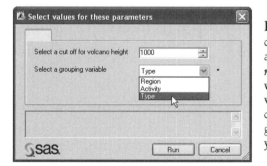

The parameters will appear in the Properties for Code window. This window shows that both the HeightCutOff and GroupVar parameters have been associated with this code. Click **OK** to save the changes and close the window.

Running the SAS Code To run the code, click the Code window to make sure it is active, and select **Code ▶ Run** *program-name* **On** *server-name* from the menu bar. When you do this, a window will open, prompting you to select values for each parameter. In this window, the cut-off height has been set to 1000 meters, and the grouping variable has been set to Type. When you are satisfied, click **Run**.

Number of Volcanoes 1000 Meters or Higher For Each Value of Type

The FREQ Procedure

	Type			
Type	Frequency	Percent	Cumulative Frequency	Cumulative Percent
Caldera	1	3.70	1	3.70
Cinder Cone	1	3.70	2	7.41
Complex	1	3.70	3	11.11
Shield	4	14.81	7	25.93
Stratovolcano	20	74.07	27	100.00

Frequency Missing = 1

Results The output from the SAS code will appear in the workspace. This report is summarized by Type, includes only volcanoes over 1000 meters, and has custom titles. Note that you could accomplish the same result without writing any SAS code by using the results of a parameterized query as the input to a parameterized One-Way Frequencies task.

APPENDIX

358

Data Used in This Book

Reading about a topic is good, but many people learn better by doing. However, before you can do the examples in the tutorials or reference sections, you need the data. One way to get the data is to type the data shown in this appendix into a SAS Enterprise Guide Data Grid, a Microsoft Excel spreadsheet, or a text file. Another way is to download the data sets from the companion Web site for this book. You can download the data sets shown in this appendix by going to

support.sas.com/companionsites

Select the title *The Little SAS Book for Enterprise Guide 4.1* to display its companion Web site, and then select the link for data.

Tours Data

Filename: Tours.sas7bdat
File Type: SAS data set

Columns:

Name	Description	Values
Volcano	Name of the volcano	
Departs	City from which tour departs	
Days	Length of the tour in days	
Price	Price of the tour in U.S. dollars	
Difficulty	Strenuousness of the tour	c (Challenging)
		m (Moderate)
		e (Easy)

Tours.sas7bdat

Tours (read-only)

	Volcano	Departs	Days	Price	Difficulty
1	Etna	Catania	7	$1,025	m
2	Fuji	Tokyo	2	$195	c
3	Kenya	Nairobi	6	$780	m
4	Kilauea	Hilo	1	$45	e
5	Kilimanjaro	Nairobi	9	$1,260	c
6	Krakatau	Jakarta	7	$850	e
7	Poas	San Jose	1	$50	e
8	Reventador	Quito	4	$525	m
9	St. Helens	Portland	2	$157	e
10	Vesuvius	Rome	6	$950	e

Tour Dates Data

Filename: TourDates.sas7bdat
File Type: SAS data set

Columns:

Name	Description
Tour	Code for tour
Volcano	Name of the volcano
DepartureDate	Date of tour departure
Guide	Name of guide for tour

TourDates.sas7bdat

TourDates (read-only)

	Tour	Volcano	DepartureDate	Guide
1	PS27	Poas	08/05/2006	Carlos
2	SH40	St. Helens	06/19/2006	Casey
3	SH41	St. Helens	07/05/2006	Casey
4	SH42	St. Helens	07/23/2006	Casey
5	SH43	St. Helens	08/15/2006	Kelly
6	FJ12	Fuji	09/12/2006	Cooper
7	ET01	Etna	08/05/2006	Cooper
8	KE05	Kenya	05/31/2006	Kelly
9	KL18	Kilauea	07/08/2006	Malia
10	KL19	Kilauea	07/15/2006	Malia
11	KL20	Kilauea	07/22/2006	Malia
12	RD02	Reventador	07/11/2006	Carlos
13	VS11	Vesuvius	07/21/2006	Cooper
14	VS12	Vesuvius	08/15/2006	Cooper
15	KJ01	Kilimanjaro	06/09/2006	Kelly
16	KK03	Krakatau	07/19/2006	Kelly

Tour Bookings Data

There are two versions of the bookings data. One is a Microsoft Excel file and the other is a SAS data set, but they both contain the same columns and data values.

Filename:	Bookings.xls	Bookings.sas7bdat
File Type:	Microsoft Excel spreadsheet	SAS data set

Columns:

Name	Description
Office	Office where reservation was made
CustomerID	Customer identification number
Tour	Code for tour
Travelers	Number traveling in party
Deposit	Amount of deposit
Deposit_Date	Date of deposit

Bookings.xls

	Office	CustomerID	Tour	Travelers	Deposit	Deposit_Date
1	Office	CustomerID	Tour	Travelers	Deposit	Deposit_Date
2	Portland	SL28	SH43	10	425	7/5/2006
3	Portland	DE27	PS27	6	75	7/11/2006
4	Portland	SL34	FJ12	4	200	7/19/2006
5	Portland	DI33	SH43	4	150	7/23/2006
6	Portland	BU12	SH43	2	75	7/23/2006
7	Portland	DE31	FJ12	3	175	7/25/2006
8	Portland	WI48	FJ12	2	100	7/26/2006
9	Portland	NG17	PS27	5	65	7/26/2006
10	Portland	RA28	PS27	2	30	7/28/2006
11	Portland	ME11	PS27	2	30	7/28/2006
12	Portland	GI08	SH43	8	300	7/31/2006
13	Portland	HI15	SH43	4	150	7/31/2006
14	Portland	MA09	SH43	2	75	7/31/2006

Bookings.sas7bdat

	Office	CustomerID	Tour	Travelers	Deposit	Deposit_Date
1	Portland	SL28	SH43	10	425	05JUL2006:12:00:00 AM
2	Portland	DE27	PS27	6	75	11JUL2006:12:00:00 AM
3	Portland	SL34	FJ12	4	200	19JUL2006:12:00:00 AM
4	Portland	DI33	SH43	4	150	23JUL2006:12:00:00 AM
5	Portland	BU12	SH43	2	75	23JUL2006:12:00:00 AM
6	Portland	DE31	FJ12	3	175	25JUL2006:12:00:00 AM
7	Portland	WI48	FJ12	2	100	26JUL2006:12:00:00 AM
8	Portland	NG17	PS27	5	65	26JUL2006:12:00:00 AM
9	Portland	RA28	PS27	2	30	28JUL2006:12:00:00 AM
10	Portland	ME11	PS27	2	30	28JUL2006:12:00:00 AM
11	Portland	GI08	SH43	8	300	31JUL2006:12:00:00 AM
12	Portland	HI15	SH43	4	150	31JUL2006:12:00:00 AM
13	Portland	MA09	SH43	2	75	31JUL2006:12:00:00 AM

Volcanoes Data

Filename: Volcanoes.sas7bdat
File Type: SAS data set

Columns:

Name	Description	Values
Volcano	Name of the volcano	
Country	Country where the volcano is found	
Region	Region where the volcano is found	Af (Africa) An (Antarctica) AP (Australia/Pacific) As (Asia) Eu (Europe) NA (North America) SA (South America)
Height	Height of the volcano in meters	
Activity	Activity of the volcano	Active Extinct
Type	Kind of volcano	Caldera Complex Shield Stratovolcano

Volcanoes.sas7bdat

	Volcano	Country	Region	Height	Activity	Type
1	Altar	Ecuador	SA	5321	Extinct	Stratovolcano
2	Arthur's Seat	UK	Eu	251	Extinct	
3	Barren Island	India	As	354	Active	Stratovolcano
4	Elbrus	Russia	Eu	5633	Extinct	Stratovolcano
5	Erebus		An	3794	Active	Stratovolcano
6	Etna	Italy	Eu	3350	Active	Stratovolcano
7	Fuji	Japan	As	3776	Active	Stratovolcano
8	Garibaldi	Canada	NA	2678		Stratovolcano
9	Grimsvotn	Iceland	Eu	1725	Active	Caldera
10	Illimani	Bolivia	SA	6458	Extinct	Stratovolcano
11	Kenya	Kenya	Af	5199	Extinct	
12	Kilauea	USA	AP	1222	Active	Shield
13	Kilimanjaro	Tanzania	Af	5895		Stratovolcano
14	Kliuchevskoi	Russia	As	4835	Active	Stratovolcano
15	Krakatau	Indonesia	As	813	Active	Caldera
16	Lassen	USA	NA	3187	Active	Stratovolcano
17	Mauna Loa	USA	AP	4170	Active	Shield
18	Nyamuragira	DRCongo	Af	3058	Active	Shield
19	Nyiragongo	DRCongo	Af	3470	Active	Stratovolcano
20	Pinatubo	Philippines	As	1486	Active	Stratovolcano
21	Poas	Costa Rica	NA	2708	Active	Stratovolcano
22	Popocatepetl	Mexico	NA	5426	Active	Stratovolcano
23	Puy de Dome	France	Eu	1464	Extinct	Cinder Cone
24	Reventador	Ecuador	SA	3562	Active	Stratovolcano
25	Ruapehu	NZ	AP	2797	Active	Stratovolcano
26	Sabancaya	Peru	SA	5976	Active	Stratovolcano
27	Santorini	Greece	Eu	367	Active	Shield
28	Shishaldin	USA	NA	2857	Active	Stratovolcano
29	St. Helens	USA	NA	2549	Active	Stratovolcano
30	Vesuvius	Italy	Eu	1281	Active	Complex
31	Villarrica	Chile	SA	2847	Active	Stratovolcano
32	Warning	Australia	AP	1125	Extinct	Shield

Eruptions Data

There are two versions of the eruptions data. One is a text file and the other is a SAS data set, but they both contain the same columns and data values.

Filename:	Eruptions.csv	Eruptions.sas7bdat
File Type:	Text file with comma-separated values	SAS data set

Columns:

Name	Description	Values
Volcano	Name of the volcano	
StartDate	Date the eruption started in MMDDYY10. format	
EndDate	Date the eruption ended in MMDDYY10. format	
VEI	Volcanic Explosivity Index	0–8

Eruptions.csv

```
Volcano, StartDate, EndDate, VEI
Barren Island, 12/20/1795, 12/21/1795, 2
Barren Island, 12/20/1994, 06/05/1995, 2
Erebus, 12/12/1912, . , 2
Erebus, 01/03/1972, . , 1
Etna, 02/06/1610, 08/15/1610, 2
Etna, 06/04/1787, 08/11/1787, 4
Etna, 01/30/1865, 06/28/1865, 2
Etna, 12/16/2005, 12/22/2005, 1
Fuji, 12/16/1707, 02/24/1708, 5
Grimsvotn, 10/31/1603, 11/01/1603, 2
Grimsvotn, 01/08/1873, 08/01/1873, 4
Grimsvotn, 12/18/1998, 12/28/1998, 3
Kilauea, 05/30/1840, 06/25/1840, 0
Kilauea, 05/24/1969, 07/22/1974, 0
Kliuchevskoi, 09/25/1737, 11/04/1737, 2
Kliuchevskoi, 03/25/1931, 03/27/1931, 4
Kliuchevskoi, 01/20/2005, 04/07/2005, 2
Krakatau, 05/20/1883, 10/21/1883, 6
Krakatau, 07/04/1938, 07/02/1940, 3
Krakatau, 05/29/2000, 10/30/2000, 1
Lassen, 05/30/1914, 06/29/1917, 3
Mauna Loa, 06/20/1832, 07/15/1832, 0
Mauna Loa, 03/25/1984, 04/15/1984, 0
Nyamuragira, 11/07/1907, 12/05/1907, 3
Nyamuragira, 02/06/2001, 04/05/2001, 2
Nyiragongo, 06/21/1982, 10/17/1982, 1
Nyiragongo, 01/17/2002, 02/03/2002, 1
Pinatubo, 04/02/1991, 09/02/1991, 5
Poas, 12/29/1898, 12/31/1907, 1
Poas, 04/08/1996, 04/08/1996, 1
Popocatepetl, 10/13/1663, 10/19/1665, 3
Popocatepetl, 12/21/1994, 08/05/1995, 2
Reventador, 12/12/1856, 12/13/1856, 3
Reventador, 02/24/1944, 03/01/1944, 3
Reventador, 11/03/2002, 01/10/2003, 4
Ruapehu, 02/13/1861, 05/16/1861, 2
Ruapehu, 06/17/1996, 09/01/1996, 3
Sabancaya, 05/01/1997, 05/02/1997, 3
Santorini, 09/27/1650, 12/06/1650, 4
Santorini, 05/23/1707, 09/14/1711, 3
Santorini, 01/26/1866, 10/15/1870, 2
Santorini, 01/10/1950, 02/02/1950, 2
Shishaldin, 03/13/1999, 05/27/1999, 3
St. Helens, 03/26/1847, 03/30/1847, 2
St. Helens, 03/27/1980, 10/28/1986, 5
St. Helens, 10/01/2004, . , 2
Vesuvius, 12/15/1631, 01/31/1632, 5
Vesuvius, 12/25/1732, 06/04/1737, 3
Vesuvius, 12/18/1875, 04/22/1906, 4
Vesuvius, 07/05/1913, 04/04/1944, 3
Villarrica, 11/07/1837, 11/21/1837, 2
Villarrica, 08/05/2003, 01/01/2004, 1
```

Eruptions.sas7bdat

	Volcano	StartDate	EndDate	VEI
1	Barren Island	12/20/1795	12/21/1795	2
2	Barren Island	12/20/1994	06/05/1995	2
3	Erebus	12/12/1912		2
4	Erebus	01/03/1972		1
5	Etna	02/06/1610	08/15/1610	2
6	Etna	06/04/1787	08/11/1787	4
7	Etna	01/30/1865	06/28/1865	2
8	Etna	12/16/2005	12/22/2005	1
9	Fuji	12/16/1707	02/24/1708	5
10	Grimsvotn	10/31/1603	11/01/1603	2
11	Grimsvotn	01/08/1873	08/01/1873	4
12	Grimsvotn	12/18/1998	12/28/1998	3
13	Kilauea	05/30/1840	06/25/1840	0
14	Kilauea	05/24/1969	07/22/1974	0
15	Kliuchevskoi	09/25/1737	11/04/1737	2
16	Kliuchevskoi	03/25/1931	03/27/1931	4
17	Kliuchevskoi	01/20/2005	04/07/2005	2
18	Krakatau	05/20/1883	10/21/1883	6
19	Krakatau	07/04/1938	07/02/1940	3
20	Krakatau	05/29/2000	10/30/2000	1
21	Lassen	05/30/1914	06/29/1917	3
22	Mauna Loa	06/20/1832	07/15/1832	0
23	Mauna Loa	03/25/1984	04/15/1984	0
24	Nyamuragira	11/07/1907	12/05/1907	3
25	Nyamuragira	02/06/2001	04/05/2001	2
26	Nyiragongo	06/21/1982	10/17/1982	1
27	Nyiragongo	01/17/2002	02/03/2002	1
28	Pinatubo	04/02/1991	09/02/1991	5
29	Poas	12/29/1898	12/31/1907	1
30	Poas	04/08/1996	04/08/1996	1
31	Popocatepetl	10/13/1663	10/19/1665	3
32	Popocatepetl	12/21/1994	08/05/1995	2
33	Reventador	12/12/1856	12/13/1856	3
34	Reventador	02/24/1944	03/01/1944	3
35	Reventador	11/03/2002	01/10/2003	4
36	Ruapehu	02/13/1861	05/16/1861	2
37	Ruapehu	06/17/1996	09/01/1996	3
38	Sabancaya	05/01/1997	05/02/1997	3
39	Santorini	09/27/1650	12/06/1650	4
40	Santorini	05/23/1707	09/14/1711	3
41	Santorini	01/26/1866	10/15/1870	2
42	Santorini	01/10/1950	02/02/1950	2
43	Shishaldin	03/13/1999	05/27/1999	3
44	St. Helens	03/26/1847	03/30/1847	2
45	St. Helens	03/27/1980	10/28/1986	5
46	St. Helens	10/01/2004		2
47	Vesuvius	12/15/1631	01/31/1632	5
48	Vesuvius	12/25/1732	06/04/1737	3
49	Vesuvius	12/18/1875	04/22/1906	4
50	Vesuvius	07/05/1913	04/04/1944	3
51	Villarrica	11/07/1837	11/21/1837	2
52	Villarrica	08/05/2003	01/01/2004	1

Recent Eruptions of Etna Data

Filename: Etna.csv
File Type: Text file with comma-separated values

Columns:

Name	Description	Values
Volcano	Name of the volcano	
StartDate	Date the eruption started in DDMMYY10. format	
EndDate	Date the eruption ended in DDMMYY10. format	
VEI	Volcanic Explosivity Index	0–8

Etna.csv

```
Volcano, StartDate, EndDate, VEI
Etna, 17/07/2001, 09/08/2001, 3
Etna, . , 30/10/2002, 1
Etna, 26/10/2002, 28/01/2003, 2
Etna, 08/03/2003, 09/11/2003, 1
```

Latitude and Longitude Data

There are two versions of the latitude and longitude data. One is a text file and the other is a SAS data set, but they both contain the same columns and data values.

Filename: Latlong.txt   Latlong.sas7bdat
File Type: Fixed-width text file   SAS data set

Columns:

Name	Description
Volcano	Name of the volcano
Latitude	Latitude
Longitude	Longitude

Latlong.txt

```
Volcano        Latitude Longitude
Altar          -1.67    -78.42
Barren Island  12.28     93.52
Elbrus         43.33     42.45
Erebus         -77.53    167.17
Etna           37.73     15.00
Fuji           35.35     138.73
Garibaldi      49.85    -123.00
Grimsvotn      64.42    -17.33
Illimani       -16.39   -67.47
Kenya          -0.09     37.18
Kilauea        19.43    -155.29
Kilimanjaro    -3.07     37.35
Kliuchevskoi   56.06     160.64
Krakatau       -6.10     105.42
Lassen         40.49    -121.51
Mauna Loa      19.48    -155.61
Nyamuragira    -1.41     29.20
Nyiragongo     -1.52     29.25
Pinatubo       15.13     120.35
Poas           10.20    -84.23
Popocatepetl   19.02    -98.62
Puy de Dome    45.50      2.75
Reventador     -0.08    -77.66
Ruapehu        -39.28    175.57
Sabancaya      -15.78   -71.85
Santorini      36.40     25.40
Shishaldin     54.76    -163.97
St. Helens     46.20    -122.18
Vesuvius       40.82     14.43
Villarrica     -39.42   -71.93
```

Latlong.sas7bdat

	Latlong (read-only)		
	Volcano	**Latitude**	**Longitude**
1	Altar	-1.67	-78.42
2	Barren Island	12.28	93.52
3	Elbrus	43.33	42.45
4	Erebus	-77.53	167.17
5	Etna	37.73	15
6	Fuji	35.35	138.73
7	Garibaldi	49.85	-123
8	Grimsvotn	64.42	-17.33
9	Illimani	-16.39	-67.47
10	Kenya	-0.09	37.18
11	Kilauea	19.43	-155.29
12	Kilimanjaro	-3.07	37.35
13	Kliuchevskoi	56.06	160.64
14	Krakatau	-6.1	105.42
15	Lassen	40.49	-121.51
16	Mauna Loa	19.48	-155.61
17	Nyamuragira	-1.41	29.2
18	Nyiragongo	-1.52	29.25
19	Pinatubo	15.13	120.35
20	Poas	10.2	-84.23
21	Popocatepetl	19.02	-98.62
22	Puy de Dome	45.5	2.75
23	Reventador	-0.08	-77.66
24	Ruapehu	-39.28	175.57
25	Sabancaya	-15.78	-71.85
26	Santorini	36.4	25.4
27	Shishaldin	54.76	-163.97
28	St. Helens	46.2	-122.18
29	Vesuvius	40.82	14.43
30	Villarrica	-39.42	-71.93

Portland Flights Data

Filename: Portland.sas7bdat
File Type: SAS data set

Columns:

Name	Description
Origin	City from which flight departs
Destination	City in which flight arrives
FlightNo	Flight number
FlightPrice	Price of flight in U.S. dollars

Portland.sas7bdat

Portland (read-only)

	Origin	Destination	FlightNo	FlightPrice
1	Portland	Catania	L469	$679.00
2	Portland	Hilo	HA25	$603.00
3	Portland	Nairobi	KLM6034	$1,733.00
4	Portland	Rome	D1576	$544.00
5	Portland	San Jose	CA1210	$394.00
6	Portland	Tokyo	UA383	$605.00

Seattle Flights Data

Filename: Seattle.sas7bdat
File Type: SAS data set

Columns:

Name	Description
Origin	City from which flight departs
Destination	City in which flight arrives
FlightNo	Flight number
FlightPrice	Price of flight in U.S. dollars

Seattle.sas7bdat

Seattle (read-only)

	Origin	Destination	FlightNo	FlightPrice
1	Seattle	Catania	BA48	$702.00
2	Seattle	Hilo	HA21	$577.00
3	Seattle	Jakarta	AA119	$1,715.00
4	Seattle	Nairobi	KLM6034	$1,661.00
5	Seattle	Quito	CA1086	$733.00
6	Seattle	Rome	USA6	$496.00
7	Seattle	San Jose	CA1100	$380.00
8	Seattle	Tokyo	UA875	$621.00

Appendix A

Northwest Weather Data

Filename: NWweather.sas7bdat
File Type: SAS data set

Columns:

Name	Description	Values
City	City	
Month	Month	1–12
AvgTemp	Average high temperature in degrees Fahrenheit	
FromNormal	Change from normal temperature in degrees Fahrenheit	
InchesRain	Amount of rain in inches	
Bookings	Number of tours booked for that month	

NWweather.sas7bdat

	City	Month	AvgTemp	FromNormal	InchesRain	Bookings
1	Seattle	1	45.8	4.9	8.39	32
2	Seattle	2	41.7	-1.6	1.76	19
3	Seattle	3	46.8	0.6	6.34	23
4	Seattle	4	48.9	-1.3	2.74	18
5	Seattle	5	54.8	-1	1.16	21
6	Seattle	6	62.8	2.1	0.51	18
7	Seattle	7	67.9	2.6	0.06	17
8	Seattle	8	66.4	0.8	0.32	17
9	Seattle	9	62.6	1.5	0.89	22
10	Seattle	10	54.3	1.6	8.96	20
11	Seattle	11	42.8	-2.4	6.77	25
12	Seattle	12	41.8	1.1	3.88	31
13	Portland	1	44.8	4.9	7.64	22
14	Portland	2	44.3	1.2	2.37	19
15	Portland	3	49	1.8	5.75	17
16	Portland	4	50.8	-0.4	4.37	18
17	Portland	5	57.3	0.2	1.49	21
18	Portland	6	66.1	3.4	0.31	19
19	Portland	7	71.6	3.5	0	13
20	Portland	8	70.1	1.6	0.19	15
21	Portland	9	66.8	3.2	0.85	23
22	Portland	10	58.2	3.9	3.01	24
23	Portland	11	45.2	-0.6	4.09	27
24	Portland	12	42.5	2.3	7.45	33

On-Time Status of Flights Data

Filename: OnTimeStatus.sas7bdat
File Type: SAS data set

Columns:

Name	Description	Values
Month	Month	Dec Jan Feb
Departure	Whether delayed 15 minutes or more	OnTime Late
TimeOfDay	Whether before or after 12 p.m.	BeforeNoon AfterNoon
NumOfFlights	Number of flights in that category	

OnTimeStatus.sas7bdat

	Month	Departure	TimeOfDay	NumOfFlights
1	Dec	OnTime	AfterNoon	25
2	Dec	Late	AfterNoon	33
3	Dec	OnTime	BeforeNoon	80
4	Dec	Late	BeforeNoon	13
5	Jan	OnTime	AfterNoon	15
6	Jan	Late	AfterNoon	12
7	Jan	OnTime	BeforeNoon	30
8	Jan	Late	BeforeNoon	13
9	Feb	OnTime	AfterNoon	20
10	Feb	Late	AfterNoon	8
11	Feb	OnTime	BeforeNoon	43
12	Feb	Late	BeforeNoon	1

Advertising Results Data

Filename: AdResults.sas7bdat
File Type: SAS data set

Columns:

Name	Description	Values
City	City	
Month	Month	1–12
AdDollars	Money spent on advertising in U.S. dollars	
Bookings	Number of tours booked for that month	

AdResults.sas7bdat

	City	Month	AdDollars	Bookings
1	Seattle	1	350	30
2	Seattle	2	330	19
3	Seattle	3	525	32
4	Seattle	4	400	18
5	Seattle	5	375	21
6	Seattle	6	325	18
7	Seattle	7	150	17
8	Seattle	8	250	17
9	Seattle	9	250	22
10	Seattle	10	325	20
11	Seattle	11	400	25
12	Seattle	12	500	31
13	Portland	1	325	25
14	Portland	2	290	19
15	Portland	3	250	17
16	Portland	4	300	18
17	Portland	5	300	21
18	Portland	6	275	19
19	Portland	7	200	13
20	Portland	8	225	15
21	Portland	9	325	23
22	Portland	10	350	24
23	Portland	11	425	27
24	Portland	12	400	33

Ages Data

Filename: Ages.sas7bdat
File Type: SAS data set

Columns:

Name	Description	Values	
Difficulty	Strenuousness of the tour	c	(Challenging)
		m	(Moderate)
		e	(Easy)
Age	Age in years		

Ages.sas7bdat

	Ages (read-only)	
	Difficulty	**Age**
1	e	45
2	e	38
3	e	65
4	e	43
5	e	29
6	e	72
7	e	66
8	e	57
9	e	39
10	e	33
11	m	26
12	m	37
13	m	42
14	m	27
15	m	31
16	m	39
17	m	35
18	m	30
19	m	41
20	m	55
21	c	65
22	c	39
23	c	59
24	c	55
25	c	50
26	c	47
27	c	42
28	c	60
29	c	58
30	c	67

Index

Special Characters